Container Gardening

FOR

DUMMIES®

2ND EDITION

**by Bill Marken, Suzanne DeJohn, and
The Editors of the
National Gardening Association**

WILEY

Wiley Publishing, Inc.

Container Gardening For Dummies®, 2nd Edition

Published by
Wiley Publishing, Inc.
111 River St.
Hoboken, NJ 07030-5774
www.wiley.com

Copyright © 2010 by Wiley Publishing, Inc., Indianapolis, Indiana

Published by Wiley Publishing, Inc., Indianapolis, Indiana

Published simultaneously in Canada

No part of this publication may be reproduced, stored in a retrieval system or transmitted in any form or by any means, electronic, mechanical, photocopying, recording, scanning or otherwise, except as permitted under Sections 107 or 108 of the 1976 United States Copyright Act, without either the prior written permission of the Publisher, or authorization through payment of the appropriate per-copy fee to the Copyright Clearance Center, 222 Rosewood Drive, Danvers, MA 01923, (978) 750-8400, fax (978) 646-8600. Requests to the Publisher for permission should be addressed to the Permissions Department, John Wiley & Sons, Inc., 111 River Street, Hoboken, NJ 07030, (201) 748-6011, fax (201) 748-6008, or online at http://www.wiley.com/go/permissions.

Trademarks: Wiley, the Wiley Publishing logo, For Dummies, the Dummies Man logo, A Reference for the Rest of Us!, The Dummies Way, Dummies Daily, The Fun and Easy Way, Dummies.com, Making Everything Easier, and related trade dress are trademarks or registered trademarks of John Wiley & Sons, Inc. and/or its affiliates in the United States and other countries, and may not be used without written permission. All other trademarks are the property of their respective owners. Wiley Publishing, Inc., is not associated with any product or vendor mentioned in this book.

For general information on our other products and services, please contact our Customer Care Department within the U.S. at 877-762-2974, outside the U.S. at 317-572-3993, or fax 317-572-4002.

For technical support, please visit www.wiley.com/techsupport.

Wiley also publishes its books in a variety of electronic formats. Some content that appears in print may not be available in electronic books.

Library of Congress Control Number: 2009942824

ISBN: 978-0-470-57705-9

Manufactured in the United States of America

10 9 8 7 6 5 4 3 2

About the Authors

Suzanne DeJohn loves plants, botany, and nature. She's worn a variety of hats in her 13 years at the National Gardening Association (NGA), including working in the education, editorial, and IT departments. She coordinated NGA's online question-and-answer service and has answered thousands of gardening questions, giving her insight into just what information people are looking for. She's also written more than 200 columns on environmentally friendly food and flower gardening for NGA's Regional Reports, a biweekly online publication and eNewsletter. Convinced that gardeners are curious and love to learn, she created the *Exploring the Garden* series of in-depth, online courses that teach the principles of botany in the context of the garden.

Suzanne's varied background also includes a BS in geology from Tufts; university courses in botany, soils, and plant pathology; a stint as a research technician in plant pathology; and several years as a self-employed artist and graphic designer. She's worked on a landscape crew, an organic farm, and spent several years as a cook at a natural foods store. The common themes running through these seemingly disparate vocations are plants, beauty, nature, and healthy food. In addition to her writing and other work at NGA, she and her husband recently opened a small, pet-friendly B&B in Cambridge, Vermont.

Bill Marken is an editor and writer who lives in the San Francisco Bay area. He served as editor in chief of *Sunset, the Magazine of Western Living,* for 15 years. In his career with *Sunset,* he also worked as a writer for the magazine's garden section, pitched in on several editions of the best-selling *Western Garden Book,* and generally nurtured his interest in subjects related to gardening, landscaping, travel, and other aspects of the good life in the western United States. He is also the founding editor of *Rebecca's Garden* magazine and has served on the board of the League to Save Lake Tahoe, the major watchdog of the threatened lake.

The National Gardening Association (NGA) is committed to sustaining and renewing the fundamental links between people, plants, and the earth. Founded in 1972 as "Gardens for All" to spearhead the community garden movement, today's NGA promotes environmental responsibility, advances multidisciplinary learning and scientific literacy, and creates partnerships that restore and enhance communities.

NGA is best known for its garden-based curricula, educational journals, international initiatives, and several youth garden grant programs. Together, these reach more than 300,000 children nationwide each year. NGA's Web sites, one for home gardeners and another for those who garden with kids, build community and offer a wealth of custom content.

To find out more about the National Gardening Association, write to 1100 Dorset St., South Burlington, VT 05403, or visit its Web site at www.garden.org or www.kidsgardening.org.

Dedication

Suzanne dedicates this book to her husband, Dale Lane. "Your energy, encouragement, and enthusiasm make everything I do easier and better. Thank you."

Acknowledgments

I would like to thank author Bill Marken for providing so much sound, in-depth information in the first edition of *Container Gardening For Dummies*. I'm grateful to Charlie Nardozzi for helping out with the writing and editing, especially when deadlines were looming. A round of applause goes to Wiley project editor Vicki Adang and copy editor Christy Pingleton for asking the right questions, helping refine text, and livening up sections that sorely needed it. My appreciation also goes to technical editor Marie Iannotti for keeping me on my toes. Thank you, Stacy Kennedy, for getting the project going. And finally, thank you to the National Gardening Association for giving me the opportunity and time to work on this project.

—Suzanne DeJohn

Publisher's Acknowledgments

We're proud of this book; please send us your comments at http://dummies.custhelp.com. For other comments, please contact our Customer Care Department within the U.S. at 877-762-2974, outside the U.S. at 317-572-3993, or fax 317-572-4002.

Some of the people who helped bring this book to market include the following:

Acquisitions, Editorial, and Media Development

Project Editor: Victoria M. Adang
  (Previous Edition: Tim Gallan)

Acquisitions Editor: Stacy Kennedy

Copy Editors: Caitlin Copple,
  Christine Pingleton
  (Previous Edition: Linda Stark)

Assistant Editor: Erin Calligan Mooney

Editorial Program Coordinator: Joe Niesen

Technical Editor: Marie Iannotti

Editorial Manager: Michelle Hacker

Editorial Assistant: Jennette ElNaggar

Art Coordinator: Alicia B. South

Cover Photos: iStock

Cartoons: Rich Tennant
  (www.the5thwave.com)

Composition Services

Project Coordinator: Sheree Montgomery

Layout and Graphics: Joyce Haughey

Special Art: Ron Hildebrand

Proofreader: Evelyn C. Gibson

Indexer: Cheryl Duksta

Publishing and Editorial for Consumer Dummies

  Diane Graves Steele, Vice President and Publisher, Consumer Dummies

  Kristin Ferguson-Wagstaffe, Product Development Director, Consumer Dummies

  Ensley Eikenburg, Associate Publisher, Travel

  Kelly Regan, Editorial Director, Travel

Publishing for Technology Dummies

  Andy Cummings, Vice President and Publisher, Dummies Technology/General User

Composition Services

  Debbie Stailey, Director of Composition Services

Contents at a Glance

Table of Contents

Introduction

*I*n this book, we want to share with you the many pleasures of growing plants in containers. While it's fun and rewarding to grow plants in the ground, growing in containers offers even greater options and opportunities. You'll discover an amazing number of plant possibilities and an equally amazing variety of pots, both purchased and improvised.

Containers make it possible for those without outdoor garden space to create beautiful gardens and grow some of their own food — on the front stoop, on an apartment balcony, or in a sunny windowsill. And even if you do have a yard, you'll find good reasons to consider growing some of your plants in containers.

About This Book

Growing plants in containers is a lot like growing plants in the ground. Except when it's not. This book takes you step by step through the process of growing plants in pots, from choosing soil mixes and containers, to deciding what to grow, to taking care of plants using environmentally friendly techniques. The information is organized in a logical way that's easy to access — you can read the book cover to cover, flip through pages to see what catches your eye, or use the detailed table of contents and index to hone in on just the information you need. If you're new to container gardening, or new to gardening altogether, this book introduces you to what we're sure will become a most rewarding pastime. And if you're an experienced gardener, you can find enough in-depth information and creative ideas to help you take your container gardens to the next level.

Conventions Used in This Book

When we refer to a plant's hardiness — its ability to survive cold winter temperatures — we use the U.S. Department of Agriculture's Plant Hardiness Zone map, which you can check out in Chapter 2, and all temperatures are given in degrees Fahrenheit.

We also use the following conventions throughout the text to make things consistent and easy to understand:

- All Web addresses appear in monofont.

- New terms appear in *italic* and are closely followed by an easy-to-understand definition. Italics are also used for the two-part botanical names of plants.

- **Bold** is used to highlight keywords in bulleted lists and the action parts of numbered steps.

Foolish Assumptions

We don't expect you to know much at all about gardening. This book is useful for both novice and experienced gardeners. We expect that you enjoy growing plants and will do the work that's necessary to plant and maintain them.

How This Book Is Organized

The book is divided into six major parts that are intended to lead you through all stages of container gardening. The parts are grouped according to topic to make it easier for you to find related information.

Part I: Getting Started with Container Gardening

Why bother growing plants in pots? By the end of the first chapter you'll be convinced to give container gardening a try. The next chapter describes the climate and garden conditions important to container growing. Based on this information, you can decide whether you want to stick with plants that you discard at the end of the growing season or try your hand at perennial plants. Then we get down to the nitty-gritty: How to choose containers and soil mixes, followed by step-by-step planting instructions.

Part II: Enjoying a Summer Fling with Single-Season Containers

Most gardeners opt for plants that grow for a single growing season and are replaced with fresh plants each spring. This eliminates the challenge of figuring out how to get plants to survive during cold winter weather and lets you redesign your container plantings every year. We describe the best annual flowers, vegetables, and bulbs for container growing. If you're a beginner gardener, single-season containers are a great place to start — they offer the most bang for the buck when it comes to beautiful flowers and a nutritious harvest.

Part III: In It for the Long Haul: Permanent Plantings

Ready to step up to the next challenge? In this section you find a wealth of information on climate considerations and overwintering techniques for permanent plantings. These are the plants that give year-round impact — especially woody plants like trees and shrubs. We look at hardiness ratings and how they relate to plants growing in pots. When it's time to choose plants, check out the chapters on perennials; trees, shrubs, and vines; and fruits and berries for suggestions on the best plants for specific garden situations. You also find ideas and techniques for growing plants indoors.

Part IV: Keeping Your Plants Healthy

This part is all about taking care of your container plants to keep them healthy and growing strong. Like plants growing out in the garden, plants growing in pots need watering, fertilizing, and occasional pruning. But container-grown plants also require some specialized care, which we describe in detail here. To help prepare you for troublesome situations, you find details on managing diseases, insects, and animal pests.

Part V: Designing and Decorating

If you need some ideas and inspiration for your container gardens, look no further. In this part you find help in determining your garden style, a primer on color theory, and some thoughts on texture and form, as well as a handful of "recipes" for sure-fire container combinations. We finish off the section with special container plant opportunities, including cactuses and succulents, bonsai, and water gardens.

Part VI: The Part of Tens

If you think you can't garden, not because you have a black thumb, but because you're physically limited in some way, Chapter 21 dispels those thoughts. It offers ten ideas to make playing in the dirt possible. And if you think you do have a black thumb, Chapter 22 can help. This chapter has handy lists of the easiest plants, the most beautiful edibles, deer-resistant options, and more. It's a handy reference to turn to when you're choosing plants. And if after reading *Container Gardening For Dummies* your interest in plants has mushroomed, check out the appendix where we list some of our favorite resources for plants and information.

Icons Used in This Book

We've sprinkled icons in the margins of this book to draw your attention to important ideas. Here's what each one means:

This icon flags information that you ought to read carefully so that you retain it.

When we provide a tidbit of advice that will save you time, save you trouble, or help keep your plants healthy, we use this icon.

We use this icon to indicate that what we're about to say will save your life, or at least the life of your plant.

Where to Go from Here

Whatever level your gardening skill happens to be, feel free to skip around and look for ideas that match your needs and interests. If you're new to gardening, start with Part I to get a sense of what's involved in growing container plants and the ways your climate affects how, what, and when you grow.

If you want ideas on plants to try, check out Parts II and III. If you're unsure of what soil mix to use, flip to Chapter 4. If you've grown flowers in containers but want to try your hand at vegetables, jump to Chapter 8. You can wait until you see signs of pests and diseases before looking at Chapter 18 or read it ahead of time so you're prepared.

Finally, if you need some real-life inspiration, turn to the color section in the middle of the book to get an idea of how much you can do with container plants.

Part I
Getting Started with Container Gardening

The 5th Wave   By Rich Tennant

"I never meant it to be a planter. It just hadn't been washed in so long that stuff started growing out of it."

In this part . . .

So, how does *your* garden grow? If your response is a slightly wry, "In the ground, of course," you may want to hold that thought until we dig a little deeper into the possibilities. Your favorite plants — whether they promise you the pleasures of blooms, herbs, fruit, flowers, or other sensory delights — can take on fresh charm when displayed in containers. And better yet, your plants' new digs don't have to stay put; you can pick up and move your mobile gardens, for their benefit or yours.

This part opens the doors to exploration beyond the garden path and provides some of the nuts-and-bolts information you need to be a successful container gardener.

Chapter 1

Why Grow Plants in Containers?

*E*veryone has the time and the space to have a garden. No matter how busy you are or how small your yard — or even if you don't have a yard at all — you surely have room for a plant-filled container or two.

Container gardening is quickly becoming one of the most popular growing techniques. And it's not just for apartment dwellers with limited space. Even gardeners with room for an in-ground garden opt to grow some or all of their plants in pots.

If you're new to gardening, growing plants in containers is one of the easiest ways to get started. Place a potted geranium or two on the front stoop, grow some herbs in a pot by the kitchen door, or sow a few salad greens in a barrel planter — before you know it you'll be bitten by the container gardening bug.

Are you an experienced gardener? Growing plants in containers allows you to cultivate a larger selection of plants than you could in your garden. You can push hardiness limits, build a water garden in a pot, or, if you're ready for a real challenge, try your hand at bonsai.

Whatever your skill level and garden situation, we're here to help you grow terrific plants in containers. We show you how to match the right plants with the right pots and give them the kind of care that produces beautiful results. It's time to get growing!

Getting a Closer Look at Container Gardening

Containers bring plants up close and personal. You can choose the plant, the container, and the location. And when you put them all together, you can stand back and marvel at what you've created. But container gardening is more than just a pretty planter. Here are some of our favorite reasons to surround yourself with container gardens.

Expressing your creative side

Combining plants and pots brings the art of gardening to a whole new level. Need convincing? Check out the color photos in the center of this book and observe how the size, shape, color, and material of the containers complement the artful arrangements of plants within them. Containers can enhance plants by echoing colors, providing contrast, and drawing the eye to a focal point. Now, multiply that effect by combining several containers, and you have the makings of true horticultural art.

Containers are an easy and inexpensive way to dress up a drab house exterior — think window boxes, hanging baskets, and stately urns flanking the front door (see the color photos in the center of the book for an example of this). They can make your outdoor living spaces more inviting, decorate your deck for a party, and provide privacy.

Getting the ultimate in gardening convenience

More and more people are growing edibles (vegetables and herbs; see Chapter 8) in addition to flowers, and containers make it easy and convenient. Step over to your windowsill to snip a sprig or two of rosemary, basil, sage, or any other herb to liven up meals. Hang a basket filled with cherry tomatoes on the back porch for a quick, nutritious snack. Even if you have a full garden out back, consider adding planters filled with your favorite edibles or mixing in veggies and herbs with your ornamentals. Find out more about mixing plants in containers in Part V.

Extending the vegetable gardening season

Because containers sit above ground level and are exposed to the spring sunshine, the soil mix in them warms up faster than garden soil, letting you start planting earlier. There's no need to wait until garden soil dries out enough to rototill — you can sow cool-season crops like spinach and lettuce in containers weeks before you could plant them in the ground.

Containers also let you grow crops later into autumn. If an early light frost threatens, you can easily cover containers with old sheets or blankets. If a hard freeze or prolonged cold spell is predicted, you simply move containers to a protected location. When it warms up again, move the containers back into the sunshine. Early cold snaps are often followed by weeks of mild weather, so you can continue harvesting even after in-ground plants have succumbed to the cold. Chapter 2 has more details on climate considerations.

Taking your garden with you

If you've ever planted gardens at a rental property and then had to move away, you know how disappointing it can be to leave your favorite plants behind. In this era of high mobility and frequent moves, container gardening lets you bring your plants with you wherever you go. New, lightweight containers and wheeled dollies make moving plants easy. (In Chapter 17 you find techniques for moving large planters.)

Making gardening more accessible

Does the mere thought of spending an hour on your knees weeding make your back ache? Well, put those aches and pains behind you. Plants in containers are easier to reach and need little weeding and no tilling, raking, or hoeing.

Containers allow people with physical challenges to continue (or start) to enjoy all the benefits of gardening, including fresh air, exercise, healthy food, and beautiful flowers, plus the intangibles, like connecting with nature and nurturing the soul. Growing plants in containers is a great idea for all gardeners, but it's a must for gardeners with limited mobility. You can locate containers in convenient places, such as near doorways and water spigots or on porches and decks. Turn to Chapter 21 for more ways to use containers to make gardening more accessible.

So Many Choices! Knowing What to Grow

If you look around your neighborhood, you may think that you're limited to planting the same things your neighbors are growing in their gardens. But when you plant in containers, your plant options expand so much that you may be overwhelmed by the available choices.

Fortunately, there's an easy way to begin narrowing down your choices. Your first step is to consider what kind of commitment you want to make. Is a short-term relationship more your style, or do you want to devote your attention to a plant for several years?

Testing the waters with annual flowers and vegetables

Most people fill their containers with plants that grow for a single season; at the end of the season they toss the plants and start with fresh plants for the next round of growing. This is the easiest way to grow plants in containers because you don't have to worry about the temperature extremes that challenge many plants, especially in regions with cold winters. Fear not: Choosing this option doesn't mean you sacrifice anything. Some of the biggest, brightest, and longest-blooming flowers are ideal for single-season containers, as are most vegetables. For example, petunias, impatiens, beans, and tomatoes are grown as *annuals* and enjoyed for a single growing season. They require just a few months of commitment from you.

Promising to nurture and protect in summer and in winter

Permanent container plantings — those that last for a few years or longer — require more commitment from you, but they also reward you in ways single-season plants can't. If you want to pick peonies for bouquets or harvest peaches for pie, you need to think long-term. Plants for permanent plantings include perennials, trees, shrubs, fruits, and berries. Most plants in these categories adapt readily to growing in containers; the biggest challenge lies in helping them survive cold winter weather. Container-grown plants are more vulnerable to temperature extremes than plants growing in the ground, so you need to take steps to protect them. However, with some careful planning and diligence on your part, you can have that vase filled with peonies and plenty of peaches for pie.

Helping Your Container Plants Thrive

Caring for plants in containers has its ups and downs. On one hand, container gardening is easier than traditional gardening — you don't have to do any weeding; you can leave the heavy tools in the garage; you can pluck the plant out of the container and toss it in the compost pile at the end of its growing season.

But the catch is that plants in containers need a little more ongoing attention than plants in the ground. Container plants depend on you for their water and nutrients. They can't send their roots out beyond the container to find what they need to survive. The following sections take a closer look at some of the pros and cons of caring for plants in containers.

Meeting a plant's exacting requirements

Containers let you grow plants with very different requirements side by side because you can give individual plants the exact conditions that they need — conditions that may be impossible to achieve in your garden.

Consider azaleas and cactuses, for example. With containers, you can plant azaleas in acid soil and cactuses in sandy soil (see Chapter 4 for the dirt on soil). You can water azaleas abundantly and cactuses sparingly (see Chapter 15 when you're ready to wet your plant's whistle). You can relocate plants as necessary to provide optimum sunlight levels — part shade for azaleas, full sun for cactuses.

Container growing also improves the productivity of some vegetable crops. For example, northern gardeners often get a larger, earlier harvest of eggplants and peppers when they grow them in containers because the sun warms the soil, speeding the growth of these heat-loving plants.

Minimizing pesky pest problems

Garden soil often harbors microbes that cause plant diseases. For example, fusarium wilt and early blight are two soil-borne diseases that can infect tomato plants when raindrops splash soil onto plant foliage. By growing plants in sterile potting mix, you eliminate the source of these diseases (Chapter 4 talks about soil mixes).

Insects that pass from plant to plant in the garden are less likely to find potted plants up on a deck or porch. And when you discover a pest problem, you can isolate affected plants by moving their pots away from those of other plants until the problem is under control. Chapter 18 covers prevention and treatment of pests and diseases.

Facing the challenges of growing in containers

Something that we can't stress enough is that a container is not a natural place for a plant to grow. Because of this, container plants usually involve more of a time commitment than the same plants in the ground.

A plant growing in the ground develops an extensive network of roots to take in water and nutrients, and the ground insulates the roots from wide temperature swings. In a container, on the other hand, roots are confined, so the plants need a constant supply of water and nutrients. Plus, the soil mass in a container is small, so it heats up faster in the sun, chills down more quickly during cold spells, and dries out much sooner on a sunny day. (Flip to Chapter 2 for more insights on how climate influences container growing.)

A container garden may need daily tending, depending on the size and type of container, what's growing in it, and the weather. Plus, you may need to tackle a few chores that don't apply to in-ground plants — repotting plants and cleaning and preserving containers, for example. (Part IV is all about how to care for container plants.)

But overall, we think the extra effort is worth it, or we wouldn't be writing this book!

Matching Plant to Location

Some plants need full sun to thrive, but any place that has sufficient light to read by is a suitable location for some type of potted plant. The key is choosing the right plant for the spot. An open, sunny area on your patio calls for something dramatic, such as a fruit tree or big pot of petunias; indoors, the corner of your desk may be a perfect spot for a small philodendron or spider plant. The great thing about growing plants in containers is that you're not limited by climate, how much space you have, or the plants commonly available at most garden centers. Read on for details.

Growing plants in impossible places

Don't have yard space for a garden? Use containers, and you can grow plants anywhere — on a rooftop, a small condominium patio, the porch of a mobile home, or the deck of a houseboat.

Perhaps you want to grow tomatoes, but your entire yard is shaded except for one spot by the front porch. Pot up a few plants and you'll have your tomatoes and eat them, too.

Maybe you have acres of space for a garden, but the soil is rocky, or hard clay, or otherwise uninviting to plants. When you grow in containers, you choose the soil mix that best suits your plants' needs. (Find out more about soil in Chapter 4.)

Expanding your gardening palette with plants outside your hardiness zone

Containers let you grow a greater variety of plants than you ever thought possible. You can push the limits dictated by your hardiness zone because you can move plants to a protected area during winter, letting you grow oranges in Minneapolis and avocados in Vermont.

Fabulous figs, beautiful bougainvillea, luscious lemons and limes — the possibilities are endless, even in frosty climates, once you know how to protect plants from the cold. (In Chapter 2 you can read more about the challenges of climate and techniques to overwinter plants.)

Inviting nature into your indoor and outdoor living spaces

Shopping malls, office buildings, and urban parks are filled with plants for a reason: Plants make people happy! They're beautiful, they're fragrant, and they provide a subliminal connection with nature that both inspires and calms. (The color green is considered soothing — one explanation for the term *green room,* where actors wait before going on stage.)

Indoors, not only are houseplants decorative, but many also cleanse the air of toxins. Be bold! In addition to a few window plants, use a line of tall plants, such as bamboo or palms, as living screens between rooms. Use containers to reinforce your decorating style — minimalist, baroque, or country-casual. (Explore more possibilities in Chapter 14.)

Use container plants in the landscape to define outdoor "rooms" by creating a visual separation between areas with different uses (the grilling and eating areas, for example). Use containers to control traffic flow, to temporarily block unsightly views, or to define a private reading nook.

Designing with Container Plants

To whet your appetite for what's to come in this book, imagine a few of the following containers in your landscape. We give you the "recipes" for these and others in Chapter 19:

- ✔ **Nature's bounty:** Grow the tastiest and most nutritious fruits right on your deck or patio. Start by planting a dwarf peach tree in a wooden half barrel. Add three strawberry plants, and then dress it all up with a border of annual flowers. Sit back and enjoy luscious strawberries in spring, peaches in summer, and flowers all season long.

- ✔ **Shade-lover's delight:** Forget trying to get grass to grow under that big maple tree. Instead, plant a rustic planter box with shade-loving fuchsia, ferns, and impatiens. Then sit back in a comfy chair with a glass of lemonade and watch your neighbors mow their lawns.

- ✔ **Suspended animation:** Does your porch lack pizzazz? Fill a moss-lined wire basket to overflowing with trailing ivy, bright-faced pansies, sapphire lobelias, and wine-red geraniums. In just a few weeks, the basket will be blanketed with blooms, enticing passersby to stop and admire your creativity.

When you're ready for something different or more challenging, we offer ideas for specialty plants, like cactuses, holiday plants, water gardens, and bonsai, in Chapter 20. You can delight yourself and your friends with your newfound green thumb.

One Last Thing: Plant Names

Every plant has a two-part botanical name, identifying its genus and species. The botanical name always appears in italics with the genus name (which appears first) capitalized. For example, *Tagetes erecta* is the botanical name for American marigold. The genus name *(Tagetes)* refers to a group of closely related plants found in nature — all the marigolds. The species name *(erecta)* refers to a specific member of the genus — such as the tall, orange-flowered American marigold. (The term *species* is shorthand for *specific epithet*, which may help you remember that it refers to a specific plant within a *genus,* or general group.)

Of course, most plants also have common names. But common names can vary from place to place and from time to time. *Nemophila menziesii* will always be the botanical name for the same plant, no matter where in the world you find it. But when it comes to this plant's common name, some people call it California bluebell, while others know it as baby blue eyes. To add to this confusion, different plants may share the same common name. For example, various kinds of butterfly flowers exist, in addition to butterfly bush and butterfly weed. Sometimes, the common name is the genus name. For example, the botanical name for the petunia is *Petunia hybrida*.

Some specialized plants have an additional name tacked on to their botanical names, which indicates that it is a variety or cultivar (cultivated variety) of that species. A variety or cultivar differs from the species in some particular way, such as flower color. For example, *Tagetes erecta* Snowbird is a white-flowered variety of the tall American marigold.

Once a genus name has been mentioned, it is sometimes abbreviated to its first letter. For example, if you see the names *Tagetes erecta* and *T. patula,* it's implied that the *T.* stands for *Tagetes.*

You can see why people who want to be precise stick to botanical names, but for most of us and for most of the time, common names work fine. However, there are times when it pays to double-check — such as when you're talking about salvias and sages (see the sidebar on salvia for more info).

Salvia: One genus, many species

The genus *Salvia* includes a remarkable number of plants with very different characteristics, although all have similar flower spikes topped with asymmetrical flowers, and many have fragrant foliage.

Annual salvia *(Salvia splendens)* is widely grown in beds and containers and produces abundant spikes of large, colorful flowers in shades of red, purple, and white. Although perennial in tropical regions, it's most often sold as an annual.

Common sage, the herb essential to Thanksgiving stuffing, is *Salvia officinalis.*

Meadow sage *(Salvia nemorosa)* is a popular perennial that is hardy to zone 4.

Pineapple sage *(Salvia elegans)* is a tender perennial with fragrant foliage that really does smell like fresh pineapple when you rub it. Although it has striking, brilliant red flowers, they're not as abundant as those of *S. splendens*; instead, *S. elegans* is grown for its fragrant foliage.

Autumn sage *(Salvia greggii),* scarlet sage *(S. coccinea),* Mexican sage *(S. mexicana* and *S. leucantha),* mealycup sage *(S. farinacea),* anise-scented sage *(S. guaranitica),* and clary sage *(S. scalerea)* are other relatively common salvias with varying degrees of hardiness.

Chapter 2

Considering Climate

. . . .

In This Chapter

▶ Understanding the impact of climate, for hotter or colder

▶ Discovering why container plants are vulnerable to extremes

▶ Considering winter survival tactics for permanent plants

▶ Zooming in on microclimatic conditions

. . . .

Most gardeners grow *single-season* container plants, and if you're new to container growing, this is a good place to start. You plant them in the spring, enjoy them all summer (a single growing season), and discard them in the fall. Then you start with fresh plants the following spring — eliminating the need to overwinter plants. Annual flowers and most vegetables and herbs are ideal for single-season planting.

Permanent plantings, on the other hand, are those that keep growing year after year. Perennials, shrubs, and trees fall into this category. While many adapt to growing in containers, they can pose challenges in cold-climate regions. You need to be aware of each plant's tolerance to cold temperatures.

Whether you're growing single-season or permanent plantings, it's important to match the plants to your garden's *microclimate* — conditions that are unique to your container's precise location in your yard. The degree of sun or shade, the amount of wind, the slope of the terrain, and reflected heat all affect plant growth. Take the time to evaluate your landscape's microclimates *before* choosing plants.

This chapter explains how your region's climate influences what plants you can grow and helps you understand how your yard's microclimates may affect your container plants.

Cluing In to Climate

The degree that climate plays a role in container gardening depends on what you're growing and when you're growing it. If you're growing single-season containers to enjoy in summer and discard in the fall, you don't need to worry about winter's chill. However, you still need to know when the weather has warmed up enough in spring so it's safe to set out tender plants that can't tolerate frost.

If your containers are filled with permanent plants — perennials, trees, and shrubs — then you need to tune in more carefully to your region's climate. In most cases, winter temperatures are the deciding factor in what will survive in your climate. Intense summer heat can also play a role in your plants' ability to thrive.

Growing plants in containers allows you to grow plants that otherwise may not survive in your climate, as long as you're willing to take steps to protect them from temperature extremes — like moving containers to protected spots.

The following sections won't turn you into an amateur meteorologist, but after reading them, you'll have a better understanding of how climate — specifically, hot and cold temps — affects plants, and you'll know where to turn for more information about the climate in your neck of the woods.

Caring about climate's effect on container plants

Container plants are more vulnerable to extreme temperatures (especially the cold) than the same type of plant growing in the ground. Even plants that most of us think of as hardy — pine trees, for example, because they thrive when planted in the ground — may not survive really cold winters in containers.

In many cases, plant roots aren't as hardy as the upper growth, and they don't need to be. Although the ground may freeze down a few inches or even a few feet, it doesn't reach the extreme cold of the air temperature. A few inches down, the soil temperature may drop into the 20s (degrees Fahrenheit), but it rarely gets colder than that because of the soil's residual heat, its insulating qualities, and its sheer mass — even if the air temperature is below zero for an extended time.

The soil in containers, on the other hand, freezes solid when exposed to prolonged freezing temperatures and, because of its limited mass, it may get nearly as cold as the air temperature. Plant roots that can withstand the 20-degree temperature of garden soil may be killed in containers where the soil gets colder than that. And in most of the country, winter temperatures regularly drop below 20 degrees.

Temperatures that alternate between freezing and thawing pose another challenge. On sunny, mild winter days the soil in containers may thaw. Then, during the next cold snap the soil freezes again, and, as it expands, it can push plants up out of the soil. Gardeners refer to this as *heaving*. Soil thawing during a warm spell can also entice roots to break dormancy too early. The new roots and tender top growth freeze when the weather chills again.

Plants in containers are also more vulnerable to extreme heat than plants growing in the ground. The soil in containers heats up more, and this heat can damage roots. Black plastic and metal containers absorb heat and provide little insulation; they're fine for use in shady spots but avoid them in sites with full sun, especially in regions with very hot summers. Wood, terra-cotta, and resin containers offer more protection from heat, especially if they're white or a light color. Containers placed on surfaces that reflect heat, such as pavement, are also more prone to overheating. You may need to move containers out of full sun during spells of extreme heat, and you'll definitely want to keep an extra close eye on soil moisture so plants don't dry out.

Factoring frost dates into your growing season

Knowing the frost dates for your region is kind of like peering into a horticultural crystal ball. The term *frost dates* is shorthand for the *average last spring frost date* and *average first fall frost date* for your locale. These dates are based on decades of weather data, but keep in mind they're just averages. Your actual last spring frost or first fall frost may occur days (or even weeks) before or after the average.

When you're growing frost-tender plants, including many annual flowers and vegetables, it's important to know your region's average last spring frost date because it dictates when you can set out most plants. In a place like North Dakota, the average last spring frost may be as late as June; in Georgia, it could be as early as February.

Knowing your region's frost dates is helpful even if you're growing hardy plants (more on hardiness in the next section). For example, if you move your containers to a sheltered place for the winter, the plants may begin sprouting earlier in spring than they would have had they wintered outdoors. Then, if you bring the plants outdoors before the last spring frost date the chances are good that the new growth will be nipped by frost. To be on the safe side, if overwintering plants have begun to sprout in their sheltered location, wait until after the last frost date to bring them outdoors.

Knowing the date of the average first fall frost is helpful, too, so you can be ready if you plan to move tender plants to a sheltered place. A gardening neighbor or your Cooperative Extension service can provide this information, or you can consult the maps on this National Climatic Data Web page: www.ncdc.noaa.gov/oa/climate/freezefrost/frostfreemaps.html.

Protecting plants from a chill

Experienced gardeners keep a close eye on the weather, especially in spring and fall when cold snaps can threaten warm-season plants. If temperatures are predicted to drop into the 40s, take measures to protect your plants.

Move small containers into a garage or enclosed porch, where temperatures stay a few degrees warmer than outdoors. Move them back out when the threat has passed.

Cover large planters with old sheets, row covers, cardboard boxes, or anything else that will hold in the heat. Use stakes to prop up the covers to avoid breaking stems on delicate plants. If frost is predicted, cover plants in late afternoon before the temperature drops. Extend the covering all the way to the ground, and secure it around the base of the container to help hold in the heat. Remove covers the next morning once temperatures warm up to the 50s.

Growing plants in containers allows you to take some liberties. You can plant before the last frost date in the spring (or keep them out for a few more nice days in the fall) if you can move them under cover when you expect cold nights.

Getting a handle on hardiness

If you're growing annual flowers and other single-season plants, you don't need to worry about winter hardiness because the plants won't be overwintering. However, if you're growing perennials, trees, and shrubs in permanent plantings, you'll want to choose plants that are adapted to your climate. Although all kinds of conditions determine what plants can grow in a certain region's climate, how cold it gets — rather than the heat or humidity — is usually the key consideration.

All plants are able to tolerate cold to a certain degree. Below that minimum temperature, a plant's tissues are damaged or destroyed; if cold temperatures are prolonged, the plant may die. A plant's ability to withstand a certain minimum temperature is called its *hardiness* (a fuchsia, for instance, is said to be hardy to 28 degrees Fahrenheit). Most seed packets and plant tags provide hardiness information.

The United States Department of Agriculture (USDA) publishes maps showing plant hardiness zones. The zone boundaries are based on one factor: the average winter minimum temperatures collected from 125,000 weather stations. North America is divided into 11 zones, the warmest (zone 11) having an average winter minimum temperature above 40 degrees Fahrenheit. Each succeeding zone, from zone 10 to zone 1, averages 10 degrees colder. Zones 1 through 10 are further divided into *a* and *b* in order to distinguish zones where average winter minimum temperatures differ by 5 degrees. Check out the map in Figure 2-1.

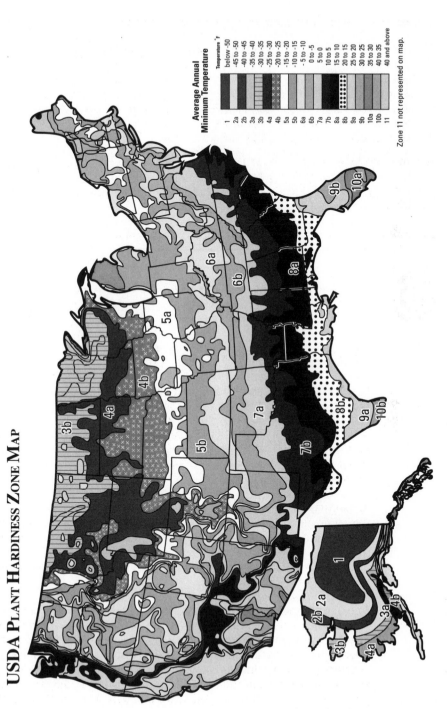

Figure 2-1:
The USDA
Plant
Hardiness
Zone Map
indicates
each zone's
average
winter
minimum
temperature.

USDA PLANT HARDINESS ZONE MAP

Average Annual
Minimum Temperature

Temperature °F	
1	below -50
2a	-45 to -50
2b	-40 to -45
3a	-35 to -40
3b	-30 to -35
4a	-25 to -30
4b	-20 to -25
5a	-15 to -20
5b	-10 to -15
6a	- 5 to -10
6b	0 to -5
7a	5 to 0
7b	10 to 5
8a	15 to 10
8b	20 to 15
9a	25 to 20
9b	30 to 25
10a	35 to 30
10b	40 to 35
11	40 and above

Zone 11 not represented on map.

When the heat is on: Heat tolerance

The USDA hardiness zone recommendations are handy, but in regions with long, hot summers, heat tolerance is often just as important in determining whether plants will thrive. The American Horticultural Society developed the AHS Heat Zone Map to help gardeners in warm climates choose plants. The map divides the United States into 12 zones based on the average number of *heat days* each year, which they define as days that reach 86 degrees Fahrenheit or higher. The lower the zone number, the fewer the heat days — zone 1 averages less than 1 heat day per year, while zone 12 gets more than 210. If you live in a hot climate you may want to research the heat tolerance of the plants you plan to grow. To be on the safe side, choose plants that are somewhat more heat tolerant than your climate dictates.

You can download the AHS Heat Zone Map at www.ahs.org/publications/heat_zone_map.htm.

You can view a color version of the USDA Hardiness map online at www.usna.usda.gov/Hardzone/ushzmap.html, as well as get a closer look at the hardiness zone that covers your region of the country.

Any attempt to divide all of North America into zones is bound to have limitations, and the hardiness map is no exception. Individual plant hardiness can vary depending on growing conditions and climate factors in addition to winter cold. But the hardiness map is a good starting point. Zone systems based on average minimum temperatures are also available for western Europe, South Africa, Australia, New Zealand, Japan, and China.

Plants mentioned in this book are identified by climate zone according to the lowest winter temperatures that they can withstand — when growing in the ground, that is. For example, a tree recommended as hardy for USDA zone 5 can reliably grow in that zone and milder ones (higher numbers) — areas where temperatures do not fall below –20 degrees Fahrenheit. As you read elsewhere and often in this book, these hardiness zone recommendations need to be interpreted differently for plants in containers because they're more affected by temperature extremes. See the previous section "Caring about climate's effect on container plants" for details on why this is so.

When it comes to cold hardiness, a rule of thumb is to subtract one or two hardiness zones for plants growing in containers. For example, figure that if you live in zone 6, you should choose plants that are hardy to zones 4 or 5. If you live in zone 8, look for plants hardy to zones 6 or 7. Of course, this advice changes if you're willing and able to move container plants into a sheltered spot or otherwise provide protection during cold weather.

Gardeners in zones 4 and colder should plan to provide winter protection for all of their container plants because even the most cold-hardy plants may not survive extreme winters if left unprotected. Chapter 10 has more details on how to protect container plants over the winter.

In regions with mild winters, like Southern California and Florida, gardeners can plant cool-season annual flowers and vegetables in fall and enjoy them into winter — more on that in Chapters 7 and 8.

Determining Your Garden's Microclimate

In addition to the overall climate, your own outdoor spaces have particular conditions that you need to take into account when planning to grow container plants. Factors like the amount of sun and wind, the location on a slope, and whether there's reflected heat combine to create conditions at a particular spot that differ from those in the rest of your landscape. These localized conditions are called *microclimates*. We cover factors that influence microclimate in the following sections.

Portability expands the climate tolerance of container plants. You can bring them indoors for protection from the cold, move them into more sun if they're not getting enough, or move them into a shadier spot if they're getting sunburned.

Shedding a little light on sun and shade

Plants have natural attributes that cause them to perform better in different amounts of sunlight. Think about a plant's native habitat. What's the best garden location for a vine that's native to the jungle? One that provides some protection from the sun, like the shade it gets in nature from a high canopy of trees. Give the plant too much sun and it burns like a fair-skinned redhead on the beach in Cancun. Conversely, think about a plant with a sunny habitat. Zinnias, originally from Mexico, thrive in full sun. In too much shade, they grow spindly and develop mildew on their leaves.

Light conditions are classified as shade, part sun, or sun. Plants growing in different locations are exposed to different amounts of sunlight, depending on their orientation with respect to houses, hillsides, and other man-made and natural structures. The exposure of the plant's location generally determines its light conditions:

✔ **A northern exposure** probably is blocked from the sun all day. This is *full shade*.

✔ **An eastern exposure,** unless it's blocked by trees or buildings, receives sun in the morning and shade for the rest of the day. This is a typical *part sun* (or *part shade*) exposure. The same goes for an area that receives dappled shade, such as the space under a tree with a high or thin canopy.

✔ **A southern exposure** gets the most hours of sun. This is *full sun,* and it's usually defined as at least six hours of sunlight during the middle of a summer day. Most annuals and vegetables do best in full sun.

✔ **A western exposure** may get shade in the morning and full sun in the afternoon — this is usually considered a *sunny* location because of the intensity of the light. Shade plants will probably cook in this location.

Definitions of sun and shade also depend on your climate. Near the coast, where it's cool and often overcast, plants described as preferring part sun may do better in a full sun location, and plants that normally love shade may flourish in full sun. The converse is true, too. Plants growing in hot, sunny climates may need more shade than those same types of plants growing in cool climates.

Note how the shadows change throughout the growing season. An area that was full sun in June may be in part shade by August because the sun is lower in the sky and nearby trees, buildings, or structures may block it. However, one of the great things about containers is their portability. Move a full-sun-loving container into a brighter location whenever you notice shadows blocking the light.

Pay attention to the sun/shade requirements specified for each plant, and watch plants for responses after planting. A sign of too much sun is white or light brown, burned spots on the leaves. Giveaways for too much shade are spindly foliage growth and weak blooming. If you notice those signs, move the container or experiment with different plants next time.

Watching out for wind

What about wind exposure? Wind can dry out the soil quickly and rob plants of moisture. Stiff breezes can topple tall plants and break brittle ones.

If you're placing containers in a windy spot, be sure they're made from a heavy material like clay, use a soil-based planting mix to add even more weight, and choose short plants that are less likely to be blown over. (See Chapter 3 for advice on choosing containers and Chapter 4 for information on soil mixes.)

Surveying slope

Hilly terrain can affect weather conditions. You may find that a sunny hillside garden is several degrees warmer than a neighbor's garden at the bottom of the hill. Low spots collect cold air and can be decidedly chillier than nearby sloping spots. Hilltops, on the other hand, are often windy. If you live on a slope, put frost-tender annuals and marginally hardy perennials midslope, rather than at the top or bottom of a hill.

Recognizing reflected heat

Paving, house walls, and other reflective surfaces can warm up a garden. These warming effects may be positive if you're growing marginally hardy plants or you're growing full sun plants in a part shade location. However, they can cause problems when reflected heat burns up plants, as can happen to plants placed around a swimming pool. Even sun lovers like cactuses can be burned by reflected light.

Chapter 3

Choosing a Pot to Plant In

Among the joys of gardening is the opportunity to express your creativity, and container gardening doubles the pleasure because you get to choose both plants and pots. As container gardening has increased in popularity, so has the variety of shapes, sizes, colors, and materials available among containers. Add to that the abundant opportunities for homemade and improvised pots, and the possibilities are endless.

However, keeping in mind the needs of the plants is vital. In this chapter you find lots of info about the benefits and challenges of growing plants in different types of containers.

Selecting from All Sorts of Materials

Containers are available in a wide variety of materials, and you can add to your options by making your own pots or repurposing other household items for use as containers. As you consider pots, keep three key factors in mind: drainage, porosity, and weight:

✔ **Drainage:** For healthy plant growth, roots need oxygen, and that means that excess water in the soil must be able to drain properly. No matter what container you choose, be sure it has drainage holes. And keep in mind when you're displaying plants that the drainage holes can't be blocked. (Flip to Chapter 15 for more on water and drainage.)

- ✔ **Porosity:** Porous materials allow moisture and air to pass through them. Pots made of unglazed terra cotta, wood, peat, and paper pulp are relatively porous. Plants in these containers dry out faster than those in nonporous containers, which means you have to water them more often. The upside is that porous containers "breathe," allowing air to reach plant roots. Plus, as soil moisture evaporates through the sides, it cools the soil and helps draw away any excess water.

- ✔ **Weight:** It's easy to forget just how heavy moist soil can be. Combine that with a heavy container, and you may find yourself with a potted plant that's impossible to move. Container materials vary widely in weight, so if mobility is important to you, choose lightweight materials or plan to place containers on casters before planting. On the other hand, a heavy pot is desirable for top-heavy plants or windy sites, to keep plants from toppling.

In the following sections, we discuss materials that are commonly used for containers, along with their strengths and weaknesses.

Your basic clay pot

Clay pots are probably what you think of when someone says "flower pot." Clay pots range in size from teeny-tiny to huge. The bigger they are, the heavier they are, and all clay pots are breakable. They come in two varieties: unglazed and glazed. (You can find color photos of both in the color pages in the middle of this book.)

Remember that in cold climates, terra-cotta and glazed clay pots can crack when moist soil freezes and expands inside them. Empty containers before storing them for the winter.

Terra cotta or unglazed clay

Picture a flower pot, and you probably see a plain clay container — the kind Peter Rabbit tipped over while he was sneaking into Mr. McGregor's garden. Terra-cotta ("baked earth" in Italian) pots are usually reddish-orange in color but are available in other colors as well, including tan, cream, black, and chocolate brown. The pots lack a decorative, waterproof glaze. If you're unsure whether a pot is glazed, moisten the surface — if the pot is unglazed, it will absorb water and the surface will darken.

Terra-cotta pots generally offer good value for the money. Their earthy colors and natural surface make them look comfortable in almost any garden situation, from rustic to formal. Unglazed clay's porosity allows plant roots to breathe and excess moisture to evaporate — desirable traits for many plants. However, porosity also means that the soil dries out quickly.

If you like the look of aged, moss-covered, terra-cotta pots, here's a trick to accelerate the aging process. Take a handful of moss from your yard (or someone else's, with permission), remove as much soil as possible, tear it into small pieces, and mix it with some buttermilk. Use a paintbrush to apply the resulting slurry to the sides of an unglazed terra-cotta pot. Place moist soil in it (with a plant if you like) and place it in a shady spot, watering as often as necessary to keep the soil damp. Moisture will seep through the sides of the pot, encouraging the moss in the slurry to colonize the damp clay surface.

Glazed clay

Glazed clay pots are fired with a glass-like coating that makes them waterproof. They're available in just about every color and shape imaginable, so they offer endless opportunities for creatively mixing and matching plants and containers. Glazed pots are waterproof, so they hold moisture better than unglazed ones.

Wouldn't a wood container be wonderful?

Recycled oak whiskey half-barrels are popular planters, although wooden containers made specifically for garden purposes are becoming more common. Most are made of rot-resistant redwood and cedar. Their appearance is usually rustic, making them at home on decks and in other informal places, although fancier designs are available. Wood containers provide good soil insulation, helping to keep roots cool. How well they hold water depends on the type and thickness of the wood, as well as how tight the joints are. Thicker lumber — at least ⅞ inch — is better. Container bottoms may rot if they stay too moist, so these pots need to be raised at least an inch off the ground with stands or saucers, as we describe later in this chapter.

Wood containers are heavy, relatively unbreakable, and stand up well to cold weather (though emptying them each winter in cold climates is still a good idea). If the sides leak water and cause the soil to dry out too quickly, you can line the pots by stapling heavy plastic on the inside. Just be sure to punch drainage holes in the bottom to match the ones in the container.

Avoid growing edibles in containers made from pressure-treated wood. The old chromated copper arsenate (CCA) type contains arsenic, a poison which has been shown to leach into soil. This type is no longer sold, but it's still around. The new pressure-treated wood uses copper compounds as a preservative, which is considered safe. But I recommend erring on the side of caution and avoiding pressure-treated wood altogether.

Cachepots: Gardening's quick-change artists

Hide an ordinary-looking container in a fancy outer pot, and — voilà — you've got a cachepot. A fancy word for a simple idea, cachepots can save you money and let you display your best-looking plants. Here's how: Grow a variety of flowers in inexpensive plastic pots. As each plant comes into peak bloom, display it in your fancy cachepot. When it begins to flag, swap in another plant. Just be sure the plastic pots fit comfortably in the decorative pot so you can easily swap them in and out.

Cachepots also let you display plants in less-than-ideal settings. For example, say you have a beautiful container in a shady spot and you want to grow sun-loving petunias in it. Have two or three individually potted petunia plants and keep one in the cachepot for a week or two before moving it back into the sun and swapping in another plant.

Some cachepots lack drainage holes, so they can be used on surfaces that may be damaged by water. In this case, add a layer of pebbles in the bottom to catch excess water as it drains from the plant, and empty any water that accumulates in the cachepot frequently.

Decorative containers such as woven baskets that can't withstand constant moisture or aren't tight enough to hold soil are also good candidates for using as cachepots.

Picking from a plethora of plastic pots

In addition to the plain-looking, green and black nursery pots, plastic containers are now available in a wide range of styles and colors. Some are made to resemble clay pots and do a good job of this, at least from a distance. However, plastic won't develop the attractive patina of weathered clay.

Plastic is easier to clean and lighter in weight than clay. It's also nonporous and doesn't dry out as quickly. Avoid cheap, poor-quality plastic pots, which can fade in the sun and become brittle.

 Some plastic pots, like the one shown in Figure 3-1, can help you with your watering chores. These self-watering containers contain a hidden reservoir that you fill with water, and a delivery system makes it available to plants. Most often, there's a wick that draws moisture up into dry soil. The self-watering feature is most helpful for smaller pots that might otherwise need daily or twice-daily watering. Self-watering containers can be made out of other materials as well, but be careful if yours is lightweight plastic: If the reservoir in the bottom of the pot gets too low, plants can become top-heavy and tip over. You can also purchase inserts that turn a regular pot into a self-watering one, or you can create your own self-watering system, as we explain in Chapter 15.

The imposters: Fiberglass, polypropylene, and resin

Fiberglass, polypropylene, and resin are synthetic materials that are usually made to look like terra cotta, clay, or wood. They're long-lasting, lightweight, and waterproof. Some types feel like heavy-duty Styrofoam and are easily dinged and dented. Others have a harder shell and stand up to reasonable abuse. If you pick up a container and it weighs much less than you expected, it's probably made of one of these materials.

Fabulous fabric pots

Some of the newest and most ingenious containers on the market are made of fabric. Offering the ultimate in portability, these small fabric containers have handles for easy carrying and fold flat when not in use. They're constructed from heavy-duty fabric, usually rot-proof polypropylene, and have drainage holes in the sides and bottom. You can also get long, compost-filled tubes that you can arrange in different shapes in your garden. You simply cut holes in the top where you want to plant. Check out the color photos in the middle of this book for a look at a fabric planting bag and a compost-filled fabric tube.

Making your own planter from scratch

Use hypertufa to make your own lightweight, faux stone trough planter. Hypertufa is a mixture of cement, sand, and peat moss that you can mold into various shapes. It's commonly used to create shallow planters that resemble old, weathered stone troughs. Here's what you need and instructions for constructing this easy-to-make container:

1 bag of Portland cement

1 bag of coarse sand

1 bag of peat moss

2 rectangular cardboard boxes (The boxes will make up the mold. One box should fit inside the other with a 2-inch or larger gap in dimension — you'll be filling the gap between the two boxes with the hypertufa mixture.)

Note: *Wear gloves and a dust mask when working with dry Portland cement.*

1. Place equal parts cement and sand in a wheelbarrow. (For a small planter, start with a half-gallon of each, using a half-gallon milk jug with the top cut off to measure.) Then add two parts peat moss. Mix these materials, and then add water until you get a stiff "dough."

2. Place 2 inches of the mix in the bottom of the larger box. Then place the smaller box inside the larger box, centering it so the gap is even all around. Begin filling in the space between the sides of the boxes with the mix, packing firmly as you go. Fill it as high as you want your planter to end up. (If this is your first effort you may want to start with a planter that's no more than 8 inches deep.) When you're done, place the box in a dry spot.

3. After two weeks, pull a corner of the inner box away to determine whether the trough is hard and dry. If so, fold the box inward and pull it out.

4. Cut or peel away the outer box carefully, taking care to avoid damaging the walls. Moisten stubborn pieces and then remove them. Smooth sharp corners with a wire brush. If you like, add texture to the sides by brushing the surface so that it mimics weathered stone.

Containing plants in cast concrete

Whether you purchase concrete planters or make your own, you'll find them to be durable, heavy, and cold-resistant. They can be simple troughs or ornate urns, and you can dye the mix before molding them or paint them when they're done. Ready-made concrete containers may closely resemble natural stone.

Making a statement with metal

Metal is a favorite choice for antique and Asian planters. Look for brass, copper, iron, aluminum, and other metal containers at boutiques and antique shops. Metal containers can get very hot in full sun, so you may want to consider using them as decorative cachepots to prevent the soil from touching the hot metal. Metal containers that don't have drainage holes also function well as cachepots.

Sowing seeds in biodegradable pots

Many gardeners use purchased plastic six-packs or flats made just for start-ing seeds, but biodegradable pots are even better, especially for plants with sensitive roots, like lupines. Biodegradable pots made from peat, coconut fiber, and compressed paper pulp are designed to be planted, pot and all, in the ground or in a larger container. The roots grow through the sides, the pot decomposes, and root disturbance is minimized.

Reaping the benefits of raised beds

Elevated planting beds made with lumber, brick, or other materials may be considered a form of container. Gardeners use raised beds for a variety of reasons. Made from attractive materials, raised beds can be decorative and add height and interest to a flat landscape. Raised beds also dry out and warm up faster in spring, allowing for earlier planting. And if garden soil is rocky, thin, or of poor quality, raised beds can be filled with purchased top-soil. Although raised beds aren't the focus of this book, much of the informa-tion applies. (Flip to the middle of this book to see a photo of a raised bed.)

Using a Container with the Right Size and Shape

When choosing containers, keep two things in mind: what's good for the plant and what looks good. A pot that's too small for a plant crowds its roots, cutting off moisture, oxygen, and nutrients that are vital for healthy growth. If a pot is too big, the superfluous soil may stay too wet and can smother the roots. Very shallow containers inhibit root growth; containers in odd sha may make repotting a challenge.

Rules regarding what constitutes the ideal container size differ a season and permanent plants. Single-season, ornamental plan and bulbs can be crowded together more closely than pla ground, providing much more impact quickly. They ca conditions forever, but you can satisfy their tight-q water and food for the short duration of a single

As a rule for spacing plants, figure that if planting is 10 to 12 inches, container (You can find more advice on spa Part II.) As a general rule of sca tall, provide a pot with a di plants grow 2 or 3 fe

The tall and short of it

It may be counterintuitive, but technically speaking, for a given diameter, the taller the pot, the better the drainage. To some extent, water drains through soil in relation to the height of the soil column. In effect, the weight of the soil pushes the water through the soil. Practically speaking, however, a shallow container has more of its surface area exposed to sunlight and therefore dries faster than a deeper one of the same volume.

For permanent plants like fruit trees, conifers, and perennial flowers, think longer term and choose a pot that looks in scale with the plant when you buy it and allows room for a year or two of root growth. As a rule, when buying a nursery plant, transplant it to a container that is 2 inches deeper and wider than its nursery container. Refer to Part III for more detailed guidelines.

If you live in a region with cold winters, take that into consideration when choosing containers because you may need to move plants into a protected place. Refer to Chapter 10 for more on overwintering plants.

The following se_____ _____ features of common styles of pots.

_____ld standby

_____ra-cotta pots with rims or plastic ver-
_____y are wide, allowing the roots to grow
_____to slip out more readily for repotting.

_____e, sometimes called azalea or fern
_____be used for shallow-rooted plants —

_____e even shallower — not much
_____planting bulbs in such a small
_____ts, need little soil, and are
_____her drought-tolerant plants are
_____heck out the sidebar "The tall
_____ container depth affects soil

Strawberry jars (also known as pocket planters)

Strawberry jars, sometimes called pocket planters, can be spotted at many nurseries and garden centers. They're tall pots with "pockets" scooped out of the sides all the way around at different levels. Originally designed to hold strawberry plants, they work for other types of plants, too. Traditionally made from terra cotta, these planters are now available in other materials.

Create a striking display by planting the top and each pocket with annual flowers — when the growth fills in, the entire planter will be covered with foliage and blooms. Plant each pocket with a different herb, and you'll be ready for any culinary creation. For details on how to plant these pots, turn to Chapter 5.

Perhaps you yearn for an urn

Urns are typically made of solid, one-piece construction with a base, pedestal, and decorated bowl. You'll find them made from various materials. Urns are available with lots of decorative touches and finishes in all kinds of styles. Sizes range from table-top miniatures to massive estate planters. For the best results, choose a deep urn that offers ample space for roots. You can check out a photo of two urns flanking a front door in the color section in the middle of this book.

Urns are usually tall and potentially top-heavy, which makes them prone to toppling. Choose heavy ones or plan to carefully secure them to prevent a mishap.

Improvised containers: Choosing the unusual

All kinds of things can be and have been made into containers for plants: retired wooden and metal wheelbarrows, old canisters, watering cans, bathtubs, well-loved but retired garden boots. The sky's the limit: Just make sure that the improvised container has proper drainage holes and room for roots to grow.

Where to find potential containers? Try thrift stores, farm supply stores, barn sales, garage sales, antique shops, your grandmother's toolshed, or estate sales. The key is to keep your eyes open and get the word out among friends and fellow gardeners who may run into exactly what you're looking for. Figure 3-2 shows some interesting improvisations.

Figure 3-2:
You can turn all kinds of stuff into containers for plants.

Choosing a Container for a Specific Spot

Plants don't have to be ground-bound. You can also think vertically when it comes to container gardening. You can create a delightful display by planting a trailing plant in a container that's placed a few feet off the ground. The following sections give you some options for containers that are suited to these higher-up locations.

Keeping plants in suspense: Hanging baskets

Among the most popular and versatile types of containers, hanging baskets liven up porches, bring plants to eye level, and in some cases make use of the only available gardening space. For the sake of lightness, hanging baskets are usually made of plastic or moss-lined wire. Before choosing baskets, evaluate where you'll be hanging them to ensure that the site can accommodate them. Can you attach strong, screw-in hooks? Is the wood solid and in good shape?

You can choose from the following types of baskets:

- **Plastic baskets:** The most common type, plastic pots are lightweight. The pots have drainage holes and may or may not include an attached saucer. Small baskets dry out quickly in full sun, so choose the largest basket your situation permits.

- **Self-watering baskets:** These pots are usually plastic with a built-in reservoir. Water drains into the reservoir and is drawn up into the soil as it dries out — great for baskets that you can't water daily.

- **Traditional wire baskets:** Typically made of galvanized or plastic-coated metal, these baskets are available in a variety of shapes and sizes. They're typically lined with sphagnum moss or coconut fiber; some may include a plastic liner to keep them from drying out so quickly. The open-frame style enables you to plant through the sides so that plants can cover the entire basket.

Refer to Chapter 5 for details on how to plant hanging baskets.

The latest twist on hanging baskets is the upside-down planter. The subject of countless late-night infomercials, upside-down planters boast all sorts of miraculous benefits, some of which are actually true. Usually sold for growing tomatoes, they're really just modified hanging baskets (most are wire cages lined with heavy plastic sheeting) with a hole in the bottom. You set the plant in from the bottom, fill the container with soil, and hang it up. Tomato plants grown upside-down don't need staking, caging, or weeding, and because they're growing in midair, they're less likely to contract soil-borne diseases. Flip to the middle of this book for a photo of an upside-down planter.

Taking a look-see: Window boxes

Picture a traditional farmhouse with window boxes overflowing with petunias and geraniums, and you can see the appeal of these containers. Like hanging baskets, window boxes like the one pictured in Figure 3-3 provide additional garden space and dress up living spaces both indoors and out. Plant your window boxes with fragrant flowers and as the breeze wafts in through the open window, it'll perfume the room. Window boxes also add curb appeal and break up visually drab home exteriors. In addition to installing them beneath windows, you can attach the boxes to porch and deck rails.

Because the planters are narrow and have limited space for soil, window boxes tend to dry out quickly. Traditional wooden boxes look beautiful but tend to leak water, so line them with plastic, poking a few drainage holes before planting. Or, look for self-watering types to help with watering chores.

Figure 3-3:
Window
boxes can
dress up the
exterior of
any home.

It's easiest to attach window boxes before planting them, because they're lighter and more easily maneuvered into place.

Trailing over a railing

Designed with flanges that fit securely over standard deck rails, these planters make it even easier to dress up your home's exterior. Simply drop them in place over the rail and plant away! There's no need for drilling holes or using screws, so there's no damage to deck rails. These planters are also easy to remove to a sheltered location if bad weather threatens, and easy to take down at the end of the season. Most railing planters are made from plastic; look for self-watering types because these planters can dry out quickly, especially if they're on a sunny, breezy deck. (Flip to the middle of this book for a photo of a railing planter in action.)

Well, hang it! Wall-mounted pots

Perfect for flanking a doorway or dressing up a fence, most wall-mounted pots are flat on one side. Planted with colorful annual flowers, they bring beauty and scent right up to eye level. The most common types are plastic and moss-lined wire.

Green roofs

Picture dozens of living walls mounted on a roof, and you'll get a good image of what a green roof looks like. Sometimes called *living roofs,* green roofs are becoming popular in urban areas to capture rainwater and to insulate buildings to reduce heating and cooling costs. Most green roofs start with a watertight membrane topped with a soil-less planting medium. Small, drought-tolerant, low-maintenance plants like sedum are planted to cover all or most of the roof's surface. Although more commonly used on commercial buildings, green roofs are gaining popularity for use on private homes.

Another variation on this theme are portable, plastic pocket planters (say that three times fast!). Essentially, this type of planter is a tall bag made from heavy plastic sheeting, with holes for planting and a handle for carrying and hanging on the wall. Plants quickly grow to hide the plastic and create an easy, inexpensive, and eye-catching display.

A variation on the wall-mounted pot, *living walls* are shallow, gridded panels you plant with succulents or other small, easy-care plants, then hang on a wall or privacy fence as you would a picture. You can create your own living art by planting different plants in different grids. (For a photo of a wall-mounted pot, check out the photo insert in the middle of this book.)

Accessories, at Your Service

To take full advantage of the benefits of growing in containers, you'll probably want a few handy accessories. They help you prevent damage to surfaces, keep plants healthy, and move heavy containers with ease. The following sections give an overview of the most useful accessories.

Saucers: Shallow, but necessary

Placed under containers, these shallow dishes help keep water from going where you don't want it — onto a deck, table, or patio, for instance. Unwanted water can damage surfaces, cause staining, and just be a general nuisance.

A saucer looks better if it matches the container. You can find shallow dishes in terra cotta or plastic. Clear plastic saucers are inexpensive and fairly inconspicuous. Select a saucer that's at least an inch wider in diameter than the bottom of the pot so there's enough room for draining water.

Water left standing in saucers means that water can't drain from the soil in the container — a recipe for root rot. Plus, standing water also provides ideal breeding ground for mosquitoes. Be sure to empty saucers once water has finished draining.

Elevation: Giving pots a raise

Lifting containers off the ground has several advantages. A tall stand, either purchased or made, can lift plants up for eye-level viewing and nose-high fragrance. (Turn to Part V for ideas on designing and decorating with container plants.) Raising containers — even just a few inches off the ground — has practical advantages, too. Propping up containers allows water to flow more freely from drainage holes and promotes better air circulation underneath. It allows moisture to evaporate, reducing damage to surfaces. And it reduces damage to wood containers and eliminates insect hiding places.

So how do you raise containers? You can buy decorative pot feet, sold in many catalogs. You can use bricks or wood blocks (use at least three so that your pot is stable). Or, for just a little lift, you can use hose washers on masonry surfaces.

Free-wheelin' it

If you anticipate needing to move large, heavy containers, invest in some sturdy plant dollies and put the containers on them before you fill them with soil and plants. (After planting they may be too heavy to lift.) Also called plant caddies and plant trolleys, these low platforms roll on heavy-duty casters, making it a snap to move containers, both indoors and out.

Raising containers for accessibility

Containers allow gardeners of all ages and abilities to enjoy the wonders of growing plants. Raised containers — either large containers or smaller ones placed on stands — reduce the need to reach and bend and make it possible to perform all gardening chores from a sitting position or from a wheelchair. Placing containers on a smooth surface with plenty of room for maneuvering makes them even more accessible. For more information on accessible gardening, turn to Chapter 21.

Chapter 4

Getting the Dirt on Soil Mixes

· ·

· ·

*I*n the garden, plants depend on soil to provide them with a means of support — a place for roots to anchor — and a storehouse for nutrients, oxygen, and moisture. Plants growing in containers need the same things, but because their roots are growing in a confined space, their needs are more exacting.

If you want to do all your container planting with bags of soil mix bought at the garden center — without having any idea what's in the blend — you can count on reasonably good results. You really don't need to read this chapter.

But if you want to understand what plants need and why, the place to start is at ground level. The more you understand about soil and how it influences plant growth, the better equipped you are to choose and maintain the ideal soil mix for plants. Are you curious now? If so, keep reading.

Why Soil Matters

Growing healthy plants starts with building healthy soil. Although it may look inert (except for the occasional earthworm), garden soil is teeming with life. In this complex, underground ecosystem, microorganisms like bacteria and fungi are constantly breaking down organic matter, releasing nutrients that plants need in the process. Critters large and small are tunneling, opening up pathways that allow air and water to move. Building healthy soil in the garden usually involves adding organic matter like compost to feed soil microbes and adjusting soil pH to its optimal level (more on those later in this chapter).

Why is soil so critical? Because of roots. While we sit back and applaud the flowers and foliage that grow above the rim of the pot, it's the roots that are really supporting the show and that deserve our accolades. Roots work constantly to find the right amount of air, moisture, and nutrients in the soil to fuel the flowers and foliage above.

In the ground, a plant's roots may extend dozens or even hundreds of feet to find what they need. In contrast, the roots of a plant in a container must find everything within the confines of the pot. That's why providing the right soil mix is the most important thing you can do to ensure the success of your container plants.

A Quick Primer on Soil

Your local garden center may have half a dozen or more types of soil mixes labeled for container growing. They go by different names — seed-starting mix, soil-less mix, potting soil, topsoil. To make sense of all the different soil mixes, called *growing media* by horticulturists, it helps to understand some of the lingo used to describe soil. We give you the basics in the following sections.

Getting a feel for soil texture

Healthy garden soils contain a mixture of water, air, and solids (mineral particles and organic matter, or *humus*). The relative percentages of the mineral particles — sand, silt, or clay — determine the soil's *texture*. Here's a closer look at all three components:

✔ **Sand:** This gritty stuff is larger in size than the other two soil particles. Sandy soils drain well and dry out quickly, but they're unable to hold nutrients. When you try to form sand into a ball, it crumbles and won't hold its shape.

✔ **Clay:** These particles are so fine that they can be seen individually only with an electron microscope. Clay soils are sticky to the touch and drain slowly. They're high in nutrients, but the nutrients often occur in forms that are unsuitable for plants. Clay feels slippery to the touch and holds its shape when you roll it into a ball.

✔ **Silt:** Silt is similar to clay, but the individual particles are much larger, moderating its characteristics. It holds water and nutrients longer than sand, but not as tightly as clay. Dry silt feels like flour. Moist silt feels smooth but not sticky and holds its shape fairly well when rolled into a ball.

Most garden soils are composed of a combination of all three particles, in varying proportions.

Making sense of soil structure

The way in which a soil's mineral particles group together determines the *soil structure.* Healthy soil with good soil structure looks a little like crumbled chocolate cake. It's moist and airy at the same time and contains different-sized clumps. Compare this with a powdery cake mix, representing soil with poor structure, and you get a sense of what soil structure is all about. Soil scientists call the little clumps *aggregates,* and they're one of the keys to a healthy soil.

Organic matter that's in the process of decomposition and *humus,* the end product of that decomposition, are the "glue" that helps hold soil particles together into aggregates. Organic matter also acts as a reservoir of nutrients and feeds soil organisms that, in turn, slowly release nutrients in forms plants can use. Organic matter performs magic in the soil: It helps sandy soils hold moisture and it helps clay soils drain better.

When a soil has good structure, it has plenty of spaces for air and water, and lots of room for plant roots to grow in the spaces between the soil aggregates. A soil with good structure retains water without becoming waterlogged and contains a balance of the nutrients necessary for plant growth — exactly what you want when choosing a container soil mix.

Although it seems to make sense that a good soil in the garden has all the right stuff to make it a good soil in a pot or planter, it just isn't so. Soils that are terrific in the field are not so great when put in containers. When the soil is lifted, it loses its structure. And as garden soil settles in a shallow container (much different from the natural depth of the soil in a field), it forms a dense, poorly draining mass. Plus, garden soil may harbor disease-causing organisms that can devastate container plantings and it often contains unwelcome weed seeds.

Choosing sweet or sour soil: A word about pH

No discussion of soil science can be complete without a mention of pH, or the relative sweetness (alkalinity) or sourness (acidity) of the soil. The pH is measured on a scale of 0 to 14, with 7 being neutral. A soil pH below 7 is considered acidic, while one above 7 is alkaline.

The pH scale is *logarithmic.* That means that each unit represents a power of ten. Soil with a pH of 5 is ten times more acidic than soil with a pH of 6.

The reason a soil's pH is important for plants is that some nutrients are available for uptake by a plant's roots only when the pH is within a specific range.

The ideal pH for most plants is 6 to 7, though a few plants (such as acid-loving rhododendrons, azaleas, blueberries, and some perennials) prefer a slightly lower pH.

Kits for determining pH are readily available in most garden centers, and they're probably all you need for testing soil or your own potting mixes. For the definitive word on a soil's chemistry and makeup, you can order a professional test. Check with your local Cooperative Extension office for more information or for addresses of reputable soil-testing labs.

When buying commercial soil mixes for container plants, you don't have to worry about pH. Mixes in bags are formulated to the correct pH for most plants. Special mixtures are available for ferns, azaleas, or woodland plants that prefer a more acidic soil. If you decide to prepare your own mix, be sure to bring the pH to the right level for the plants you're growing.

Old soil mixes — Don't use them!

Soil mixes get worn out when they're exposed to the elements and when plants are grown in them. The organic matter degrades, the mix becomes compacted, and the nutrients get used up. Disease spores and insects find their way in, too. Plants growing in containers need a top-notch soil mix to grow their best. When it's time to replant a container, dump old mix into the garden or compost bin and start with fresh soil mix. Your plants will thank you!

What to Look for in a Container Soil Mix

Whether they're growing in the ground or in containers, plants need the same things — air, water, and nutrients. But because the nature of garden soil changes when you confine it in a pot, it's important to use a soil mix specifically formulated for containers. If you take a look at the ingredients on a bag of soil mix, you may notice that there's very little, if any, real soil listed. The following sections give you a rundown of the characteristics of a good soil mix for containers.

Good water flow, optimal drainage, and moisture retention

In garden soil, water is pulled down to the roots by gravity, capillary action, and the attraction of small clay particles. The water keeps moving down through the soil in a continuous column. Because the soil in a container is so confined and the *soil column* (depth of soil) is relatively shallow, this flow is impeded. The soil mix needs to have a looser structure to encourage this flow of water.

Good water flow helps excess water drain from the soil. Remember, plant roots need both water and oxygen. If the soil they're growing in is saturated, there's no room for oxygen. If it remains too wet for too long, the roots will begin to drown and rot, and if enough roots die the entire plant will die, too. For healthy plant growth water must move through the soil, moistening it without leaving it waterlogged.

On the other hand, you don't want *all* the water to run right through the soil and out the drainage hole. Plant roots need a consistent supply of both water *and* oxygen. They can't go without one or the other for very long. A soil mix that dries out too quickly multiplies your watering chores. Like we do in so many other facets of life, we're looking for a balance — in this case between drainage and water retention. In a nutshell: The ideal soil mix drains freely but also retains some moisture.

You may have been told to put a layer of pea gravel or pot shards in the bottom of your container to improve drainage. Don't do it! Although it may sound logical, using pea gravel in the bottom of a pot actually results in less air for the plant's roots because it shortens the soil column. Instead, fill the entire container with the same soil mix, covering the drainage holes at the bottom with screening to hold in the soil as needed.

Plenty of pore space

One of the ways a soil mix can both drain freely and also retain moisture is by having both large and small pores (*macropores* and *micropores*). When the mix is watered, the water drains quickly through the macropores but is held in the micropores. The pores are in between individual soil particles, and also between the soil aggregates — those little clumps of particles described earlier in the chapter. Picture a water glass filled with ping pong balls. There are big spaces in between the balls — those represent macropores. Now imagine a glass filled with small marbles. The spaces between the marbles — representing micropores — are smaller than the spaces between the ping pong balls. Mix the ping pong balls and marbles in a single glass, and you see that the spaces around them vary in size. In a soil mix, the larger the pores the more quickly water will drain through and the less water will remain behind.

Don't worry; you don't need to know the specific pore spaces of different soil mixes. Just know that a mix formulated for plants that need excellent drainage and tolerate dry soil, like cactuses, will have plenty of macropores. That means this soil mix will also be a good choice for other plants that need excellent drainage — succulents like agave and sempervivum ("hens and chicks"), for example. If you're growing plants like rosemary and lavender that need very good drainage but more moisture than cactuses, you may combine a cactus mix 50:50 with a regular soil mix. Now that you understand the principles you can mix and match soil mixes to suit the plants you're growing.

Lack of contamination

Container mixes need to be free of diseases, insects, and weed seeds. Garden soil loses out on all counts for container planting. In the garden ecosystem, beneficial microbes help keep harmful ones in check. Placing garden soil in a container disrupts this balance. You can pasteurize the soil with heat to kill disease organisms, but this is not an easy task and the odor produced by the process is not pleasant.

With garden soil, you're also getting insects in various stages of development as well as weed seeds, both of which can flourish in the environment of many container plantings. Rather than use backyard garden soil, commercial nursery growers (and most gardeners) now turn to soil-less mixes as a basis for their container potting mixtures. The concepts — drainage, moisture retention, and so on — are the same, only the ingredients differ. Read on for more information about this concept.

Bring On the Soil Mixes (For Peat's Sake)

The movement away from real soil in potting mixes in this country began more than 60 years ago, in an attempt to eliminate the soil diseases that were plaguing the nursery industry and to find an alternative to topsoil, which was being lost to urbanization and herbicide contamination. Today, you can find dozens of variations of soil-less "soil mixes" for sale in your local plant nursery or big-box store, as well as some that list soil as an ingredient. The term *soil mix* is used as a catch-all term to describe the brown stuff you put in your containers and plant your plants in — whether or not it contains any actual soil.

In the following sections, you find out what ingredients go into soil mixes. We also give you some pointers on matching soils, plants, and containers, as well as tips on buying and storing soil mixes, modifying a store-bought soil, and mixing your own.

Unearthing the contents of soil mixes

The soil mixes that you find on the shelves of your local nursery, garden center, or superstore today are based on a combination of organic and mineral components.

The following list gives a sampling of what you may find in different mixes:

- **Charcoal:** Charcoal is used to absorb toxic agents in the mix.

- **Coir fiber:** A by-product of the coconut industry, coir is typically shipped in compressed bricks, which expand when wetted. Coir is sometimes used as an eco-friendly alternative to sphagnum peat moss (see the bullet "Sphagnum peat moss" later in this list for more info).

- **Dolomitic limestone:** Added to peat-based mixes, it corrects the acidity of the peat. It also supplies some calcium and magnesium to plants.

- **Organic matter:** Organic matter consists of decomposed vegetative matter, such as composted wood products (pine bark or wood shavings) and aged manure. It adds nutrients, beneficial microorganisms, and weight. It also holds moisture and may have disease-suppressive qualities. The quality of organic matter varies widely.

- **Perlite:** The roundish, whitish bits you see in soil mixes are perlite. Perlite is a granite-like volcanic rock that pops like popcorn and expands to 20 times its original volume when heat treated at 1500 to 2000 degrees Fahrenheit. Unlike vermiculite (see the "Vermiculite" bullet later in this list), perlite doesn't absorb water. It improves drainage and aerates and lightens soil mixes.

- **Rock powders:** Greensand and crushed granite provide slowly released nutrients and may be a useful addition to permanent plantings.

- **Sand:** Washed, screened sand (often called builders' sand) primarily adds weight to the mix and aids water flow.

- **Sphagnum peat moss:** A high-quality peat, sphagnum peat moss acts like a sponge when moistened, retaining water while also aerating the mix and improving drainage. It's a basic component of soil-less mixes.

   Some people worry that sphagnum peat moss is being harvested at an unsustainable pace. It's true that vast expanses of peat-rich land in Europe have already been harvested, much of it for use as fuel. Most sphagnum peat moss now comes from bogs in Canada using sustainable practices, according to the Canadian Sphagnum Peat Moss Association. Coir (see the "Coir fiber" bullet earlier in this list) is sometimes used as a more environmentally friendly ingredient in soil-less mixes because it's a by-product of coconut production.

✓ **Topsoil:** Topsoil may be found in soil-based potting mixes. It adds weight to the mix and provides nutrients.

✓ **Vermiculite:** Vermiculite is composed of processed mineral flakes that expand to 20 times their original volume under heat treatment. It retains water and aerates the mix. Vermiculite breaks down more quickly than perlite (see the earlier bullet for more on perlite).

✓ **Water-absorbing polymer:** These crystals absorb many times their weight in water, slowly releasing it back to plants as the soil mix dries. They help maintain even soil moisture and reduce watering chores. See Chapter 15 for more on these polymers.

✓ **Wetting agents:** Wetting agents are used to help wet peat moss, which is naturally water-resistant when dry. Note that some wetting agents aren't approved for use in organic growing.

Some container mixes also contain synthetic or organic fertilizers to give plants an initial boost. Turn to Chapter 16 for more on fertilizers.

Look on the label of a potting mix described as organic, and you may find a fascinating array of ingredients, such as shrimp meal, bat guano, earthworm castings, crushed oyster shells, kelp (seaweed), feather, fish, and bone meal, and even beneficial microbes. These materials are added to improve the structure of the mix as well as add sources of nutrients. However, even if you start off with a mix containing lots of organic matter, you may need to apply additional nutrients throughout the growing season. You can find out more about plant nutrients in Chapter 16.

Choosing the right soil mix

Picking the most appropriate mix for your planting needs depends on knowing what you want to grow. For starting your own plants from seed or growing in very small (under 4-inch) pots, for example, you're best off buying *seed-starting mix* or *germinating mix*. These mixes are screened to be very fine, which makes them ideal for starting small seeds. But they're not a good choice for growing plants in larger containers through the season because they hold too much water and eventually compact, providing too little air for good long-term root growth.

For container gardening in hanging baskets or medium-size containers, you need a coarser mix that has better porosity, sometimes labeled *general-purpose mix*. These formulations often include composted bark for better drainage.

Larger containers that hold large shrubs or small trees require an even heavier mix (to anchor the pot and keep it from blowing over), but one with adequate drainage and air space for root growth. Such mixtures, sometimes labeled *nursery mix,* often have sand and composted bark added to the peat mix. Some also include high-quality topsoil.

Also look for soil mixes formulated for plants that require specific conditions: African violets, bulbs, cactus, orchids, and others.

Buying and storing soil mixes

You can find soil mixes at most places that sell potted plants, including nurseries, garden centers, and big-box stores. Soil mixes for container growing are sold in plastic bags, either loose (in a size range from 1 quart up to 40 pounds) or in compressed bales (weighing about 70 pounds). Compressed bales yield almost twice the volume on the label when you dig out the mix and fluff it up. If you have a large number of plants to pot, buying the bales can be more economical than purchasing individual smaller bags of mix.

Whatever you buy, keep the bag tightly closed (so it doesn't dry out or become infected with disease organisms) and protected from rain. The plastic covering on commercial-size bags and bales is usually treated with ultraviolet light inhibitors, giving the material about a one-year shelf life when stored out in the open. You can store the mix in an enclosed shed or in a dry, well-aired basement, though, if you want to keep it for more than one season.

Doctoring up a mix

Professional nurseries often buy wholesale mixtures of a general peat-based growing mix and then customize it to meet their needs. You can do the same thing. For example, you can save money by purchasing a large bale of compressed seed-starting mix at the beginning of the season. Use as much as you need to start seeds; then, when it's time to grow plants in larger pots, mix in some sterilized compost (or composted manure or composted bark mulch) to add nutrients and lighten the mix. If you're growing trees and shrubs in containers, mix in some builder's sand or purchased topsoil for added weight.

You can also add fertilizers to a mix. Slow-release formulas, such as Osmocote, that break down and release nutrients when they're exposed to water are a common choice. Organic options include kelp, alfalfa, and fish meals, which break down slowly, releasing their nutrients to plant roots. You can find out more about slow-release fertilizers in Chapter 16.

If you add garden soil to your potting mixture, you run the risk of introducing disease-causing organisms to your container mixture. For best results, use only bagged, commercial topsoil, not the backyard garden fare.

Getting into the nitty-gritty: Mixing your own

With a little knowledge of what to look for, you can't really go wrong with buying a commercial mix. If you can't find a growing mix that suits your needs, however, and you really want to get down and dirty, you can mix your own blend. If you decide to take this route, be aware that you may need to experiment to achieve just the right mix.

Here's a recipe that creates one cubic yard of mix. A cubic yard is a pile measuring 3' by 3' by 3'. That's a lot of mix! You can make a smaller amount as long as you maintain the proportions.

First combine the following:

½ cubic yard of sphagnum peat moss

½ cubic yard of vermiculite

Dump the ingredients in a pile on a smooth, clean surface like a concrete patio or driveway, or on a plastic tarp where you won't contaminate the mix (for smaller proportions, use a wheelbarrow or garden cart). Break up the peat moss as needed so it isn't clumped. Mix, adding warm water as necessary to lightly moisten the material, and continue mixing until thoroughly combined.

Now add:

10 pounds bone meal

5 pounds dolomitic limestone

5 pounds blood meal

Mix thoroughly. If you don't plan to use the mix immediately, store it tightly closed in plastic garbage bags or in a clean plastic garbage can.

For more information on mixing your own growing media, including 35 "recipes," visit the National Sustainable Agriculture Information Service's Web page at http://attra.ncat.org/attra-pub/potmix.html#appendix3.

Chapter 5

Putting It All Together: Planting Your Container Garden

In This Chapter
▶ Choosing healthy plants
▶ Organizing your planting tools
▶ Getting down to business
▶ Starting plants from seeds

You have your container (see Chapter 3) and your soil mix (Chapter 4). What's next? Planting, of course.

In this chapter we tell you how to identify a healthy plant at your local nursery. We also cover the essential tools you need when potting plants, and finally, we give you basic planting techniques that work for most plants and pots. For more specialized information, refer to Parts II and III.

What You Need to Know Before Planting

If you're new to gardening, a trip to the garden center can be overwhelming. There are so many types of plants sold in so many different ways! This section helps you navigate your way through the aisles so you can feel confident you're choosing the best plant. If you're an experienced in-ground gardener, you can probably skip this section and jump down to our step-by-step guide to planting. However, read on and you may just find some nuggets of wisdom! In the following sections, we explain the plant types you'll find when you go shopping for your container plants, and then we give you advice on what to look for in a plant so you're sure to bring home a healthy one.

Seeing how plants are sold

Transplants are the most popular choice for containers. These seedlings of annual flowers, vegetables, and, occasionally, perennial flowers are usually grown by large wholesalers and sold at local garden centers in cell-packs and small pots (up to 3 or 4 inches or so). They've been growing for six weeks or more, giving you a jump on the growing season. Although transplants are the most sought-after plants for containers, you can buy plants several other ways as well:

- **Seeds:** Mail-order catalogs and nursery racks offer seeds of countless varieties of annuals and perennials, and even some trees and shrubs. Growing plants from seeds takes time, but offers one of the most rewarding ways to garden. Not only is it fun to watch a tiny seed sprout into a beautiful plant, but you also find a much larger variety of plants sold as seeds as compared with transplants. Some plants are easier and faster to grow from seed than others; look to "If at First You Want to Seed" later in this chapter to find out more and get seed-starting advice.

- **Bulbs:** Most bulbs grow well in containers, especially if you're growing them for a single season. You can order from catalogs or check your local nursery in fall and spring. See Chapter 9 for details.

- **Container-grown plants:** Shrubs and trees, along with some larger annuals and perennials, are offered in familiar quart, 1-gallon, 5-gallon, and 15-gallon plastic pots or, occasionally, paper pulp pots. Their large size and advanced stage of growth provide instant gratification.

- **Bare-root:** Deciduous trees and shrubs, especially fruit-bearing types and roses, are typically sold bare-root when they're dormant and leafless. (Many perennials also are sold bare-root, particularly by mail-order companies.) The plants are dug from growing fields, and their roots are washed of soil, then packed in moist newspaper or peat moss. Although they may look dead upon arrival, don't worry: Their survival rate is high as long as the roots don't dry out. If you can't plant them right away, store bare-root plants in a cool, dark place and keep the packing material moist.

  Bare-root is one of the more economical ways to buy good-sized plants, and it's a sure way to start plants off right: You can ensure that roots are properly spread out in the right growing medium.

- **Balled and burlapped:** Evergreen shrubs and trees, along with deciduous types that can't be successfully handled bare-root, are dug from growing fields with a ball of soil around the roots. Then they're wrapped with burlap and sometimes an outer wire basket. Because field soil is so heavy, balled and burlapped plants can be difficult to transport and plant but usually offer good results.

Choosing healthy plants

The longer you garden, the better you become at recognizing healthy plants that are ready to take off for a long and productive life in a container. Here are some general signs to keep in mind:

- ✔ Younger is often better than older, smaller better than bigger. The longer plants stay in nursery containers, the more likely they are to become root-bound, where roots become overcrowded and begin to circle around the sides of the container.

   Don't hesitate to gently slip plants out of their containers and look for white roots woven through dark soil, rather than a tight tangle of dark roots and little loose soil.

- ✔ Deep green is better than yellow or a dull color — realizing, of course, that we're not talking about plants that naturally have yellow foliage or dull leaves.

- ✔ Look for plenty of young, healthy new growth rather than lots of woody branches.

The following sections provide specific pointers for the different categories of plants to help you select healthy specimens.

Annual flowers

Look for short, stocky plants with healthy green foliage. Bare lower stems, floppy growth, and yellowing leaves indicate the plant may not have been watered or fertilized properly. The size of the plant should be in proportion to the pot. Large plants in small cell packs are almost certainly root-bound and probably have been kept alive on a diet of constant watering and fertilizing. They'll adapt poorly, if at all, to a new container.

What about annuals in bloom? To make seedlings as appealing as possible for sale at the nursery, plant breeders tinker with genes and growers use special techniques to create plants that pop into bloom at an early age, sometimes before the plant is strong enough to support the energy-intensive blooming process. The result is a plant that blooms for a few days when you get it home, and then goes into foliage- and root-growing mode for a few weeks until it's strong enough to bloom again. Look for plants with healthy green foliage and perhaps a few buds, rather than annuals in full flower.

Vegetables and herbs

Much of the advice on annual flowers holds true for vegetables and herbs. Avoid plants in small containers that sport flowers or developing fruit (tomatoes, peppers, squash, and so on), because premature flowering and fruiting are signs that the plant has been stressed. Plants in gallon-sized or larger containers may be further along in development; however, transplanting them may cause enough stress that they drop their flowers and fruit anyway.

Bulbs

Look for firm bulbs that show no signs of rot. A loose *tunic* — the papery outer covering — is usually fine, but soft spots are definitely trouble. Bulbs that haven't yet sprouted are preferable to those with growing shoots.

Perennials

Most perennial plants are sold in quart- and gallon-sized containers. At this size, they've probably been growing for at least a year, if not longer. If you're buying plants in early spring, the top growth may still be small. Pop the plants out of their pots and look for healthy white roots coursing through the soil mix. A dense, tangled mass of roots often indicates the plants have been growing too long in the same pot and should have been transplanted to a larger container. Few or no visible roots in a container-grown plant may indicate that the plant has just been repotted in a larger container and hasn't developed a healthy root system yet. Unfortunately, if you can't see the roots you can't tell if the plant is adapting well to its new pot so it's best to avoid plants that have no signs of roots in the soil. Some perennials are sold bare-root in early spring (see more on bare-root plants in the next two sections).

Shrubs and trees

When buying shrubs and trees, avoid the temptation to buy the largest size. Instead, look for thick branching and sturdy, well-shaped plants (as opposed to one-sided growth). Inspect for vigorous new growth at the branch tips and healthy bark with no wounds, deep scars, or splits. In general, small trees and shrubs adapt more readily to their new growing conditions than larger ones, often catching up to or outpacing larger trees planted at the same time.

Most importantly, avoid a root-bound plant. If the roots fill the container and are circling the sides, the plant is seriously root-bound and may never settle properly into its new home.

When shopping for bare-root trees and shrubs, look for plump, firm, moist roots. Avoid plants with shriveled, dry, and brittle roots. Likewise, avoid plants with mushy, moldy roots or those that smell foul, indicating decay. Ideally, bare-root plants should be kept in a cool, moist place; plants that have been out in a store display may prematurely sprout — this isn't ideal, but it's not necessarily a cause for rejection.

With balled and burlapped plants, check for splits in the ball of soil, which can cause roots to dry out. Make sure that the soil ball hasn't dried out because remoistening it thoroughly can be difficult.

Hardening off

Plants purchased straight from a greenhouse benefit from a short period of *hardening off,* which simply means gradually acclimating them to their new surroundings. Plants grown in greenhouses are accustomed to warmth, high humidity, and protection from direct sun and wind. You can harden off plants before or after planting them in their new containers. Here's how:

1. As soon as you get seedlings home, place them in a bright, protected place in part shade, and water them well. Keep them there for a few days, moving them indoors at night if temperatures drop to below 50 degrees Fahrenheit.

2. After a day or two, move them to full sun for a few hours, gradually increasing their exposure to sun, wind, and cool temperatures over the course of a week to 10 days.

3. Place plants in their new home, keeping an eye out for signs of sunburn (which looks like bleached areas) or chill damage (which often appears as blackened areas), both of which usually show up on the upper, exposed leaves. If inner leaves are also affected, the plants may have another problem — turn to Chapter 18.

Hardening off also gives you a chance to keep an eye on plants for pest problems.

Fruits and berries

Often sold bare-root in early spring, fruit and berry plants should be fully dormant, with no sprouts or developing leaves. If you can't plant them right away, store them in a cool, dark place and keep packing material moist.

Houseplants

The same overall rules apply when choosing houseplants. Look for healthy new growth, an attractive shape, healthy roots, and a plant that is in proportion to its pot.

Examine plants carefully for signs of insects or disease before purchasing them. Some gardeners go so far as to quarantine new plants, keeping them separate from other plants for a week or two to be sure they're pest-free.

Your Well-Stocked Planting Tool Kit

Here's a quick checklist to make sure that you have all the tools you need before you start planting:

✔ **Container:** Double-check to make sure it's the right size (see Chapter 3 and Parts II and III).

✔ **Potting mix:** Choose a potting mix appropriate for the plants (see Chapter 4).

✔ **Drain hole cover:** Cut a piece of window screen large enough to cover the drainage hole(s).

✔ **Shears and knife:** You may need to cut up root-bound roots or trim top growth a bit.

✔ **Scoop or trowel:** Use this to move soil mix. You may want a shovel for big jobs.

✔ **Gloves:** Handling soil dries out your hands, and you may want leather, cloth, or rubber gloves to protect them.

✔ **Water:** Your plant needs it as soon as you plant it. Use a watering can or hose (a bubbler attachment helps soften the flow). Room-temperature water is best.

✔ **Miscellaneous:** Stakes, plant ties, trellis — anything else you may need right after planting.

A Step-by-Step Guide to Planting a Basic Container

Follow these steps to plant most shrubs, trees, annuals, and perennials in most of your standard containers. Later in this chapter we give you planting tips for different types of containers. Refer to Parts II and III for details on specific types of plants.

1. Getting the container ready

Make sure that the container is the right size for your plants (see Chapter 3 for specifics). For permanent plants, choose a container that's 2 inches wider and deeper than the nursery container, as shown in Figure 5-1. Bare-root plants need a container that's several inches wider and deeper than the stretched-out, trimmed-up roots. Annuals and perennials can be crowded together more closely in containers than in the ground. Refer to Parts II and III for more details.

Some containers need a bit of preparation. Soak new terra-cotta pots in water for 10 or 15 minutes before planting to prevent clay from drawing moisture out of the soil mix.

If you're using old pots, you may want to clean them as we describe in Chapter 17 to remove salt deposits and reduce chances of disease. And, as logic dictates, applying preservative to wood containers before you plant is easier than doing so afterwards (see Chapter 17 for how-tos).

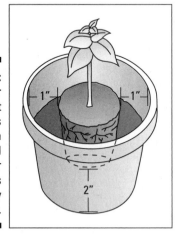

Figure 5-1:
Give your plant about 2 inches more in depth and diameter than its nursery container.

Most commercially made pots have drain holes to allow water to flow out of the container. Often these holes are so large that they allow soil to flow out with the water. To prevent this, use a piece of window screen large enough to cover the hole, as shown in Figure 5-2.

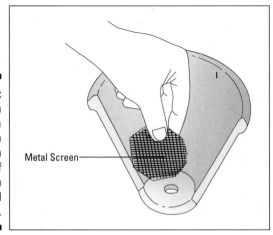

Figure 5-2:
You can cover a large drain hole with a piece of fine-mesh metal screen.

Metal Screen

If your container lacks a drain hole, you need to make one. Drilling holes in the base of a wooden box is easy: Drill one ½-inch hole for a box up to 12 square inches; two to four ½-inch holes for larger boxes or a half barrel. For clay pots, use an electric drill with a masonry bit. Support the pot on a block of wood, and start drilling with a smaller bit, eventually reaching the final size of ½ inch. Adding water to the drill hole may help.

2. Preparing the soil mix

Many peat-based soil mixes are bone dry in the bag, and moistening them before planting is vital. Pour enough mix to fill your container into a pail. (If you're using the whole bag, you can moisten it right in the bag.) Now's the time to mix in a slow-release fertilizer; see Chapter 16 for details. Pour warm water over the mix, stirring as you go. Let the water soak in for at least a half-hour, stirring the mix occasionally and adding more water as needed so the moisture is evenly distributed. (You may be surprised at how much water you have to add to moisten dry peat moss.)

Strive for the moisture level of a wrung-out sponge — damp, but not sopping wet. The soil mix should be moist enough that you can form it into a loose ball in your hand. If your soil mix comes out of the bag this moist, you can skip this step.

3. Prepping the plant

Whatever the plant's original residence — nursery pot, cell-pack, or paper pulp pot — you need to pay attention to a few key matters before you start the actual planting.

First, make sure that the nursery plant's soil is moist enough to hold the roots together when you plant. If the soil is dry, give it a good soaking and let it drain for at least an hour. Place bare-root plants in a bucket of water for an hour or so before planting.

Next, you need to remove the plant from the nursery container. Here are some tips for getting plants out of their pots:

✔ **Plastic cell-packs:** Turn the pack upside down and wiggle and squeeze the base of each cell. Gently tug on the plant, holding it by the leaves rather than the stem. (If a leaf breaks, others will grow; if the stem breaks, the plant's a goner.) If the plant resists coming out of the cell, use scissors to cut the plastic off.

✔ **Small pots:** Support the root ball by placing your hand over the soil surface with the stem between your fingers, as shown in Figure 5-3. Turn the plant over and tap on the pot to loosen the root ball. If it sticks, squeeze or gently shake it, or, if necessary, use scissors to cut away the pot.

✔ **Larger containers, such as 1- and 5-gallon pots:** Tip a plastic container on its side or upside down, taking care not to break branches, and let the root ball slip out, catching it with one hand. If the root ball doesn't slip out easily, tap the rim of the upside-down container on a hard surface. If the root ball really resists, cut off the pot with shears, taking care not to damage the roots. Paper pulp pots can be treated like plastic — they're easy to cut apart if plants resist slipping out.

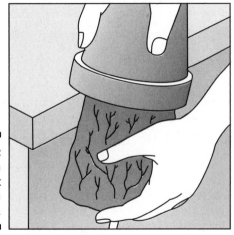

Figure 5-3:
Getting a
plant out
of a plastic
container.

After the plant is free from its original pot, inspect the root ball. Is it root-bound? Do roots protrude from the drain hole? Or are roots twined around into a dense mass that repels water? For small plants, such as annuals, that may be a bit root-bound, gently loosen the mat of roots with your fingertips. For larger plants, such as 1- or 5-gallon shrubs, use a knife to score some vertical scratches in a tight root ball.

4. Planting

Start adding some moist soil mix to your container. Your goal is to end up with the soil about an inch below the rim of the container for small plants (2 inches or more for large containers), so there's enough space to hold plenty of water as you apply it. The amount of soil and planting technique varies for different types of plants:

✔ **For small plants in cell packs or little pots:** Fill the container almost to the level that you want to end up with. With your hands or trowel, scoop out a little hole for each root ball, slip in the plant, and firm down around its edges with your fingers. If the soil level starts to rise too high, remove some soil. Match the soil level to your plants' previous growing conditions — don't bury plants too deep or allow their root balls to rise above the soil level. Figure 5-4 shows the ideal position.

Figure 5-4:
This one's
planted just
right.

✔ **For plants in gallon pots and larger:** Place an inch or two of soil mix in the bottom of the container. Then place the plant in the container to see how much, if any, more soil you need to add to raise the plant to the desired height. Add enough soil mix to raise the top of the root ball to the desired level in the pot, usually 2 to 4 inches below the rim. Then set the root ball on top of the soil mix and begin filling in with more soil mix, tamping it down with your hands, a trowel, or a shovel handle for large containers. Tamping down is important to establish firm contact between the root ball and the new soil mix and to remove air pockets. Keep adding soil mix until it levels up with the top of the root ball.

✔ **For balled and burlapped plants:** Place the root ball on soil mix at the bottom of the container, just as you would for plants grown in 1- or 5-gallon nursery pots (see the preceding bullet). Cut away the twine holding the burlap in place at the top of the root ball. Fold back and trim away the top several inches of burlap with heavy scissors or a knife. Then slash the remaining burlap down the sides to allow for root growth. The buried part gradually decomposes. (Make sure all the burlap is buried in the soil mix; any exposed burlap will wick water away from plant roots.) Fill with soil mix around the root ball, tamping it down as you go to remove air pockets, until it is level with the top of the root ball.

In the old days all burlap was biodegradable. Now, sometimes it's made with plastic fibers or treated with chemicals to keep it from degrading. If this is the case or you're unsure, gently cut away as much of the burlap as possible and remove it from the container.

✔ **For bare-root plants:** Remove the plant from the bucket where it has been soaking, and trim off any broken or damaged roots. Check the instructions that come with the plant for more specific pruning advice. Examine the plant to find the former soil line (usually indicated by a faint, discolored ring around the trunk). Mound the soil mix at the bottom of the container, spreading the roots evenly over the mound. Adjust the level of the mound until the plant's soil line matches up with the desired soil level in the container. Fill around the roots and up to the soil line, tamping gently as you go.

5. Watering

Even though you've planted a well-watered plant into moist soil, you still need to water after planting to help soil settle around plant roots and eliminate any remaining air pockets. Watering a just-planted container is trickier than you may imagine. Water tends to follow the path of least resistance, and drains quickly through the loose soil mix, bypassing the denser root ball. You walk away thinking that your watering job is done. Days later, you realize that the root ball never really got wet, and the plant is desiccated. Protect against this by watering thoroughly the first time.

The secret to successful watering is a slow and gentle stream. Drip irrigation or gently trickling hoses are ideal. Or, if you're patient, apply water slowly using a watering can or a hose, taking care not to wash soil out of the container. Slowly fill the pot to the rim, and repeat several times. Probe with your fingers to find out whether the root ball has absorbed water — if you don't detect moisture, try soaking it again.

6. Finishing up

Just a few more steps and you're done! The first two steps are universal; the last two apply only to certain types of plants:

✔ Apply mulch to improve the appearance, keep soil from washing away during watering, help conserve water, and keep weed seeds from sprouting. Bark chips are decorative and help insulate the roots from hot sun. Some gardeners prefer the look of stone mulch, and it's a fine choice, too.

✔ Hose off the container if it got muddy during the planting process.

✔ Stake and tie trees or tall annuals or perennials.

✔ Add a trellis to the container for vines that need support.

Potting Plants in Specialized Containers

Special containers need special planting techniques, either because of their shape or the way they'll be displayed. For example, you want lightweight soil and strategically placed plants in a container that you'll mount on a wall or hang from a porch roof. Here's a rundown of some of the more commonly available options.

Planting hanging baskets

Plastic baskets are the easiest to plant; wire baskets involve a few extra steps. (Refer to Chapter 3 for an explanation of different types of baskets.) Start by gathering all your materials together in a comfortable place to work.

Choosing a soil mix

A successful soil mix for hanging baskets has two characteristics. First, the mix needs to be lightweight. Second, the soil must retain moisture, because hanging baskets dry out faster than most other containers.

One way to achieve a suitable mix is to start with a bag of high-quality potting mix and add perlite or vermiculite at the ratio of three parts soil mix to one part additive. Perlite and vermiculite both lighten the mix; vermiculite also absorbs and retains water. Both are available at garden supply stores. Mixing in timed-release fertilizer granules is a good idea, too. If hangers will be displayed in full sun, consider adding water-absorbing crystals, which absorb water and turn gel-like, releasing moisture slowly as the soil dries. Add to the soil mix according to package directions. Refer to Chapter 4 for more on soil mixes and additives.

Planting a solid basket

The steps for planting a solid basket are similar to those for planting any small container:

1. **Place a piece of window screen over the drain holes in the bottom of the basket.**

2. **Fill the container with potting mixture.**

3. **Plant the upright plants toward the center, firming the soil around them.**

4. **Add the fillers, if you have room for them, near the plants in the center, and finish with the spillers along the rim.**

5. **Hang and water the basket immediately.**

6. **Water daily for the first few days, and then ease off if the soil is staying moist.**

   Step up watering if the weather turns hot and as the plant roots fill the basket.

Planting a wire basket lined with sphagnum moss

These popular baskets dry out quickly and require extra care, but will reward you with remarkable displays for your efforts. Baskets lined with flexible plastic in place of the moss are planted using a similar technique.

1. **Start by soaking sphagnum moss in water for at least 10 minutes.**

   Support a round-bottomed basket on a large pot or bucket to keep it upright.

2. **Begin to line your basket by laying sheets of dampened moss — about 1 inch thick — along the bottom and halfway up the sides.**

3. **Loosely fill the basket with soil to just below the moss level, and then resume lining the sides with moss.**

   Continue right up to the top until the moss covers the rim area, as shown in Figure 5-5. Use plenty of moss so you don't have any gaps, and fill loosely with more soil until you reach the top.

4. **Begin planting the sides by starting near the bottom, as shown in Figure 5-6.**

   Carefully open a space between the wires and through the moss. Loosen any tangled roots, and insert the roots through the hole and into the moist soil. Use more wads of moss to tuck the plant in securely, and gently bend the wires together above and below the plant.

5. **Continue planting the sides.**

   Allow at least 3 inches between plants as you stagger them evenly around the sides. The more plants you place here, the quicker things can grow together and the less basket you'll see later on.

Figure 5-5:
Lining a basket with sphagnum moss.

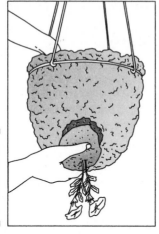

Figure 5-6:
Begin
planting
from the
bottom.

6. **Plant in the top of the basket, as shown in Figure 5-7.**

   Space plants evenly with the tallest in the center, allowing at least 3 inches between plants. Set them so that the soil level is slightly below the rim. Again, the fuller you plant the top, the quicker your basket can become a mass of color and texture. Be careful not to plant right over the roots of side plants near the rim. Firm the top plants in, adding more soil as needed but keeping the level below the top of the moss.

7. **Attach the supports and hang the basket.**

8. **Water gently and thoroughly until water drains freely.**

Figure 5-7:
After you've
planted
along the
sides, you
can plant
on top.

9. **Replace any moss that may have fallen out, tucking new moss securely around the plants.**

10. **Water daily as plants become established.**

Planting a strawberry pot or pocket planter

Strawberry jars and pocket planters have holes cut into the sides as well as an open top. They come in a range of sizes, but most jars have between 8 and 15 pockets sized for small plants like herbs or annuals — or strawberries. Follow these easy steps for designing and planting an impressive strawberry jar:

1. **Decide what you want to grow in the jar.**

   You can plant herbs, strawberries, or small flowers. Or, you can mix sunny annuals with tasty herbs and have the best of two worlds.

2. **Buy enough plants for all the pockets, including one to four plants for the mouth at the top.**

   Six-pack plants are the ideal size for the side openings.

3. **Decide where you want each plant to go.**

   Alternating themes or repeating patterns work well if you don't want a different plant in each slot.

4. **Place a piece of window screen over the bottom drain hole, and add potting mix to the level of the lowest openings (see Figure 5-8).**

Figure 5-8: Cover the drainage hole with a piece of window screen, and then add soil to the level of the lowest pocket.

5. **Carefully slip the roots through the opening, pulling from inside the jar.**

6. **Fill in with soil up to the level of each pocket as you plant, as shown in Figure 5-9.**

   Firm soil around the roots, and pack it down around the plant in the mouth of each pocket. Repeat for all pockets.

Figure 5-9:
Add soil
to each
pocket.

7. **Plant the top of the jar with the remaining plants.**

8. **Immediately water the top and each pocket, and replace any soil that washes away (see Figure 5-10).**

Figure 5-10:
Water
the top
and each
pocket.

Planting a window box or railing planter

You have three options for planting your window box or railing planter:

- ✔ You can plant directly in the container.

- ✔ You can drop in plants, pots and all, and fill around them with moss, bark, or another lightweight material.

- ✔ You can put plants in a plastic or metal liner that fits inside the box. With this method, you can rotate liners, removing a liner when the plants in it are past their prime and swapping in a liner with fresh plants. This technique is especially good if the planters are located in less-than-ideal conditions — too much shade, for example. You can swap liners in and out, rotating them to a sunnier spot every few weeks to rejuvenate the plants.

Basically, you plant the same way you do in any container. Cover the drain holes, fill with soil mixture, and firm soil around plants, leaving at least 1 inch at the top for watering.

If at First You Want to Seed

Very few types of plants do well if started from seeds sown directly in the containers where you want them to grow. Often, they just grow too slowly and are better off started indoors a month or two before being planted in the container. Some seedlings grow better if they're started in small containers and then "moved up" — transplanted into gradually larger containers. They just don't perform well if grown in an excessive amount of soil mix.

The following annual flower and vegetable seeds are good choices for direct sowing into large containers: beans, lettuce, marigolds, nasturtiums, sunflowers, and zinnias. Follow seed packet directions for sowing in the ground.

You can easily start many types of seeds indoors and gradually transplant up to your final containers. Seed-starting kits and equipment are available at garden centers and in catalogs. Mainly, you need trays or flats, cell-packs, or other small containers, along with special seed-starting soil mix. Then follow these steps:

1. **Fill containers to the top with moist, sterile, soil-less mix (see Chapter 4).**

   Level the top by sweeping across it with your hand or a table knife.

2. **Use your fingertip or a pencil to make small depressions for seeds.**

   Seeding depth need not be exact, but try to plant your seeds at the depth recommended on the seed packet — usually about three times as deep as the seeds are wide.

3. **Drop one or two seeds into each depression, cover with pinches of seed-starting mixture, and dampen thoroughly with plain water.**

   To keep from flooding out the planted seeds, either use a pump spray bottle to mist the containers repeatedly, or place the containers in small pans or trays and fill the pans with 1 inch of water. The containers will absorb the water from the pans in about an hour.

4. **To keep the surface of the planted containers from drying out, cover them lightly with plastic wrap or enclose the whole tray in a large plastic bag.**

   Place the containers in a warm place.

5. **Start checking for germination after three days.**

   As soon as the first sprouts emerge, remove the plastic and move the seedlings to good light.

6. **Thin your seedlings.**

   Most of the time, you end up with way too many seedlings. If left alone, they become so crowded that they can't grow well. Retain only one or two seedlings in a container that's 2 inches across.

   To thin to the proper number, keep the strongest-looking ones, and use scissors to snip the others off at the soil line. (You can pull out the extra seedlings with your fingers or tweezers and gingerly transplant them to individual containers, but you risk damaging the roots of the remaining ones.)

7. **When seedlings are about two weeks old, they're ready for a little fertilizer.**

   Use a fertilizer that can be mixed with water, and mix it at half the strength recommended on the package. Fertilize seedlings about once a week, or every other time you water them.

8. **After four to six weeks, your seedlings are big enough to move outside.**

   To help them get ready for the big move, spend a week or two hardening them off — refer to the sidebar earlier in this chapter for details.

Part II

Enjoying a Summer Fling with Single-Season Containers

The 5th Wave   By Rich Tennant

"Aside from a little beginner's confusion,
I've done very well with my bulbs."

In this part . . .

*I*f your heart quickens at the sight of bountiful displays of brilliant geraniums and petunias overflowing their containers, or if you have your heart set on harvesting your own sun-warmed, vine-ripened tomatoes, you've come to the right place. Growing annual flowers, vegetables, and herbs gives you the most bang for your container buck. The smallest seeds and the skimpiest transplants will transform right before your eyes into overflowing abundance. Enjoy it all, then toss the plants at the end of the season and start fresh next spring — learning from the past season's successes and challenges and experimenting with color and plant combinations to your heart's content.

Chapter 6

A Short but Sweet Relationship with Annuals

In This Chapter

▶ Looking at the various types of annuals

▶ Taking seasonal changes into account

▶ Combining the best of two worlds: Food and flowers

*W*hat's the first thing that you think of when you picture container plants? Probably a hanging basket overflowing with annual flowers and maybe a tomato plant on the deck. If you're new to container gardening, single-season plants like these are definitely the way to go.

In this chapter you find an overview of the types of plants suitable for single-season containers, a rundown of the benefits of growing annuals in containers, information about making the most of seasonal weather, and some general information on mixing different types of plants in containers. The next three chapters go into details on growing annual flowers, vegetables and herbs, and bulbs in containers.

Evaluating Your Options

The plants used in single-season containers are often, but not always, annual plants. That's because they tend to grow quickly and produce the desired result — flowers or edible parts — within months of planting.

Some perennial plants can be grown as annuals — they'll just have a shorter lifespan than what nature originally intended. In the following sections, we explain the three categories of plants typically grown in single-season containers.

Sizing up annuals

Botanically speaking, an annual (from the Latin *annus*, meaning year) is a plant that undergoes its life cycle in one growing season. For example, a marigold or bean seed sprouts in the spring, grows quickly, blooms in summer, sets and disperses its seeds, and dies when frost hits in fall. The seeds sprout the next year to repeat the process. Contrast this with a perennial, which lives for at least a few years.

The nursery definition of annual is different, and in some ways more practical: Annuals are plants that gardeners purchase or sow in spring and enjoy for one growing season, with the expectation that they'll need to replace them with fresh plants the following spring. (In mild climates, you can plant annuals in fall and winter — more on this later.)

What's the difference in the definitions? Some plants that nurseries label as annuals are, botanically speaking, perennials that, in a suitable climate, will live for more than one year.

TIP

For your single-season containers, look for flowers labeled as annuals or bedding plants. Most vegetables and herbs are suitable for container growing, too.

Perusing perennials that pretend to be annuals

If left in the ground in regions with mild winters, some plants that are sold as annuals will overwinter and resprout the following spring (meaning they're actually perennials). The petunia is a classic example. Surprisingly, many of the most common so-called annuals are really perennials, including alyssum, bacopa, calibrachoa (also known as million bells), cleome, lantana, snapdragon, twinspur, and verbena. However, these plants won't survive the cold winter temperatures that affect much of the country, so for most of us it's perfectly reasonable to consider them annuals.

To further confuse the matter, some plants are biennials: They produce foliage their first season, then flowers and seeds the second season, after which they die. Several familiar vegetables and herbs are biennials, including carrots and parsley. However, gardeners usually harvest them during their first growing season, before they flower. Biennial flowers include foxglove, sweet William, and hollyhock; however, plant breeders have developed varieties of these that bloom their first growing season, blurring the distinction.

You can plant perennials in single-season containers; however, they may take longer to flower. If a perennial is already blooming when you buy it, it's fine for a single-season planting.

Tending toward the tropical

Truly tropical plants won't survive temperatures below freezing, and some may be damaged if temperatures dip into the 50s Fahrenheit. Begonia, coleus, impatiens, sweet potato vines, zonal and ivy geraniums — even peppers and tomatoes — are perennial in their native tropical to subtropical regions. They'll overwinter in only the mildest climates, so for all practical purposes you can consider them annuals — unless you live in the tropics or want to overwinter them indoors.

Why Grow Single-Season Containers?

Why, you might wonder, would someone grow annuals — plants that must be replaced each year — instead of long-lived perennials? One reason is that some of the most beautiful and easiest to grow flowers are annuals. Plus, most vegetables and many herbs grow quickly and produce their harvest in one growing season. Then, at the end of the season you can discard the plants and start fresh next spring with the same old favorites or experiment with something new.

Contrast this with permanent plantings — perennials, trees, and shrubs — that need extra care if they're to survive cold winter temperatures, even if those same plants are hardy when they're growing in the ground. That means moving them to a sheltered spot or protecting them with a thick mulch and crossing your fingers that the plants survive.

The only downside to growing single-season containers is that you must replant each year, and that involves some effort and expense.

Matching Plants to the Season

For the most part, the plants your local nursery sells each season should withstand all but the most extreme seasonal conditions in your region of the country. But that doesn't mean you can buy them the first week they're for sale, plant them, set them outside, and expect them to thrive. Nurseries often display plants for sale weeks before the plants can tolerate the up-and-down temperatures of changing seasons.

So you have to know a little bit about the frost dates in your area and the plants' preferred temperatures. The following sections help you out in both regards. (And if you want even more information about climate and container plantings, flip to Chapter 2.) We also introduce the idea of planting a container so it looks good season after season.

Planting by the calendar

Before you plant, you need to know when your average last spring frost occurs (see Chapter 2 for more on frost dates). Ask a gardening neighbor, inquire at a local nursery, consult with your Cooperative Extension office, or take a look at the climate maps at www.ncdc.noaa.gov/oa/climate/ freezefrost/frostfreemaps.html.

Keep in mind that this is only an average — if your average last spring frost is May 1, half the time the actual date is earlier than this and the other half it's later.

Although the average last frost date isn't exact, it does provide a good guideline for determining when you can set out frost-sensitive plants — just be prepared to protect them if a late cold spell threatens. You can set out frost-tolerant plants a few weeks before your average last frost date. (See Chapter 2 for ways to protect plants.)

Plants that have been raised in a greenhouse should be hardened off — slowly acclimated to outdoor conditions over the course of a week or 10 days. Flip to Chapter 5 for details.

Cool-season or heat lover?

Plants vary in their temperature preferences. Some, like larkspur and spinach, are described as *cool-season* plants: They grow well in cool temperatures and tolerate light frosts, but begin to languish when summer heats up. At the other extreme are *warm-season* plants, like celosia and basil: They may suffer chill damage and stunted growth if temperatures drop below 45 degrees, but they love the sun and heat of midsummer.

Seed packets and plant tags usually provide information about a plant's temperature preferences, and we also include it in the plant descriptions in the next few chapters. When in doubt, assume a plant is vulnerable and don't expose it to freezing temperatures.

Cool-season and warm-season are, of course, relative terms. Where summers are cool, like along the foggy California coast or in other overcast climates, you can grow cool-season plants all summer. Where winters are warm and nearly frost-free (as in low-elevation Arizona and much of California), fall through spring is an ideal stretch for growing cool-season plants like Iceland poppies and lettuce.

Truly tropical climates like those found in Hawaii and southern Florida are in a separate category and have their own special rules for growing annuals. We recommend checking with local nurseries for exact timing.

Success (ion) in planting

You can make the most of plants' different temperature preferences with *succession planting*. Start out in spring with frost-tolerant, cool-season plants. By early summer when they begin to fade, replace them with heat-lovers. Come fall, as temperatures cool, go back to cool-season plants.

For example, sow spinach in early spring — it prefers cool temperatures and can tolerate frost. As the weather heats up in early summer, the spinach will begin to bolt (send up flower stalks) and get bitter tasting. Pull it out and plant a heat-loving crop, like beans. As the weather begins to cool in fall the bean harvest will slow; then it's time to pull out the bean plants and go back to a cool-season crop.

The same concept holds true for flowers. Pansies are a classic early spring flower but will begin to flag in early summer. Replace the pansies with heat-lovers, like zinnias. Come fall, it's time to go back to pansies or another cool-season flower.

This method is familiar to gardeners in regions with very hot summers, where fall planting is as common as spring planting and cool-season plants will grow all through the winter. However, gardeners everywhere can take advantage of different plants' preferences. This is especially true for container gardening, where environmental conditions have a magnified effect on plants.

Look to individual chapters for examples of succession planting options.

Mixing Edibles and Ornamentals

Edibles traditionally are relegated to a separate, backyard garden. And this still makes sense if you use pesticides on your ornamental plants that aren't appropriate for use on plants you'll be eating. But as more and more gardeners move toward the least-toxic and organic pest controls, they're also beginning to mix and match ornamentals and edibles in the same garden. This is sometimes referred to as *edible landscaping,* and the concept is ideal for container growing, too. Here are a few reasons to consider mixed plantings:

- ✔ **Beauty:** Adding a few flowering plants to a veggie planter makes it prettier.

- ✔ **Pest-repellent properties:** Some flowers, notably marigolds, are reputed to repel insect pests.

- ✔ **Convenience:** Add a few herb plants to the flower planter on your front stoop, and you can harvest a few sprigs just steps from the kitchen.

- ✔ **Space conservation:** If your garden space is limited to a deck or balcony, you can still grow lots of beautiful *and* tasty plants.

The Nature's Bounty container design in Chapter 19 includes both flowers and edibles.

When you're mixing plants in a container, be sure they're compatible — they should have similar requirements for sunlight and soil moisture. And make sure the container is large enough to accommodate the plants' mature sizes.

Chapter 7

Adding Pizzazz with Colorful Annual Flowers

*P*opular, fun, easy to grow, and universally loved, annual flowers are just the right plants to start with when talking about container gardening. They're apt to be the first plants that you grow in containers, yet annual flowers are so varied and abundant that even the most experienced gardeners never tire of growing them.

Nothing's simpler than planting annuals in pots: Go to the nursery, put whatever looks good in the shopping cart, buy a pot and a bag of potting mix, take it all home, and put it together. That's often plenty good enough. But that doesn't have to be all there is to it. There are endless ways to combine plants and pots to create unique designs. You may be surprised at how much you enjoy the process and the results.

In this chapter, we point out the many reasons to grow annual flowers in containers, describe the special care needed that's a bit different from growing the same plants in the ground, and then look at annuals that are particularly well-suited to container life.

Defining Annual Flowers

Annual flowers are one-season plants, typically sold in six-packs and small pots. Although many vegetables and herbs are annuals, the term *annuals* usually refers to purely decorative plants — those grown for their flowers or attractive foliage. If you ask for annuals at a nursery, they'll direct you to annual flowers. Sometimes, they're also called bedding plants because they're traditionally used to add color to planting beds.

In addition to the familiar geraniums and petunias, plant breeders have introduced a remarkable number of new annuals over the last few years, as well as new varieties of old favorites. Endless combinations of colors, sizes, and forms are possible!

Seeing What Makes Annuals So Popular

People grow annual flowers in containers for a variety of reasons, and not just because they don't have a place to grow them in the ground. First and foremost, annuals are just plain fun to grow. They have some of the brightest, most appealing flowers, which attract children, butterflies, and just about anyone who wanders past. Here are some other reasons to give them a try:

- ✔ Annuals are movers. They grow fast and bloom when young, even while they're still in the nursery packs, which is not always such a good thing (more on this later).

- ✔ Annuals give you the longest season of abundant bloom of any plants.

- ✔ Annuals are relatively inexpensive, especially if you buy small plants. If you make mistakes, you can pull out the plants, and you may even have enough time to replant.

- ✔ With containers, you can put your favorite annuals where they can be best appreciated: sweet peas on your deck where you can smell their fragrance; Johnny-jump-ups in an eye-level pot where you can view their tiny splotched faces.

- ✔ With containers, you can display plants at their peak. Then you can move them out of site for some R and R and replace them with others that are reaching their peak.

- ✔ You can rotate blooming containers of flowers by the season. Start with spring bloomers like pansies, follow with summer petunias, and then try fall asters.

- ✔ Nothing dresses up a deck or patio faster for a party than blooming annuals brimming from decorative pots.

Understanding Annuals' Ideal Growing Seasons

In typical cold-winter climates, annuals are grown from spring to fall. In mild-winter climates, annuals can thrive year-round. So when do you shop for annuals and plant them? That depends on your climate and the plants' temperature preferences.

The terms hardy, half-hardy, and tender describe different types of annuals. They don't refer to the plants' ability to withstand the coldest winter temperatures; rather, they're an indication of the plants' temperature preferences during the growing season.

The term *hardy annuals* describes plants that can withstand some frost. They perform best when temperatures are mild, days are short, and soil is cool, typically in early spring and early fall. Their enemies are hot weather and long days, which cause a decline in performance and the onset of seed setting — ending the bloom season. Examples of hardy annuals are calendulas, pansies, and snapdragons. Plant these cool-season favorites a few weeks before the average last spring frost date in your area. (Refer to Chapter 2 for tips on determining your frost date.)

Freezing temperature damages or downright destroys *tender annuals.* Many of these tender types thrive in hot summer weather and are considered warm-season annuals; examples are celosia, marigolds, vinca rosea, and zinnias. Plant them after the date of your last frost — and when soil and air temperatures are warming up. Count on them to reach their peak in midsummer.

The term *half-hardy* describes plants that fall between hardy and tender. They can tolerate cool soils, chilly weather, and possibly a light frost, but will continue to grow through the summer in all but the hottest places. Many of the most common annual flowers fall into this category, including cosmos and petunias.

In regions with prolonged sub-freezing temperatures in winter, plant annuals in spring, enjoy them all summer into fall, and plan to replace them with fresh plants next spring. You can plant hardy and half-hardy annuals a few weeks before your last frost date, but wait until after that date to set out tender annuals. Garden centers usually sell the various types of annual flowers when the weather is right for planting them. If in doubt, ask the staff for advice.

In mild-winter regions where temperatures rarely or never drop below freezing, you can plant cool-season annuals like pansies and Iceland poppies when temperatures begin to cool down in late summer or early fall. Blooms may appear before Christmas and peak in late winter and early spring. The plants will likely begin to fade as temperatures heat up in spring; replace them with warm-season plants.

Shopping for Annuals

When you're ready to plant your container with annuals, you'll probably decide to plant containers with nursery transplants (ranging in size from seedlings in six-packs to plants in 6-inch pots) rather than seeds. Transplants make it easier for you, and they're not expensive when used in the quantities that most people buy for containers.

Look for plants that have a good green color and are relatively short and stocky. Start with small plants — their root systems adapt quickest to growing in new conditions. If you want color right away, buy larger, blooming plants in pots, gallon cans, or even larger containers. Just be sure that the roots haven't filled the nursery container to the point of shedding water. At the nursery, don't hesitate to tip the plant out of its pot or pack so that you can inspect the roots. Avoid plants with a thick tangle of roots.

Many small transplants sold these days already come with flowers — thanks to clever plant breeders successfully developing annuals to bloom precociously and tempt you into buying them rather than the more laggardly all-green seedlings. However, blooming as a youngster may actually impede future blooming. As painful as it may be, snipping off the flowers and flower buds will help the plant get established because it can focus on growing roots rather than energy-intensive flowers.

Some annuals are easy to start from seeds sown right in containers if you're so inclined; good choices for seed sowing are cosmos, marigolds, nasturtiums, sunflowers, and zinnias.

Planting Annuals in Containers

What kind of containers are recommended for annuals? Almost anything goes, as long as it has drainage holes. There are so many kinds of annuals, so many colors, shapes, and sizes, and so many different kinds of looks that your container choices are truly wide open. In the following sections, we give you the basic features to keep in mind when picking a container for annual flowers.

Flowers from above

The rewards of growing annual flowers in hanging baskets are pretty obvious — you get beautiful flowers or greenery at eye level or overhead where you can really appreciate the spectacular view. They're ideal for dressing up places where you otherwise have no color. And remember that they can be viewed from indoors as well.

Before deciding on a location, make sure that you'll have easy access for daily watering. (Even the reservoirs of self-watering baskets need frequent replenishing.) Keep in mind that most baskets drain water freely — right on your head if you happen to be sitting under one.

When it comes to size, you need to weigh two factors. Larger baskets hold more plants and generally require less frequent watering, but they're heavy and require strong hooks or other hanging hardware. Smaller baskets limit the number and size of plants you can use and need to be watered frequently, but they're easier to hang.

Pot size matters

Keep in mind that the smaller the pot, the faster the soil will dry out and the more often you'll need to water. Following are some guidelines for container sizes:

To grow healthy annuals, the container needs to be at least 6 inches deep.

As a general rule of scale, if the annuals normally grow 10 or 12 inches tall, provide a pot with a diameter of at least 8 inches. If the plants grow 2 or 3 feet tall, go for a diameter of 24 inches or a large container like a half barrel. See Chapter 3 for more information on containers.

Transplanting annuals to their new home

Starting with a good potting soil mix — not dirt dug up from your garden — goes a long way toward helping plants thrive. Look for soil mixes formulated for container growing. They have a good balance of water-holding capacity and drainage. (Look to Chapter 4 for details on choosing a soil mix.)

Set plants so that they're at the same height in their new container as they were in their nursery pots. In other words, don't bury plant stems, and don't leave roots exposed above the soil line. (See Chapter 5 for step-by-step instructions on planting in containers.)

Seasonal plants like annuals can be crowded together in a container more closely than is suggested for ground planting. Cramped conditions can return a much greater impact quickly. Annuals can't grow in crowded conditions for long, but their season is short, and you can satisfy the demand for extra water and food that the tight quarters create (see the next section for tips on this). If the recommended spacing for ground planting is 10 to 12 inches, in a container you may space the plants 6 to 8 inches apart. In fact, as a general rule, you can safely plant most annuals 6 inches apart.

Care and feeding

An annual grown in a container needs the same things that a plant in the ground does — mainly water, air, and nutrients. Remember, though, that roots in a container are confined and can't forage for what they need, so careful watering and feeding are essential.

More than anything else, remember that annuals like to set a fast pace with no pit stops: Running out of water or food can set them back for weeks or abruptly end their seasons.

Watering is much more critical for annuals grown in the confined spaces of containers than for those growing in the ground. Never let the soil dry out. You may want to install a drip system (discussed in Chapter 15) if you have many containers. Feeding container-grown annuals is also more critical than nourishing the same plants grown in the ground. Start feeding a few weeks after planting. Chapter 16 gives you the details.

Pinching and deadheading

Pinching and deadheading are important chores. *Pinching* is simply removing the growing tips on young plants, using your fingers or small pruners. This encourages the buds along the stem to sprout and grow. Plants that form shrubby mounds, such as chrysanthemums and petunias, benefit from this because it encourages lots of side branches.

Deadheading is removing spent flowers (see Figure 7-1). When you're deadheading, don't just pick off the petals; rather, pinch or snip off the whole spent flower head, which usually includes a developing seed pod. Doing this not only gets rid of unattractive fading blooms, it also removes the seeds that are developing within the flower head. The goal of flowering plants is to reproduce by making seeds. If you keep removing flower heads before the seeds mature, the plants will continue to produce flowers in an attempt to produce seeds. Keep deadheading, and they'll keep producing flowers.

Figure 7-1:
When dead-heading, remove the entire spent flower, not just the petals.

Top Annuals for Containers

When choosing plants for containers, pay special attention to their eventual sizes and growth habits. In general, compact varieties perform better in containers (sunflowers are perhaps the most extreme example, with the 10-foot Russian Giant out of the question and the 24-inch Teddy Bear perfect for containers). Look for dwarf varieties or those specially developed for containers. Names often provide a clue to container performance. Cascade petunias, for example, are designed to spill from pots.

Garden designers have coined three terms to help you choose plants for containers:

- ✔ *Thrillers* are tall, eye-catching plants for the center or back of the pot.
- ✔ *Fillers* are shrubby plants good for surrounding the taller center plant.
- ✔ *Spillers* tumble over the sides, softening the transition between plant and pot.

You can't really go wrong if you plant a large container with a thriller in the center, surround it with a few fillers, and add some spillers around the edges. Flip to Part V for ideas and inspiration on mixing and matching annual flowers in containers, as well as specific "recipes." And in the plant descriptions in the following sections, we indicate which category the annual fits in.

Figure 7-2 shows a planter filled with a combination of both upright and trailing varieties of fuchsia plus shrubby impatiens, creating a lush planter that is suitable for a shady area of your yard. (The upright fuchsias are the thrillers; the impatiens, the fillers; the trailing fuchsia, the spillers.)

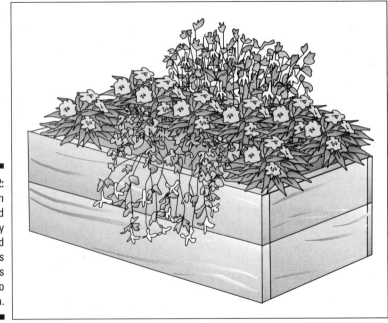

Figure 7-2:
A wooden planter filled with brightly colored annuals adds interest to any area.

We group flowering annuals by hardiness and light requirements in the following sections. Use these lists to help you design your containers and create a planting calendar. If your region has a long spring and hot summer weather, you can plan on swapping out plants as the seasons change. Choose all cool-season plants for a spring planting, and replace them with tender heat-lovers when summer hits. Then go back to cool-season plants in fall. Or you may decide to do a single planting, choosing all half-hardy plants and enjoying them spring to fall. Or, you can wait until after your last frost date and plant only heat-lovers, or a combination of half-hardy plants and heat-lovers. Lots of options! We also include sections on vines and foliage plants and ornamental grasses.

Half the fun of choosing plants is poring over beautiful photos. Go to www.hort.cornell.edu/gardening/homegardening/scenee139.html to see pictures of most of the flowers in our lists. A search engine can help you find photos of any missing ones.

Hardy, cool-season plants for sunny spots

These plants like cool weather and can tolerate light frosts, but they begin to flag as summer heats up. They're perfect for spring and fall planters, and grow right through the winter in mild climates. Plan to replace them with heat-lovers in summer.

- **Calendula:** Here's a great choice for containers early in the year. Sturdy plants and bright orange or yellow blooms stand up well to cool weather. *Thriller or filler, depending on variety/height.*

- **Iceland poppy:** A cool-season stalwart, its crinkly flowers in bright oranges, pinks, yellows, and other shades stand tall on long slender stems, but the plants are low and unprepossessing — best mixed with spreading plants that can provide some camouflage. Pansies are good container companions. *Thriller.*

- **Lobelia:** Call on the compact edging types to tuck into mixed plantings. Use the trailing types to spill from hanging baskets or pots. Flowers in light to deep blue, as well as white and lavender, lend themselves to color-combining with many other annuals. *Filler or spiller, depending on variety.*

- **Ornamental kale:** Grow it for striking, multicolored foliage — not flowers — early in the season and in fall, when colorful flowers are hard to come by. Show off a single plant in an 8-inch pot, or put several in a larger container. *Thriller or filler.*

- **Pansy and viola:** Hardy and carefree, these are often the first annuals you notice in containers each spring. Pansies have big, blotchy flowers. Violas are usually solid colors — yellow, blue, purple, and more. Combine pansies or violas with bulbs or fill pots with single or mixed colors. *Filler.*

- **Salvia:** There are many types of salvia, so read plant labels. *Salvia farinacea* sports 2-foot spikes of deep blue flowers, adding height and cooling color to containers. *Thriller.*

- **Snapdragon:** Height varies, so read plant labels. Tall varieties add drama to large containers; dwarf types are shrubbier. Cut a few spikes for indoor bouquets, too. *Thriller or filler.*

- **Sweet pea:** The familiar tall, climbing sweet pea quickly grows out of bounds in a container. Bush types make a fairly restrained container plant, growing only 12 to 30 inches tall. Flowers have a heavenly fragrance. *Filler.*

Half-hardy plants for sunny spots

These plants like the cool weather of spring and fall, and some may tolerate a light frost. However, they also continue to grow through the summer in all but the hottest regions, making them some of the best choices for single-season containers.

- **Bacopa:** Clouds of tiny white, blue, or pink flowers cover these trailing plants. They can be temperamental and will drop their flowers and buds if the soil dries out. Give them part shade in hot, sunny weather. *Spiller.*

- **Bidens:** Heat- and drought-tolerant, these plants are covered with small yellow flowers all season long. *Spiller.*

- **Calibrachoa:** A relatively new petunia relative, this plant is sometimes called million bells for its profusion of small, richly colored, petunia-like flowers. Tolerant and adaptable, this is one forgiving plant. If it starts to look ragged, cut it back and it will rebound quickly. *Spiller.*

- **Cleome:** With a height of 2 to 4 feet, depending on variety, cleome belongs in the center of the container where it can attract attention with its airy pink, purple, or white blooms. *Thriller.*

- **Diascia:** Also called twinspur, this plant's soft spikes of brightly colored flowers are ideal for informal containers, where they'll tumble every which way for a rambling, cottage-garden look. *Filler.*

- **Gaura:** With slender flower stems topped by delicate blooms, gaura adds a delicate note to plantings. Height varies, from 10 inches to 3 feet or more, so check plant labels. *Thriller or filler.*

- **Geraniums:** We can't think of any geranium that isn't a candidate for good, healthy living in a container. Put a few zonal geraniums in terra-cotta pots on your front stoop. Ivy geraniums are a favorite choice for hanging baskets. Scented geraniums have less-showy flowers but very fragrant foliage. (Note that these "annual geraniums" are in the genus *Pelargonium* and are different from hardy, perennial "true geraniums" in the genus *Geranium*.) *Filler.*

- **Lantana:** This adaptable, shrubby plant bears showy flower clusters from spring to fall. On many varieties the flower color changes with age, so the older, outer flowers of each cluster are a different color than the younger, inner ones. *Filler.*

- **Nemesia:** These plants like cool temperatures; move them to part shade when summer heats up. Flowers are richly and vividly colored in red, yellow, white, pink, and blue. Plants grow 8 to 18 inches tall — great near the rims of containers where they can spill over the sides. *Filler or spiller.*

- **Petunias:** On their own or in mixed plantings, petunias are standouts for containers with their abundant, crayon-colored flowers. They vary in height, shape, and habit depending on the variety, so check plant labels. If plants get too rangy in containers, cut stems back by about a third. *Filler or spiller.*

✔ **Scaevola:** Called fan flower for its unusual, fan-shaped blooms, scaevola can be kept shrubby with regular pruning or be allowed to sprawl and drape in hanging baskets. Give it part shade in hot, sunny weather. *Filler or spiller.*

✔ **Sweet alyssum:** Low and spreading with a profusion of tiny flowers, this is a dependable choice for filling in among mixed annuals or spilling over edges of a pot. Sweet alyssum is easy to grow from seeds or transplants. Familiar white is a great complement in mixed plantings, but rose and purple varieties are also available. *Filler or spiller.*

Tender plants for sunny spots

These plants love the heat. Wait until after the last spring frost to plant these flowers, and be prepared to cover them if temperatures drop below 50 degrees Fahrenheit. They're good candidates for replacing cool-season plants when they begin to wane as summer heats up.

✔ **African daisy (*Arctotis* and *Osteospermum* spp.):** These shrubby plants with colorful, daisylike flowers bloom profusely from spring to fall. *Filler.*

✔ **Ageratum:** These puffy little flowers most typically are blue, but white and pink also are available. Tall varieties reach 2 feet, but the most common varieties are dwarf, growing just 8 to 10 inches tall. *Filler.*

✔ **Angelonia (sometimes called summer snapdragon):** The tall flower spikes are a good warm-season replacement for cool-season snapdragons. They tolerate heat and drought. *Thriller or filler.*

✔ **Celosia:** Dramatic, fluffy plumes in the brightest yellow, orange, red, and pink adorn these plants all summer. Height ranges from 8 inches to 2 feet, depending on variety. *Thriller or filler.*

✔ **Cosmos:** Lacy and elegant, tall cosmos (up to 4 feet) stand out in borders and can also perform in large containers (half barrels, for example). For smaller containers, look for more compact or dwarf varieties. The daisylike flowers come in a range of magentas, pinks, yellows, oranges, and whites. *Thriller or filler.*

✔ **Dahlia:** You want compact bedding dahlias, not the tall, pot-toppling varieties (unless you grow them in a huge container). Dwarf dahlias grow about 12 to 15 inches tall, with flowers in bright, clear colors: orange, pink, purple, red, white, and yellow. *Thriller or filler.*

- ✔ **Euphorbia:** A recent introduction named Diamond Frost has become popular for its tiny white blooms atop wiry stems. A good filler, this plant is heat- and drought-tolerant. *Filler.*

- ✔ **Gerbera:** Look for this elegant, deeply colored daisy sold blooming in pots. Transplant a few into a larger container, and enjoy the striking flowers. They can be fussy, however, so don't take it personally if the plants are short-lived. *Filler.*

- ✔ **Marigold:** Compact French marigolds and signet marigolds (12 to 20 inches tall) are indispensable container classics. Fill a pot with a single variety or combine marigolds with other annuals. Colors include yellow and orange, plus mixes of orange, yellow, maroon, dark red, and more. These aromatic plants may help deter insect pests. *Filler.*

- ✔ **Pentas:** These mounding plants are topped with flower clusters that are absolute magnets for butterflies. They flower best in full sun but will tolerate and continue to flower in part shade. *Filler.*

- ✔ **Portulaca:** Also called moss rose, this low-growing plant has succulent leaves and abundant flowers in brilliant colors. This heat-lover needs very well-drained soil and is a good choice for sunny window boxes. *Spiller.*

- ✔ **Salvia (*S. splendens*):** Usually called annual salvia to distinguish it from its perennial cousins, this mounding plant is topped by bright spikes of red, white, or purple flowers and is an attention-getter in containers. *Filler.*

- ✔ **Strawflower:** The petals (technically, bracts) of these daisylike flowers are dry and papery, making them popular for drying. Look for dwarf varieties that grow 12 to 15 inches tall. *Filler.*

- ✔ **Sunflowers:** Bushy dwarf varieties grow only 1 or 2 feet tall and are terrific in containers. Two top choices are Dwarf Sungold and Teddy Bear. Sunflowers are easy to grow from seeds started directly in containers. *Thriller.*

- ✔ **Verbena:** With clusters of red, purple, yellow, pink, or white flowers, verbenas can take the heat and are reliable performers. Some varieties are more upright; others are trailing. *Filler or spiller.*

- ✔ **Vinca rosea:** Take a lesson from shopping centers and other public spaces where you see vinca rosea in the hottest spots. This is one tough, heat-loving annual for containers that must face hot sun. Its foliage always looks sharp and glossy. White and pink flowers bloom over a very long season. *Filler.*

- ✔ **Zinnias:** Mix the colors or use single colors for bright containers in full sun. Compact dwarfs, notably the Profusion series, work best in containers. Zinnias come in hot colors and do well in hot weather. *Filler.*

Annuals for shady locations

Color is harder to come by in shady spots, but a handful of annuals thrive in containers and will bloom well in light to medium shade.

- ✔ **Bedding begonia:** Tuberous, rex, angelwing, and rieger begonias offer some of the most dramatic flowers around, not to mention the unusual and often variegated foliage. The plants are somewhat fragile, so place them where they won't be buffeted by wind or inadvertently damaged by passersby. Some varieties are more upright; others trailing. Wax begonias are smaller and more tolerant of sun. *Filler or spiller.*

- ✔ **Browallia:** This is a beautiful trailing plant with white or blue flowers. A number of new varieties are available specifically for hanging baskets. *Spiller.*

- ✔ **Fuchsia:** Impossibly bright, bell-shaped flowers attract hummingbirds, making cascading varieties ideal for eye-level hanging baskets. Some varieties are shrubbier and more upright. *Thriller, filler, or spiller.*

- ✔ **Impatiens:** Impatiens perform brilliantly in containers, including hanging baskets. Flower colors include red, pink, rose, violet, orange, white, and bicolors. Double-flowered varieties are especially nice in containers where you can admire the blooms up close. New Guinea impatiens have larger, glossier leaves and tolerate more sun. *Filler.*

- ✔ **Torenia:** Also called wishbone flower, torenia tolerates heat and humidity and flowers all summer long in part to full shade. Read plant labels — some torenias are shrubby; others trail. *Filler or spiller.*

Flowering vines

Grow these vines on a trellis or other vertical support for a traffic-stopping display. Place them in front of a fence or lattice to hide an eyesore or add a little privacy to your outdoor living areas. If you have a large container, you can set a trellis right in it. Or set the container in front of a wall-mounted support.

- ✔ **Black-eyed Susan vine:** Also called thunbergia, this vine bears striking orange or white flowers with black centers and grows up to 8 feet tall, a manageable height for container growing. Plant in full sun.

- ✔ **Mandevilla:** This pretty, tropical vine sports large, trumpet-shaped blossoms on glossy leaves. Plant it in full sun. At the end of the growing season, trim it back and bring it indoors over the winter. Set it outside again the following spring.

- ✔ **Morning glory, cypress vine, and cardinal climber:** All plants in the genus *Ipomoea*, these are rambling vines that can reach 15 feet or more in height and need strong supports. All need full sun.

Foliage plants and ornamental grasses

Grown for their attractive leaves rather than their flowers, foliage plants can provide unusual forms and textures on their own or be used to complement flowers.

- **Alternanthera:** The common names Joseph's coat and calico plant refer to the colorful foliage, which may be any combination of green, yellow, orange, red, or purple, depending on the variety. Plant in part to full shade.

- **Coleus:** Colorful foliage brightens shady spots and adds a tropical look. Recent introductions boast an astounding range of foliage colors, from chartreuse to purple-black, with variegated varieties combining colors to rival the boldest flowers. Most coleus prefer part to full shade; some of the newer varieties tolerate full sun.

- **Dracaena:** These tall, strappy-leaved plants are commonly used in the center of large containers to add height. Most varieties prefer part shade.

- **Dusty miller:** Traditionally used as a filler and accent for bright flowers, this plant's silvery gray foliage beautifully sets off purple petunias, red impatiens, or many other annuals and colors. Plants grow 12 to 15 inches tall. Plant in full sun.

- **Fountain grass:** The strappy leaves and tall flower stalks topped with feathery plumes add a gentle, graceful movement as they sway in the slightest breeze. Plant in full sun to part shade.

- **Helichrysum:** Called licorice plant for the aroma released by its leaves, this trailing plant has velvety leaves in a range of hues from chartreuse to gray-green. Plant in full sun to part shade.

- **Plectranthus:** Also called Swedish ivy, this plant has fuzzy leaves and can be kept to a mounding habit or allowed to trail over the sides of the container. Plant in full sun to part shade.

- **Sweet potato vine:** With richly colored foliage in hues of bright yellow-green to bronze to burgundy, these plants start out shrubby but will eventually trail gracefully over the sides of containers. Plant in full sun to part shade.

- **Vinca vine:** Not to be confused with flowering *Vinca rosea*, the green or green-and-white foliage trails down the sides of pots. Plant in full sun.

Chapter 8

Plant, Pick, Eat: Vegetables and Herbs

*I*magine deep red, vine-ripened tomatoes, aromatic basil, cooling cucumbers, and lettuce so fresh it's practically still growing — all harvested from your patio. Achieving this vision isn't as daunting a task as you may expect. Growing vegetables in containers — on a patio, deck, balcony, or even out in the garden — is not that difficult. And the tasty payoff makes it especially rewarding.

With some planning, you can eat your own produce all summer long. Apartment dwellers and homeowners alike find container vegetables appealing. First, the convenience is tough to match: Just walk out on the deck and snip some lettuce for a salad or swipe a few peas for a stir-fry. And second, the flexibility yields some fresh ideas: Plant cherry tomatoes in hanging baskets or lettuce among your petunias. Move containers as necessary to give them the sunniest spot on the deck or to get them out of the way when company arrives and you need the space. With vegetables in containers, you truly have a movable feast.

And don't overlook culinary herbs for containers. Many are attractive and fit right in with ornamental plants. Usually less demanding than vegetables, many herbs are of Mediterranean origin and like it on the hot and dry side. Brush by a pot of thyme, rosemary, or sage on the way to the door, and you may imagine you're in the south of France.

In this chapter you find general information on growing vegetables and herbs in containers, as well as crop-by-crop tips. Bon appétit!

Giving Container Vegetables and Herbs What They Really Need

If you grow vegetables in the ground, you know that the number-one rule is to keep them growing vigorously — with plenty of water, nutrients, sunlight, and whatever else the specific crops require. Vegetables and herbs in containers need no less care. In fact, providing the essentials to vegetables and herbs growing in containers can be more challenging because their growing space is limited.

To ease the caretaking task, place container plants in a convenient spot where you can dote on them. Your portable garden is likely to reward your attention with tasty returns! Following is some general information; look to the sections on individual crops for specifics.

Plenty of sunlight

Sunshine is a common limiting factor in vegetable and herb gardening, especially for apartment dwellers and gardeners with small yards. Most edibles need a minimum of six hours of direct sunlight, at least some of it during midday when the sun's rays are strongest. The sunniest spot in your yard may be your front stoop or the corner of your back deck. Wherever it is, dedicate it to your veggies and herbs.

Exceptions to the full-sun rule include lettuce and spinach, which actually benefit from some shade in the heat of midsummer to keep them from *bolting* — sending up flower heads that end your salad-picking days. Root vegetables like carrots and beets can tolerate some light shade, too. So even if you don't have a spot in full sun, you can grow something for the dinner table!

The right container

First question: Can vegetables and herbs be beautiful as well as productive? Of course, if you choose attractive pots and keep your plants well tended.

If all you want is to pick the produce and you don't care what the container looks like, the requirements are pretty basic:

✔ **The container must be big enough.** As a rule of thumb, containers should be at least 8 inches wide and 12 inches deep for most vegetables and herbs, but a diameter of 12 to 18 inches and a depth of 15 inches is preferable — the larger size can accommodate the necessary volume of soil and water.

✔ **The container must have drainage holes at the bottom.** Plastic mop buckets, small garbage cans, 5-gallon buckets from delicatessens, and even plastic milk jugs are all possibilities if you poke some holes for drainage, even if they miss the boat in the beauty department.

If the containers are going to be part of your garden scene, you probably want something more presentable (but with the recommended dimensions and drainage holes). Remember that terra cotta, no matter how attractive, tends to dry out quickly — a major problem for vegetables and herbs racing full steam ahead. You may be better off planting in plastic. If you want a big container to hold a number of vegetables and herbs or a whole salad's fixings, an oak half-barrel is hard to beat. (See Chapter 3 for more details about containers.)

A good soil mix

Commercial soil mixes, as we describe in Chapter 4, can be used straight from the bag. But many vegetables and herbs benefit from additional organic matter like bagged compost or ground bark: Add one part of organic matter to each three parts of soil mix.

The benefits of growing your own veggies

There's renewed interest in home-grown foods as more and more people discover the rewards of food gardening. Here are a few:

✔ **Getting the freshest vegetables:** Hands down, the freshest, best-tasting vegetables and herbs are those you grow yourself and harvest at their peak.

✔ **Saving money:** Growing your own food saves money, especially when it comes to "gourmet" vegetables like fancy lettuce mixes and Oriental eggplant.

✔ **Using fewer pesticides:** You know exactly what's been sprayed, and you may opt for organic fertilizing and pest control techniques.

✔ **Becoming a locavore:** Eating locally produced, in-season foods is a growing trend, and nothing is more local than your own backyard!

✔ **Trying new vegetables:** Want to try the latest variety of squash or lettuce, but can't get it at your local grocery store? That's not a problem if you have the right conditions for growing it in your yard.

Water, water, water

Watering is always important with container plants, and even more so with vegetables and herbs — let them wilt once and they may never really get back on track. Containers can dry out in a day or in a few hours depending on the planter's size and the intensity of the summer heat, and even if you rewet it right away, the plants may be permanently stunted.

To avoid letting your plants get too thirsty, check pots and planters often and don't allow the soil to dry out more than an inch or two below the surface. Self-watering planters and drip irrigation can help ease your watering chores: Chapter 15 delves into these and other watering options.

Fertilizer

In general, vegetables and herbs are heavy feeders — especially when grown in containers. The need for nutrients varies according to what you're growing. Lettuce and other leafy crops need a consistent supply of nitrogen to produce those leaves, whereas tomatoes need some nitrogen to grow, but too much can inhibit flowering — no flowers, no tomatoes.

One option is to mix an all-purpose, slow-release, granular fertilizer — organic or synthetic — into the soil mix before planting. Or, plan to fertilize religiously during the growing season. Find out more about fertilizer options in Chapter 16.

Choosing Vegetables for Containers

Theoretically, you can grow just about any vegetable in a container. Questions do come up, though, about the appropriate pot for those 600-pound pumpkins — maybe the right container is the back of the pickup that hauls the monster to the county contest weigh-in. We suggest that you grow crops that can provide you with at least a few fresh meals and that don't monopolize your whole patio or life. Although some vegetables are technically perennials, the most common crops are typically grown as annuals and produce their edible harvest the first season.

Try to choose container-friendly varieties: vegetables that are naturally small-statured and bred specifically for growing in pots. When you read seed catalogs, look for varieties described with words like "compact," "good for containers," "bush-type," "baby vegetable," "midget," "dwarf," and "tiny." Think twice before choosing varieties with words like "jumbo," "gargantua," "mammoth," and "whopper" in their names.

Like annual flowers, vegetables and herbs have temperature preferences. Some grow best in the cool of spring and fall (or winter in mild climates). Others need heat to thrive. For the biggest and tastiest harvest, time your planting to coincide with the best weather for individual crops. To help you know what to plant when, we group veggies by their growing season in the following sections.

Cool-season vegetables

In cold-winter regions, sow seeds or set out transplants in early spring, a few weeks before your average last-frost date (see Chapter 2) so the plants mature while the weather is cool. In mild-winter climates, plant in fall for a winter harvest.

Broccoli, cabbage, and kinfolk

Collectively called *brassicas* or *cole crops,* plants in this group are in the Cruciferae or mustard family and include the familiar broccoli, Brussels sprouts, cabbage, cauliflower, collards, kale, and mustard. Less common kin include broccoflower (a cross between broccoli and cauliflower), Chinese cabbage, kohlrabi, and romanesco broccoli. All need similar care and cool weather.

We recommend these varieties:

- **Broccoli:** Arcadia, DeCicco, Marathon, Munchkin, Small Miracle
- **Cabbage:** Danish Ballhead, Melissa Savoy
- **Cauliflower:** Cheddar, Snowball

Lettuce and spinach

Leafy greens grow quickly: You can begin harvesting your own gourmet baby spinach and lettuce in just four weeks. Plant seeds every few weeks in spring for a constant supply into early summer. (Most salad greens turn bitter and bolt, producing flowers and seed, once the weather heats up.) Start planting again in late summer for a fall harvest. In warm-winter areas, you can grow salad greens all winter.

Spinach and loose-leaf lettuces are the easiest to grow. For an extended harvest and to keep plants attractive, cut individual leaves as you need them, rather than cutting the whole plant off at the base. (The plants resprout, but they look unattractive for a few weeks.) Buttercrunch varieties (also called butterhead and Boston lettuce) make small, loose heads. They're also easy to grow and are more tolerant of hot weather than loose-leaf lettuces. Sow seeds for some unusual greens, too, like arugula (rocket), mache, radicchio, and watercress. Or sow a mesclun mix (a combination of various greens, often including some spicy ones) for harvesting when they're just a few inches tall.

The following varieties of lettuce and spinach are good ones to try:

- **Lettuce:** Buttercrunch, Tom Thumb, Salad Bowl, Romaine, Dark Green Boston, Ruby, Bibb
- **Spinach:** Bloomsdale, Matador

Onions and their relatives

Onions, scallions, chives, and leeks are collectively called *alliums,* and they're kitchen essentials. Plant scallions every few weeks from early spring to fall for a constant supply. Sow leek seed in early spring. Leeks are slow growers, but worth waiting for when you can impress your friends with homegrown, gourmet, grilled leeks. Chives are perennials that are hardy to zone 3. Snip off leaves as you need them.

Chive blossoms are edible, and their lavender color gives a nice tint to herb vinegars.

We suggest the following varieties of scallions and leeks:

- **Leeks:** Imperial Summer, Tornado
- **Scallions:** Beltsville Bunching, Long White Bunching

Peas

Cool temperatures produce the sweetest, most tender peas. Plant seeds of edible-podded pea varieties, including snow peas and sugar snap peas, and shelling types (which you remove from the pod before eating) in early spring for an early summer harvest. Plant them again in late summer for a fall harvest. (In mild-winter regions they make a good winter crop.) Some varieties are climbers and need support; others are lower-growing bush types.

We recommend the following varieties:

- **Shelling peas:** Garden Sweet, Half Pint
- **Snap peas:** Super Sugar Snap
- **Snow peas:** Oregon Sugar Pod II, Tom Thumb

Root crops

Beets, radishes, and turnips are good candidates for containers at least 8 inches deep. Short, stubby carrot varieties like Thumbelina are also fine. For full-size carrots and parsnips, choose containers that are at least 12 inches deep. Sow seeds in early spring, in soil that is lightweight and drains freely. Harvest them while they're young and tender (with the exception of parsnips, which taste best when they've been exposed to a few fall frosts).

Potatoes are large plants, each requiring a 5-gallon pot or larger. Plant *seed potatoes* — small potatoes sold specially for planting — in early spring for a summer harvest.

Try planting any of the following varieties of root vegetables in your containers:

- **Beets:** Baby Ball, Chicago Red, Detroit Dark Red
- **Carrots:** Little Finger, Red-Cored Chantenay, Thumbelina, Short 'n' Sweet
- **Parsnips:** Hamburg, Harris Model
- **Potatoes:** Red Gold, French Fingerling, All Blue
- **Radishes:** Cherry Belle, Easter Egg, French Breakfast
- **Turnips:** Purple Top, Tokyo Cross

Warm-season vegetables

These crops need warm soil to sprout and warm air temperatures to grow. Wait until after the last frost date to plant them. Some fast-growing, warm-season crops are best started directly from seed; others require a longer growing season, so you're better off setting them in as transplants that you've grown indoors or purchased.

Beans

Beans are easy to grow and provide a nutritious, protein-rich harvest. Bush varieties stay compact, have high yields, and mature over a period of a few weeks, usually earlier than pole beans. Pole varieties can do fine in pots, as long as you provide stakes or taut strings for them to run up. The effect can be attractive, especially for a balcony. Look for yellow- and purple-podded varieties in addition to the usual green.

Plant bean seeds in spring when temperatures are reliably warm. (Bean seed will rot in the ground if planted in cool, wet soil.) After seeds sprout, thin seedlings by removing any extras so that the remaining ones stand 6 inches apart. Water and fertilize regularly, and harvest beans continually, or they'll stop producing.

We suggest the following varieties:

- **Bush:** Masai, Topcrop, Greencrop, Purple Queen, Gold Mine
- **Pole:** Kentucky Blue, Romano, Blue Lake, Purple King

Corn

Surely not! But yes, you can grow corn in containers. It's one of those crops that take a lot of room and extra care, so think twice about whether it might be easier to buy corn from a local farm and save your containers for something more manageable.

If you're determined to give it a try, provide soil mix with lots of organic matter and a deep, large container like a half-barrel. Sow seeds in spring when the weather — and the soil — warms up. (Like bean seed, corn seed sown in cold, wet soil will rot.) Plan on watering and fertilizing abundantly.

Varieties with a shorter stature are more likely to produce mature ears and less likely to topple in the wind than taller ones. Because the plants are wind-pollinated, the ears may not fill out completely as they would if you planted a large block in your garden. But if you have your heart set on homegrown sweet corn, by all means plant a big container or two.

Choose from these recommended varieties:

- ✔ **Sweet corn:** Golden Midget, Sugar Buns, Precocious
- ✔ **Popping corn:** Tom Thumb

Cucumbers, melons, pumpkins, and squash

There are bush and vining varieties of these closely related crops, collectively referred to as *cucurbits*. For containers, look for varieties described as compact. Full-sized plants, especially winter squash and pumpkins, grow quickly and will overtake your containers . . . your deck . . . maybe even your house. If you choose vining types, provide space and a trellis for climbing. All cucurbits need warm soil to germinate and hot weather to produce a good crop. Sow seeds in spring after the weather warms up, or plant transplants to get a head start.

Plant a "three sisters garden" in a pot

Native Americans planted three warm-season crops together: corn, beans, and squash. Called the three sisters, these plants help each other grow: The beans add nitrogen to the soil, corn (which needs lots of nitrogen) gives the beans something to climb, and the broad leaves of the squash plants keep weeds at bay.

Make your own "three sisters garden" by planting a dozen corn seeds in the middle of a large planter — at least a half barrel. When the corn is a few inches tall, plant eight bean seeds in a circle around it. After another week or so, plant four squash seeds around the perimeter. Keep the soil moist and fertilize regularly, and you'll be harvesting your own three sisters. Flip to the color section in the middle of this book for a picture of a "three sisters garden."

Here are some good varieties to get you started on the right track:

- ✔ **Cucumbers:** Bush Pickle, Salad Bush, Patio Pick, Spacemaster
- ✔ **Melons:** Honey Bun cantaloupe, Sugar Baby watermelon
- ✔ **Pumpkins:** Summer Ball
- ✔ **Squash:** Greyzini and Space Miser zucchini, Sunburst and Scallopini Pattypan, Table Queen Acorn

Eggplant and peppers

Warm, rich soil mix and hot sun are the ingredients for successful eggplants and peppers. They're particularly well-suited to container growing. The plants are compact, and they're beautiful when laden with colorful fruit. They require a long growing season, so start seeds indoors in spring or purchase transplants. Set plants out when the weather turns warm for the season.

Hot peppers are sometimes rated using Scoville heat units (SHUs) based on the amount of capsaicin they contain, because capsaicin gives peppers their heat. Sweet peppers contain none, so their rating is 0. Jalapeños run hotter, with a rating of around 4,000. Habaneros, on the high end of the scale, come in at a fiery 200,000 or more. Many of the pepper varieties sold as ornamental plants are of the hottest variety. Use care when handling these and other hot peppers because capsaicin can cause a painful burning sensation.

We recommend the following varieties:

- ✔ **Eggplant:** Fairy Tale, Bambino, Morden Midget, Long Tom
- ✔ **Hot peppers:** Apache, Birdseye, Cubanelle, Cheyenne
- ✔ **Sweet peppers:** Red Popper, Golden Baby Belle, Mohawk, Jingle Bells

Okra

A mainstay in Southern cooking, okra is a member of the hibiscus family and has beautiful blossoms in ivory, yellow, or red. It likes sun and heat and is an ideal crop for containers, because the soil in the pot heats up in the sun. Sow seeds when the weather has warmed up, or start with transplants for an earlier harvest.

We recommend Baby Bubba Hybrid and Little Lucy.

Summer greens

Most greens, like lettuce and spinach, grow best in cool weather, but a few types thrive in the heat and will provide a nutritious harvest all summer long. Swiss chard, Malabar spinach, New Zealand spinach, and vegetable amaranth love hot weather and are easy to grow. They're attractive plants, too, so mix them in with heat-loving annual flowers.

Try the Bright Lights or Rhubarb variety of Swiss chard.

Tomatoes

Close relatives of eggplants and peppers, tomatoes are so popular in home gardens they deserve a category of their own. A sun-warmed, vine-ripened tomato defines summer for many gardeners. Although full-sized plants can grow in 5-gallon or larger containers, new compact varieties make it easy to grow tomatoes anywhere you have a spot of sunshine.

Tomato plants are classified as either determinate (those that grow to a point and stop) or indeterminate (those that keep on growing . . . and growing). Both types need some sort of support — you can use tomato cages or tie plant stems to trellises or stakes — but determinate tomatoes are more manageable for containers.

Tomatoes need a deep container. Plant nursery seedlings in spring after the weather has warmed up. Unlike most plants, you can bury the stems of tomato seedlings — they'll develop roots along the buried portion. At planting time, prune off the lowest set of leaves and set the plant deeply in the container so the next set of leaves is just above the soil line. This technique encourages the plant to develop an extensive root system that will help it take up the abundant water and nutrients it needs.

Upside-down planters are usually advertised as ideal for growing tomatoes, and they do offer some benefits, the most important being that because the plants aren't in contact with garden soil, they're less susceptible to soil-borne diseases. You can achieve a similar effect by planting tomatoes in sterile soil mix in any hanging basket or pot raised off the ground.

There are hundreds, if not thousands, of tomato varieties, so experiment to see what varieties you like best and grow well in your climate. (Some farmer's markets offer tomato taste testings — they're a good way to try new varieties before growing them in your garden.) The following varieties are particularly good for growing in containers: Patio Princess, Celebrity, BushSteak, Tumbler, Windowbox Roma, Sugary, and Super Bush.

Trying your hand at something different

Growing your own crops means you can try vegetables and herbs not available in your supermarket. You can try out different varieties of your old favorites, like Asian eggplants and Armenian cucumbers. And you can experiment with crops you've never tasted, or even seen — perhaps tatsoi (a leafy member of the cabbage family) or jicama (a crispy, sweet root vegetable).

Other vegetables you may want to experiment with include

- **Broccoli raab:** A more pungent type of broccoli, sometimes called rapini.
- **Edamame:** Soybeans that are eaten green rather than dried.
- **Florence fennel:** The lower leaves form a bulb with a refreshing anise flavor.

The best way to find out about new and unusual crops is to browse seed catalogs, especially those that specialize in heirloom varieties and those that include crops associated with different cuisines — Asian and Indian, for example. Nichols Garden Nursery (`www.nicholsgardennursery.com`) is one good source of information — and seeds.

Selecting Herbs for Containers

Herbs make perfect sense for containers. Most herbs are easy to grow, and they look good, too. Many form compact, attractive plants that look at home in their own pots or tucked among flowers.

Place your herb pots where they're handy from the kitchen or patio. Who's in favor of jogging out past the pump house to the back 40 when you desperately need rosemary for the chicken you're barbecuing on your back patio?

Like vegetables, herbs vary in their temperature preferences — some like it cool; others need the heat. Their flavor and aroma is due to the essential oils they contain: Many herbs have the best flavor when they're watered and fertilized sparingly, which increases the concentration of these oils. The following sections group herbs by the weather conditions they prefer.

Herbs that like it hot and dry

Many of the most popular herbs are native to Mediterranean climates where they thrive in hot sun with little rainfall. In regions with lots of summer rain, containers may be your only option for growing them, because you can move them under cover to keep them from getting too much water. Plant them in very well-drained soil and fertilize sparingly. These herbs are good candidates for combining in a planter, because they like the same conditions. Herbs in this category include

✔ **Marjoram and oregano:** Aromatic, sweet marjoram is an annual that's easy to grow from seed and tolerates light frost. Oregano is similar, but is a perennial and has a more pungent aroma and taste.

✔ **Rosemary:** A shrub in its native habitat, rosemary requires a large container with a well-drained soil mix and hot sun. Rosemary is not reliably hardy below zone 8, but small plants may overwinter indoors with bright sunlight.

✔ **Sage:** More cold-hardy than rosemary, sage can survive outside to zone 4. Sage is available in many varieties: tricolor, purple, golden, and dwarf — a good bet for a container.

✔ **Savory:** With a strong peppery aroma, winter savory is a wonderful addition to a pot of beans. It's hardy to zone 6. Summer savory is an annual with a more delicate aroma.

✔ **Tarragon:** An ungainly plant, tarragon belongs in a pot with more orderly herbs (such as sage). Look for French tarragon, which can only be propagated from cuttings. If you see tarragon seeds, they're the less desirable Russian tarragon. It's hardy to zone 4, but the plant can be short-lived and may not overwinter.

✔ **Thyme:** Varieties abound, but don't pass up common thyme for any kind of cooking. Hardy to zone 5, thyme likes dry conditions and lots of sun. Have fun with unusual varieties like lemon thyme, mint thyme, and nutmeg thyme.

Herbs that like cool temperatures

These plants prefer the cool weather of spring and fall and will bolt (produce flowers and seed) during hot weather. Once the plant bolts, the flavor of the leaves gets bitter. If you're growing the plants for the leaves, grow them in spring and fall. If you're interested in the seeds, grow the plants in spring so they can produce seeds in summer.

✔ **Cilantro and coriander:** These two come from the same plant — the fresh leaves are called cilantro; the dried seed is called coriander. For a continuous supply of tender, succulent leaves, sow a small bed of seed every three weeks starting in early spring and again in fall when the weather cools down. Cilantro will bolt when temperatures heat up. If you want coriander, let the seeds mature, collect and dry them, and you'll have it.

✔ **Dill and fennel:** Sow seed in early spring and harvest the foliage ("dill weed") at any time. In summer the plant produces flowers and finally dill seed — an essential in pickling. The same goes for fennel, a close relative of dill.

✔ **Parsley:** Choose between curly-leafed and flat-leafed (sometimes called Italian) — both are pretty, bright green plants. Parsley grown in cool weather has a fresher, brighter flavor; it gets more bitter in hot weather. Parsley is biennial, growing one year, and then flowering and setting seed the next. Sow seeds every spring (even though sprouting is slow) or start with nursery transplants. Parsley has a long taproot, so be sure to use a container at least 12 inches deep. Part shade is best.

Heat- and moisture-loving herbs

These plants like the heat of summer; wait a week or two after the average last frost date to plant them outdoors so they won't be stunted by cool temperatures. Unlike Mediterranean herbs like rosemary and thyme, described above, the following plants require consistently moist soil (similar to that required by most vegetables). Don't plant them alongside herbs that like soil on the dry side or one or the other will suffer; use separate containers so you can cater to each plant's needs.

✔ **Basil:** Basil is an annual that needs hot weather to grow. Plant seed or transplants when you're sure that the overnight temperatures won't drop below 50 degrees Fahrenheit, and expect to be rewarded with fast-growing plants and lots of pesto by summer. Fertilize moderately with nitrogen. Many types are available (cinnamon, Thai, lemon, globe); all do well in pots.

✔ **Stevia:** All the rage now, stevia is called "the sweet herb," and if you've ever tasted it, you know why. In its native Paraguay, it has been used as a sweetener for hundreds of years. Grow your own stevia plants so you can drop a leaf or two in your tea, and enjoy watching your friends' faces when you give them a leaf to chew and they're hit with that super sweetness. Stevia likes warm temperatures, so wait to plant until warm weather arrives in earnest. Plants grown from seed vary in sweetness, so if you're looking for the sweetest of the sweet, start with purchased plants.

Chapter 9

Bulbs to Brighten Your Space

· ·

In This Chapter

▶ Getting a quick course in bulb botany

▶ Planting bulbs in containers

▶ Choosing bulbs for every season

· ·

*J*ust imagine a 2-foot-diameter bowl of bright red tulips all abloom against a backdrop of dark green conifers. Or what about a single, intensely fragrant hyacinth perfuming your whole kitchen . . . in February! The most spectacular container gardening that you ever do may involve bulbs. Bulbs require us to play by a different set of rules than other plants, and they take extra patience and careful timing. But the rewards are worth it!

Bulbs are perennials: They store food underground that allows them to survive a dormant period and resprout months later. So why are we grouping them with annual plants for single-season containers? Because most gardeners treat them as annuals. Many bulbs take a while to reach the bloom stage after planting, and then have relatively short bloom seasons. Tulips, for example, need months to grow roots and leaves, but then bloom for just a few weeks. When they're in bloom, they're spectacular. But after that they're just leaves that begin to yellow and wither after a month or so. When that happens, most gardeners opt to replace them with annual flowers, instead of treating them as perennials to be kept year to year.

In this chapter you find a short botany lesson on bulbs and bulblike plants, planting tips, and a rundown of some of the most popular bulbs for every season.

Brushing Up on Bulb Basics

The discussion of bulbs in this chapter (and elsewhere in this book) includes types of plants that are not, botanically speaking, true bulbs, but that perform pretty much the same. Corms, rhizomes, tubers, and tuberous roots, like true bulbs, are underground food storage systems with dormant buds that, when environmental conditions are right, sprout foliage and produce flowers. Then they die back to the ground, go through a dormant or resting period, and then resprout.

The most familiar bulbs, like tulips and daffodils, are planted in fall and bloom in spring. Some less-typical bulbs bloom at other times of the year, but are plenty worthwhile in their own right. For example, you can plant summer-blooming bulbs (including calla lily, canna, and tuberous begonia) in spring for summer or early fall bloom. Plant fall-blooming bulbs, such as colchicum and autumn crocus, in late August or September; flowers appear just weeks later.

Like other plants that have evolved to overwinter or endure a dormant period, bulbs vary in hardiness. The spring bloomers tend to be the hardiest; most will survive in regions as cold as zones 4 or 5 when planted in the garden (although they're less hardy in containers; more on that in a minute). Many summer bloomers are tropical in origin, so they must be protected from winter's cold. Fall bloomers tend to be relatively cold hardy. Because they require different care, it makes sense to categorize them according to when they're planted and when they bloom. The sections later in the chapter list bulbs grouped by season. But first, we give you some general advice that applies to all bulbs.

Containers and Bulbs: A Great Partnership

Most bulbs bloom for just a few weeks. Then, when the plants are finished blooming and the foliage begins to yellow, bulb plants start to look ragged. You can't cut off the foliage until it has fully died back or you reduce the food reserves in the bulbs. So most gardeners plant early-sprouting, fast-growing shrubby perennials like daylilies to hide the unsightly bulb foliage as it ripens.

Planting bulbs in containers solves this problem. After planting, you can store the containers out of sight during the first several months as the bulbs grow roots and begin to sprout. Then, when the flowers are at their peak, you can place the containers nearby for close-up viewing (and smelling, in the case of the beautifully scented types such as hyacinths and narcissus). After the blooms have faded, you can pull out the bulbs and replant the container with other flowers.

Planting just one bulb variety per pot ensures that all the bulbs in the pot will bloom at the same time. Mixing varieties in a container, on the other hand, results in flowers coming at different times, which has much less impact. If you want different flower colors and bloom times, grow different varieties in separate containers.

The following sections give you the lowdown on making bulbs feel and look at home in a container.

Choosing the container

Bulbs look fine in a wide variety of container shapes and styles. As a general rule, spring bulbs are planted in the ground at a depth three times their diameter, but that rule doesn't have to apply to short-term container growing. Choose containers that allow at least 2 inches of soil beneath the bulbs.

The traditional container in which to grow spring-blooming bulbs like hyacinths is a clay or plastic *bulb pan,* a shallow pot 10 inches or larger in diameter and only 5 or so inches deep. These pots don't hold much soil, so they aren't candidates for replanting with other flowers.

Shopping for bulbs

You can buy bulbs at a local nursery or garden center or by mail order. The nursery bins and bags give you a chance to personally inspect the bulbs for quality — always important! But perhaps more than any other plant, durable and compact bulbs lend themselves to mail-order delivery.

When you order from reputable suppliers, you can rest assured that you'll receive high-quality bulbs. And you know that they've been stored in the proper conditions, usually a cool warehouse, rather than sitting out in an overheated store display. Plus, mail order generally offers the widest selection of varieties.

The bulbs that you see for sale at nurseries have been dug up at their most dormant stage — with no root or top growth. Spring bulbs are dug in summer for fall planting. Garden centers begin displaying different types of bulbs right before their proper planting time. Mail-order companies encourage you to order months ahead — often with significant discounts — and then they ship the bulbs to you at the proper planting time.

The bloom season for most bulbs can be short, two or three weeks at best for daffodils and tulips. (But isn't that why we love bulbs — for their fleeting burst of beauty in the spring garden?) If you want a longer bloom season, check out the bloom dates of the bulbs you buy. Daffodil and tulip varieties, for example, are described as early-, mid-, and late-season, relative to the average bloom time for that plant. (Because daffodils bloom before tulips, even late-season daffodils may be finished blooming before early-season tulips get started.) For an extended bloom season, choose varieties with staggered bloom dates, planting each type in its own container so you can display them at peak bloom.

Keep these tips in mind as you shop for bulbs:

- ✔ **Buying earlier is better than waiting.** When you pick out your bulbs as soon as they hit the nurseries or catalogs, you get a much better selection of varieties. And at this time, the bulbs aren't picked over, with just the runts remaining. If you're not yet ready to plant, keep your bulbs in a cool dark place, with good air circulation and temperatures ideally between 35 and 50 degrees Fahrenheit.

  Don't store bulbs and fruits together in an enclosed place. For example, if you store your bulbs in the refrigerator, don't put them in the vegetable crisper alongside a bag of apples. Ripening fruits emit ethylene gas which can damage the bulbs.

- ✔ **Bigger is better than smaller.** The size of the bulb indicates the amount of food stored to provide energy for later regrowth. Bigger bulbs (graded number 1 or called *topsize* or *topgrade*) usually produce bigger flowers, more flowers, and taller, thicker stems than smaller bulbs, which are sometimes called *landscape grade* or *field grade*. Smaller bulbs at a good price may make sense if you plant them in the ground where they can develop over several years, but they aren't a good choice for containers, where the bulbs usually can thrive only for one season.

- ✔ **Plump is better than scrawny.** Follow the same rule for choosing a bulb as you do for choosing a good grapefruit: The bulb should feel heavy for its size. A bulb that feels light may have lost moisture.

- ✔ **Firm is better than squishy.** To what in the world does this rule not apply? You don't want to buy rotting bulbs.

- ✔ **Two noses are better than one.** This rule applies primarily to daffodils and perhaps some Picasso paintings. Daffodil bulbs develop *noses,* or little bulbs attached to the main bulb, each of which can produce leaves and flowers. Try to buy big fat bulbs with two or three noses.

Preparing the soil

For container-grown bulbs, you want a mix that's well drained but that holds adequate moisture. Most commercial potting mixes work well, as we describe in Chapter 4. Because the bulb itself is a food storage structure, bulbs that grow only one season need little or no fertilizer. A soil mix that contains starter fertilizer is adequate, or you can mix in a small amount of bulb fertilizer at planting time. (See Chapter 16 for more on fertilizers.)

Planting the bulbs — step by step

The following steps describe the typical way to plant bulbs. Expect the results to be containers dense with flowers. (Some bulbs require different techniques — see individual bulb descriptions for details.)

1. **Figure out which end is up.**

   If you plant bulbs upside down or sideways, you're asking them to waste time and energy taking a circuitous run to daylight. Examine your bulbs for root remnants at the base — that end goes down.

2. **Fill your pot partway full of soil mix — enough so that bulbs placed upright on this layer end up with their tops 1 inch below the rim of the pot.**

3. **As shown in Figure 9-1, space bulbs so that they're gently touching or no more than ½ inch apart, and press the base of the bulbs into the soil to keep them standing straight.**

   Place any larger bulbs at the center of the group.

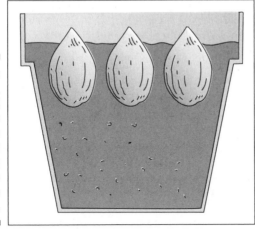

Figure 9-1:
In general, bulbs should be no more than ½ inch apart and about 1 inch below the rim of the pot.

4. **Fill in around the bulbs, and barely cover the tops of the bulbs with soil mix.**

5. **Water gently with a watering can or hose set at a trickle until the soil mix is fully moistened.**

Some spring-blooming bulbs require a special chilling period before they'll grow and bloom; you find details in the next section.

Bulbs Through the Seasons

Bulbs aren't just for spring anymore. Although spring bloomers provide extravagant color when little else is in bloom, don't overlook bulbs that bloom in other seasons. Here's a rundown of bulbs for all seasons.

Spring-blooming bulbs

The bulbs that you're most likely to be familiar with are the classic spring bloomers, such as tulips, daffodils, hyacinths, and crocuses. They create a blaze of color just when it's most welcome — late winter and early spring. Nothing else announces spring more emphatically and lyrically.

Here's their routine, whether they're growing in the ground or in containers:

1. You plant the bulbs in fall.

2. Using stored food for energy, the bulbs grow roots through the winter.

3. Top growth emerges in late winter or early spring.

4. Flowers burst into bloom in spring for a couple of weeks, and then dry up.

5. Foliage continues to grow, replenishing the underground bulb's food supply. If you dig up a bulb at bloom time, you find it scrawny compared with the plump one you planted.

6. When the foliage is done growing and replenishing the underground food supply, the leaves turn brown and die back. The bulb is plump again with stored food. It sits dormant underground, ready to sprout and bloom again the next spring.

The cold stage in Step 2 is critical for these bulbs to produce nice blooms come spring. The following section explains how you can reproduce a big chill for your container garden of spring bulbs. Then we list some spring-blooming bulbs.

Creating a bulb-chilling experience

Most spring-blooming bulbs are very hardy and will overwinter in the ground in all but the most frigid climates. In fact, they *need* this chill period to induce blooming. However, like other plants, when they're grown in containers they more readily succumb to extreme chill because soil in a container gets much colder than the soil in the garden. (Refer to Chapter 2 for more on climate and containers.) So gardeners in very cold climates need to take special steps to give their container bulbs just the right amount of chill.

After you plant the bulbs as outlined in the "Planting the bulbs — step by step" section, you need to follow the steps given here to ensure your spring bulbs will produce beautiful blooms:

1. **Place the containers where the temperature remains cool, ideally between 35 and 45 degrees Fahrenheit, to mimic the soil temperature if they were planted in the garden.**

   Where you put them depends on your climate. Where late fall and early winter temperatures stay in this 35- to 45-degree range, just move the planted containers into a cool, shady spot and leave them alone. In places where fall and winter temperatures fluctuate, rising above and falling below this range, you need to take an extra step: Wait for a spell of 40-degree weather so the soil and bulbs are at just the right temperature for proper chilling, and then mulch the containers on all sides and on top with a thick layer of straw. This will insulate the containers against temperature fluctuations and hold in the right amount of chill.

   In colder climates, providing the proper amount of chill is more challenging. You need to find a place where the containers won't freeze but will remain in that 35 to 45 degrees Fahrenheit range. This may be in an unheated garage, under a heated porch, or in a cold basement. You need to monitor the temperature and move the containers to a warmer or cooler spot if necessary. See the sidebar "Chilling out in warm-winter climates" for tips on growing spring-blooming bulbs in regions where temperatures remain above 50 degrees Fahrenheit.

   Most spring bulbs need between 8 and 15 weeks of chilling for best blooms.

2. **Inspect containers every week, watering if necessary to keep soil slightly moist.**

   You'll start to see green shoots emerging from the soil in two or three months, depending upon the type of bulb and its chilling requirements.

3. **If you live in a climate with moderate winters, the appearance of the shoots in the container may coincide with the emergence of bulbs in outdoor beds. If so, you can move the containers outdoors.**

   If you live in a cold-winter region, keep the containers in their cool place for a few more weeks — the extra chilling won't hurt them. Bring them outdoors once bulbs in outdoor beds are beginning to emerge.

4. **When flower buds start to show color, move containers into their display positions.**

5. **Water bulbs as needed to keep soil moist throughout the whole depth of the container.**

After the bulbs are finished blooming, you have a few options.

✔ You can discard them.

✔ You can move the pots to an out-of-the-way area and keep them watered and fertilized so the foliage can replenish the bulbs. When the leaves have died back cut them off an inch above the soil line. Then remove the bulbs from the pots, let them air dry, shake or brush off the loose soil, and store them in a cool, dark place for the rest of the summer. Plant them out in the garden in fall.

Use fresh bulbs in your containers every year. Bulbs that have been growing in a container typically don't do as well if you plant them in a container for a second time. If you want to keep the bulbs, plant them in the garden and use new bulbs for your container.

✔ You can carefully transplant the bulbs into the garden and let the foliage die back naturally.

Selecting spring-blooming bulbs

Here's a rundown of some popular bulbs, with specific planting instructions and suggestions for postbloom uses.

✔ **Crocus:** Welcome as the first sign of spring in many places, the small, goblet-like flowers come in many colors, including blue, purple, white, and bicolors. The look is most effective when you pack several crocus bulbs into a small container. Plant 2 inches deep, with the small corms touching. *Chill requirement: 12 to 14 weeks.*

✔ **Daffodils/narcissus:** Daffodils are the most popular spring bulbs, and for good reason. They're easy to grow and look smashing when crowded into a container. Hundreds of species and varieties are available, in a range of colors including bi-colors, but how can you pass up tried-and-true yellows? King Alfred, big-flowered and bright yellow, is an all-time hero and still a great choice. Smaller types are sometimes referred to as narcissus.

A dozen daffodil bulbs in a 12-inch-diameter clay pot make an impressive showing. Place the bulbs with their sides touching and tips level with the soil's surface. *Chill requirement: 12 to 14 weeks.*

- ✔ **Grape hyacinth (*Muscari*):** Neither hyacinths nor grapes, grape hyacinths nonetheless herald early spring with spikes topped with clusters of little blue or white flowers. The delicate flowers and foliage show off best in a small, shallow (5 or 6 inches in diameter and depth) pot. Plant the bulbs close together, and cover them lightly with soil mix. *Chill requirement: 15 weeks.*

- ✔ **Hyacinth:** Famously fragrant spikes of blue, white, or pink flowers can grow so large that they can tip over a small pot. Buy the biggest bulbs available. Plant them in a heavy clay pot that's at least 10 inches wide and about 5 inches deep. Arrange them so the sides of bulbs are almost touching; cover lightly with soil mix. Don't expect much from the bulbs in subsequent years, even if you move them into the garden. *Chill requirement: 12 weeks.*

- ✔ **Iris:** Bulbous iris (not the familiar bearded iris) are good in containers. These include Dutch, English, and Spanish types, with flowers in many colors. Wedgwood is a favorite Dutch iris with big blue and yellow blooms. Plant bulbs 1 to 2 inches deep, six or eight to an 8-inch pot. *Chill requirement: 14 weeks.*

- ✔ **Tulip:** Tulips are probably the most impressive bulbs that you can grow in your containers. They're always classy, if a bit regimental when the whole pot full blooms all at once, with the same height and color. Many, many colors and flower forms are available. Follow the directions for typical spring bulbs, and you'll find that tulips grow and bloom almost automatically in containers. But expect little from them in following years, in the ground or in containers. Tulips look best when bulbs are packed tight. Plant with sides nearly touching and tips just below soil surface. *Chill requirement: 15 weeks.*

Chilling out in warm-winter climates

In mild-winter climates (in much of California and Florida, for example), you have to simulate the conditions that spring-blooming bulbs need and naturally enjoy in cold climates. Without a certain amount of chilling, bulbs (particularly tulips and hyacinths) produce small and insubstantial flowers.

If chilling is necessary where you live, in mid-September put the unplanted bulbs in a paper bag and place it in your refrigerator, keeping the bulbs away from ripening fruit. Leave them there for about eight weeks, and then take them out of the refrigerator and plant them in your containers. After planting, water the containers and place them outdoors in a cool, shady spot so the bulbs can grow roots and finish their chilling. You should start seeing green shoots by late winter. Sometimes you can find prechilled bulbs for sale.

Force the issue with your spring-blooming bulbs

To brighten the dreariest winter days with sweet fragrance and spring colors, you can force (or trick) bulbs into blooming early indoors. Your best bets for forcing early blooms are crocuses, daffodils, hyacinths, grape hyacinths, and tulips.

Because you have to move containers indoors when you force a bloom, you probably want smaller pots than for outdoor use. For example, try half a dozen tulips or daffodils in a 6- to 10-inch pot; one daffodil or tulip or three small bulbs (such as crocus) in a 4-inch pot.

Follow the preceding steps for planting these bulbs in containers. Plant them at the usual time in fall and set them somewhere appropriate for their chilling period. After two or three months (usually after New Year's Day) you should see signs of growth. When they show 2- to 6-inch sprouts, bring the pots indoors to a cool room (60 degrees or so) to fool bulbs into "thinking" that spring is here! A week or two later, when sprouts have buds that show a little color, move the bulbs into normal room temperature in a spot that gets as much sunlight as possible. Flowers should appear within the next week or so. Continue to keep the soil moist. The cooler the room, the longer the blooms will last.

When the plant finishes blooming, discard the bulbs. Getting bulbs that have been forced into early bloom to grow and rebloom in the garden is difficult.

The bulbs of summer

Summer bulbs originate in tropical to subtropical regions and won't tolerate the cold winter weather experienced by most regions. Plant them in spring for bloom during the summer. Either discard them at the end of the season or dig up and store the bulbs in a cool-but-not-freezing place over the winter to replant the next spring.

- **Caladium:** With its big, jungly-looking leaves splotched with pink, white, and red, this bulb adds a tropical feeling to a garden. Plant tubers, one per pot, even with the top of the soil.

- **Calla *(Zantedeschia):*** Choose the common white or any of the many bright hybrids in yellow, pink, and red. All have the familiar cup-shaped flowers. Plant rhizomes 2 inches deep, 1 per 6-inch pot.

- **Canna:** Expect bright, flashy flowers and big, tropical-looking leaves. Most cannas grow tall, but for container gardening, look for dwarf varieties. Plant rhizomes 2 to 4 inches deep in containers at least 12 inches wide, 14 or 15 inches deep.

- **Dahlia:** This is a huge group of plants, from foot-tall dwarfs to strapping 6-footers, from quarter-sized flowers to dinner-plate dimensions for entering in the county fair. Dwarfs and intermediate types are best for containers; bigger plants require stakes. Plant tuberous roots 3 to 5 inches deep, 1 root to a 10- to 12-inch pot, 3 roots to a 14- to 16-inch pot.

- **Gladiolus:** Producing tall spikes of vibrantly colored flowers, gladioluses are usually grown for use as cut flowers, but the shorter "border gladioluses" are attractive in containers. Plant the corms about 6 inches deep and 4 inches apart.

- **Glory lily** *(Gloriosa rothschildsiana):* Beautiful red and yellow flowers bloom on a distinctive climbing plant. Provide a trellis to support this very tender bulb. Plant tubers 4 inches deep, 1 to each container at least 8 inches in diameter.

- **Tiger flower** *(Tigridia):* This flamboyant heat-lover comes from Mexico. Plant the bulbs 2 to 4 inches deep and 4 inches apart in a container at least 8 inches in diameter.

- **Tuberous begonia:** Great for containers (especially hanging baskets) in part shade, this plant is a favorite among hobbyist growers. Its richly colored flowers come in a variety of forms and sizes. For best results, plant begonias indoors about 8 weeks before the last spring frost date, setting the tubers concave side up about an inch deep in the soil. Keep the pot in a warm place and water sparingly, just enough to keep the soil slightly moist.

Fall bulbs

When you think about fall and bulbs, you usually think about planting daffodils and tulips, not enjoying blossoms. But there are two bulbs you can plant in early fall and enjoy their flowers just a few weeks later. Transplant them into the garden after they're done blooming.

- **Fall crocus:** Several species of crocus bloom in fall rather than spring. The foliage emerges soon after planting, followed by the familiar goblet-shaped flowers. Plant them in July and August, setting them about 6 inches deep in well-drained potting mix.

- **Colchicum:** These beautiful, vase-shaped flowers resemble crocuses but are larger. The blooms emerge just weeks after planting. Foliage appears in spring, grows for a few months, then dies back. Plant them 4 inches deep in August and September.

Winter wonders

For many gardeners, the winter holidays wouldn't seem right without regal amaryllis and fragrant paper whites. Plant these tropical bulbs indoors in fall for winter bloom. Neither requires a chilling period.

- **Amaryllis *(Hippeastrum):*** Monster-size flowers, up to 8 inches across, sit atop tall stems. Plant a single bulb in a heavy clay (less chance for toppling), 8-inch pot, setting it so that about a quarter of the bulb sticks out of soil. Keep it at room temperature and keep the soil moist, and expect flowers in seven to ten weeks. After the flowers fade, cut off the flower stalk and place the plant in a bright window. Keep it watered and fertilized. After all danger of frost is past, move the plant outdoors to a spot in part sun and continue to let the foliage grow. In late summer, stop watering and fertilizing to allow the plant to go dormant for a few months. Bring it indoors before the first fall frost, and in early October begin watering and fertilizing again. It should bloom again in a few months.

- **Paper white narcissus:** Unlike other narcissus (daffodils), paper whites need no prechilling, making them easy to force into bloom indoors. The flowers are fragrant, with a strong, sweet-musky scent. Plant them so that their tips are exposed above the soil line, setting them close so they're almost touching each other. Keep them in a bright, cool room; they grow quickly and will bloom in as little as four weeks. Discard after bloom.

Part III
In It for the Long Haul: Permanent Plantings

The 5th Wave   By Rich Tennant

"Something's about to die in your cactus container."

In this part . . .

Now it's time to expand your garden palette to include plants that come back year after year. We're talking perennial plants here — hostas and hellebores, coneflowers and coreopsis. In these permanent plantings, woody plants can take center stage — azaleas, hollies, Japanese maples, even dwarf fruit trees. Most indoor plants also live for several years (some for decades!) so we've included them here, too. Plants like these represent a significant investment, so you'll want to choose plants carefully and give them the care they need. Read on for details.

Chapter 10

Pondering Permanent Plantings

. . . .

In This Chapter

▶ Finding out all about perennials

▶ Working with Mother Nature

▶ Protecting your plants in cold-winter climates

. . . .

Why bother with permanent plantings — perennials, trees, and shrubs — when annuals bloom so abundantly and don't require overwintering? When vegetables grow so easily and provide a healthy harvest? The main reason is that permanent plantings expand your plant palette exponentially.

As much as we hate to resort to such a vague and overused word, we have to say that the plants you can grow in permanent plantings are *interesting*. And that's the main reason to grow them. They're interesting in the range of flowers they provide — from tiny, fragrance-packed lavender to towering blue delphiniums. They're interesting in their sheer numbers and variety — thousands of kinds are available, including grasses, shade plants, foliage plants, shrubs, trees, and vines. And they're interesting in the challenges that they present: from pruning and dividing to figuring out what to do with them in the winter — you don't just relegate them to the compost pile at the end of the season as you do annuals.

This chapter gives you an overview of the different types of perennial plants you can grow. We also point out some problems that microclimates can present when it comes to keeping plants in containers year-round, but, of course, we help you with some solutions too. Finally, we offer ways to protect your permanent plantings from harsh winter weather.

Getting Acquainted with Perennials

What kind of plants go into a permanent planting? In a word, *perennial* plants — plants that grow for more than one season. In this book we describe four groups of permanent plants:

- ✔ **Herbaceous perennials:** These are plants with more or less soft, succulent growth. They die back to the ground in winter and resprout in spring. Primroses, penstemons, and peonies are examples of herbaceous perennials. When people use the term *perennials*, they're usually referring to *herbaceous perennials*. (Chapter 11 covers these in more detail.)

- ✔ **Woody plants:** Technically speaking, trees, shrubs, and woody vines are perennial plants, too, in that they grow for more than one season, but most people call them . . . well . . . trees, shrubs, and vines. These plants have hardened woody parts that persist above-ground in winter. (Woody plants are the stars of Chapter 12.)

- ✔ **Fruits and berries:** Although these fall into one of the preceding categories, they merit a special mention because they're so popular and rewarding to grow, and because they have special requirements. (Get your fill of specifics on fruits and berries in Chapter 13. Sweet!)

- ✔ **Indoor plants:** We include houseplants in the permanent plantings section of this book because they generally grow for more than one season, too. Most houseplants are tropical perennials that need warm temperatures to thrive. (Check out Chapter 14 for what you need to know to successfully grow houseplants.)

So, you have lots of choices when it comes to potting up perennials. In the following sections, we list some of the advantages and disadvantages of making a commitment to perennials.

Good reasons to grow perennials

Ask gardeners why they love permanent plantings, and here's what you can expect to hear (in addition to how interesting they are):

- ✔ **They last longer.** Many gardeners prefer to fill their pots with perennial plants simply because the plants can last a long time. There's no need to replant your containers each year, as you must do with annuals.

- ✔ **Bigger can be better.** Herbaceous perennials tend to grow larger than annuals and bulbs, so they can fill large spaces if that's what you want. And trees and shrubs grow even bigger. If you really want to make a splash with your container plantings, you'll probably want to include a few big specimens.

- ✔ **They provide year-round interest.** Annuals offer bright, short-lived flowers, but if you want something that adds interest season after season, year after year, you'll want to include something perennial.

Evergreens and woody plants with intriguing shapes and colorful bark are especially useful in these situations, because they offer something to look at year-round.

Challenges perennials pose

Alas, there *are* a few downsides to permanent plantings:

- ✔ **They have down times.** Just as we all look a little ratty from time-to-time, permanent plantings often do, too — like when perennial flowers aren't blooming or when the leaves fall off deciduous plants.

For year-round interest in perennial plantings, include at least one plant that has something pleasing to the eye in winter. This may be an evergreen plant, a woody shrub with colorful bark, an ornamental grass with attractive seed heads, or a tree with an interesting branch structure. That way, when other plants have finished flowering or have died back for the winter, you'll have something nice to look at.

- ✔ **They require a bit more care.** Unlike annuals, permanent plantings require some year-round care. In addition to watering and fertilizing, you'll be pruning them, moving them to protected spots for winter in cold-climate areas, and periodically dividing or repotting them.

- ✔ **They're more expensive upfront.** Herbaceous perennials often compare in price to annuals, but you'll spend considerably more on trees and shrubs. And larger plants mean larger containers, too, which also jacks up the final bill. Remember, though, that you won't need to replant each spring as you would with annuals, so factor in that long-term cost savings.

Taking Mother Nature into Account

Annuals are easy. When a hard freeze or other extreme weather indicates that the growing season is over, you just say goodbye to the plants and toss them into the compost pile. You're done until next spring. Perennial plantings, on the other hand, need your attention to protect them from Mother Nature's whims and cycles. After all, you've probably invested a fair bit of time and money in these plants and containers.

In the following sections, we explain how microclimates can work for or against your permanent container plants, and we offer some suggestions for helping your permanent plants survive winter weather.

Taking advantage of microclimates

One way to fool Mother Nature — or work with her instead of against her — is to make the best use of your landscape's microclimates. You may have noticed spots in your landscape that are warmer in winter, cooler in summer, or especially windy. These are *microclimates* — areas where the conditions are a little different than those in the rest of the yard. Flip back to Chapter 2 for general information on microclimates. Here we take a look at why they're particularly important for permanent plantings.

Microclimates can spell the difference between a planter that thrives during the growing season, overwinters, and comes back in full force in spring and one that succumbs to extreme heat, cold winter temperatures, or wind.

All plants have preferences for sun and shade, temperature and humidity, and other weather and climate factors. Knowing the preferences of the plants in your permanent plantings is especially important. The following sections provide a few explanations for why this is so.

Dormancy

Herbaceous perennials and woody plants take cues from nature as to when it's time to start winding down and entering dormancy at the end of the growing season. As the weather cools and daylight lessens, plants begin withdrawing food reserves from their leaves and stems and storing these reserves in their roots. Plants need enough stored energy in their roots to survive winter and begin growing next spring. Some plants also concentrate sugars in their buds to keep them from freezing solid.

Container plants placed against a sun-drenched wall receive lots of reflected light and heat. This can fool plants into "thinking" that it's still summer even when winter is fast approaching. They may continue to grow at full tilt — until they're blasted by the first hard freeze. The solution? In late summer, help plants know it's time to slow down by moving containers to a spot where they don't receive so much reflected light and heat.

Freeze/thaw cycles

Even plants in the ground are subject to alternating freeze/thaw cycles, when temperatures are very warm one day and very cold the next. Weather like this can confuse plants and prevent them from entering dormancy. And when soil repeatedly freezes and thaws, it also expands and contracts, which can heave plants, pushing them right up and out of the soil where their roots can freeze or dry out.

Because the soil in container plants is more exposed to the elements, it's more likely to be subject to these freeze/thaw cycles. The solution? Add a thick layer of insulating mulch to the soil of container plantings, and consider moving plants to a shadier spot that doesn't heat up so much on warm days.

Early bloom

Flowering trees and shrubs, especially some fruit trees, may bloom earlier when they're growing in containers because the soil in containers warms up faster than the soil in the ground. If a container is placed in a spot that receives reflected sun and heat, the plants may be fooled into blooming even earlier. If that happens, the buds and flowers may be damaged when nighttime temperatures drop, even without an unusual cold spell. This is especially true of plants that are marginally hardy in your area. The solution? Move these plants to a spot where they'll stay cooler, rather than warmer, until spring has really arrived.

Overwintering containers in cold areas

In cold-winter climate areas, many container-grown perennials, trees, and shrubs can't be left out in the elements — even if the same plants growing in the ground are perfectly hardy. When you choose perennials for containers, you need to consider their climate adaptability.

Check locally to find out exactly which plants survive outdoors all year where you live (you may also learn by trial and error). Review Chapter 2, and remember that plants that are hardy in the ground in a certain climate may not be hardy in a container. (Add roughly two climate zones. For example, if a plant is hardy to zone 5 in the ground, it may be hardy only to zone 7 in a container.) A fair prediction is that container plants in cold climates can't survive the winter outdoors without some sort of protection.

The hardiness zones for the plants we list in Chapters 11 through 13 refer to their hardiness when planted in the ground. There is no firm data for container plants that we know of.

Gardeners in cold climates take steps to *overwinter* their container plants (keep them in a protected spot) to shelter them until the milder temperatures of spring arrive. Tropical plants need to be brought indoors into room temperatures; treat these as houseplants over the winter. Plants from temperate regions (where the plants normally go dormant in winter), on the other hand, need the down time induced by cold weather. For these plants, the goal of overwintering isn't to keep plants warm but rather to keep them from getting too cold.

Individual gardeners have their own favorite method of overwintering container plants that need a cold-induced dormant period. You can try the following techniques to overwinter cold-sensitive plants that aren't hardy to your region. But we'll be honest: Not all of these suggestions are simple, and none of them are foolproof.

  ✔ After plants are dormant (after herbaceous plants have died back and woody deciduous plants have dropped their leaves), water them one last time and place the pots in an insulated garage or cool basement. Look for a spot that will stay in the range of 32 to 45 degrees Fahrenheit. Check the plants occasionally, and water them if the soil dries out. Move the plants back outdoors in spring.

If the storage area is likely to drop below freezing, place the containers in a large cardboard box and fill it with hay, packing peanuts, or anything else that will provide insulation.

✔ For small shrubs and herbaceous perennials, wait until the first hard frost. Then bury each plant, still in its pot, in the middle of your mulch pile, tilting the pot to make sure water from rain and melting snow will drain off. When the weather warms in spring, move the plants back to their regular spots.

✔ For small to medium-sized plants, wait until they've entered dormancy, and then create a tall cylinder around the container and plant (using chicken wire, wire fencing, or hardware cloth; see Figure 10-1). Fill it with chopped leaves, straw, or bark mulch. This will prevent the soil and plant from freezing and thawing in winter.

✔ In colder zones, you can use the "tip and bury" method on a deciduous tree that is normally hardy only to zone 7 (such as a fig tree): Tie the branches of the plant together after it loses its leaves, lay it on its side in a trench that is 14 inches deep and wide enough to hold the entire plant (including the pot). Cover it with burlap, and then cover the plant — container and all — with soil. When the soil starts to thaw out in April or later, dig out the plant, stand it up, start watering, and see whether it responds.

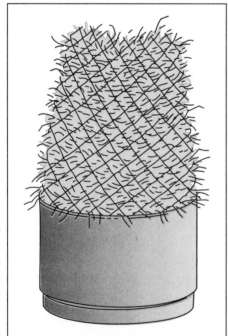

Figure 10-1:
A plant
insulated
with straw
and chicken
wire.

Even in regions where winters are chilly but not severe, hardy plants benefit from some protection. Group container plants together in a protected area out of strong winds and bright sunshine. They'll shield each other from the elements and create their own slightly warmer microclimate. Or, after plants have entered dormancy, wrap pots with bubble wrap to help insulate soil against freeze/thaw cycles.

If you live in a cold climate, remember that winter temperatures can affect your containers as well as your plants. If left outside, terra-cotta, concrete, and ceramic pots with soil in them can crack when moist soil expands as it freezes; move these pots into protected areas for the winter. Refer to Chapter 3 for more details.

Chapter 11

Picking and Potting Perennials

In This Chapter

▶ Identifying perennials

▶ Planting for repeat performances

▶ Maintaining this year's growth

▶ Dividing plants that outgrow their containers

▶ Selecting outstanding perennials

Why bother with perennial flowers when annuals bloom so abundantly and don't require overwintering? That's a good question. After all, most perennials die back in winter, have a comparatively short bloom season, and take a while to get growing in spring. With annuals, you get instant color in spring that lasts all summer long.

The short answer to the "why bother" question is that perennials offer a huge range of colors, forms, and textures not available in annuals. The longer answer is that perennials are fun to grow. In spring, you watch your pots with anticipation and rejoice at that first green shoot, knowing your plants made it through the winter. And when you grow perennials, you get to be, well, different. Potted annual flowers are everywhere — even at the gas station. Perennials broaden your plant palette and challenge you as a gardener. If you're still not convinced perennials are worth the trouble, read on. This chapter covers the basics of growing perennials and then offers some plants for your consideration.

Defining Perennials

In this chapter we're talking about a specific type of perennial: *herbaceous* flowering perennials. These perennials have soft fleshy stems (as opposed to a sturdy, woody trunk like an oak tree) and live for several years under the right conditions. Perennials represent a huge and storied population of plants, and you can find information about them everywhere from magazine racks and library shelves to Web sites, discussion groups, and online retailers.

Some of these perennials are *deciduous*. They lose their leaves at some point in the year, usually in winter, or they die back completely to the ground.

Other perennials are evergreen, especially in mild climates. In cold climates, the above-ground parts may die back. In mild places, such as Southern California, "annuals" like the popular red-flowered geranium thrive as permanent shrubs. So is the geranium an annual or a perennial? Technically, it's a perennial, but because it isn't winter-hardy in most of the country, we treat it as an annual in this book — refer to Chapter 7. Here we focus on plants that are perennial in cooler parts of the country, too.

Perennials generally have one main bloom season, usually in spring or summer, that can be as brief as a few weeks or as long as a couple months. Plant breeders continue to develop varieties with especially long bloom times, but even so, expect perennials to have shorter bloom seasons than annuals.

So, what can *you* do with perennials?

- **Grow the unusual:** Everyone and his brother grow petunias and impatiens in their containers. Be the talk of the town by planting something different, say, Green Envy echinacea or Caramel coral bells.

- **Grow the temperamental:** If your garden beds are too sunny for hostas or your soil is too cold and wet for lavender, try growing them in containers so that you can customize their environments.

- **Mix and match:** Want the best of both worlds? Combine unique perennials with favorite annuals.

Putting Perennials and Pots Together

Because of perennials' longevity, you need to put some thought into the containers you want to display them in. You may need to plan for a succession of containers, and, of course, you have to make sure the perennials are planted properly. We give you the lowdown in the following sections.

Matching plants with pots

Imagine those daylilies brightening up your front porch, their silky trumpets heralding a soft summer breeze — but what kind of pot shows off their multicolor magic? And how about that gorgeous Asian urn you discovered at a garage sale — what can you grow in it? Sometimes we start with the plant, and sometimes we start with the pot — either way can work.

Along with the aesthetics of matching plants to pots, perennials demand that you consider another factor: the plant's size now *and* its size at maturity. For example, a 4-inch daylily may ultimately spread out to a diameter of 2 feet — eventually, you'll need a very wide pot. But right now, introducing the 4-inch plant to a 24-inch pot doesn't make much sense — especially because you risk making your plant very unhappy when all that extra soil creates inhospitably soggy conditions. Remember that in a pot, a perennial may not get quite as big as a ground-grown plant, but it may come close.

So how do you choose the right size pot for now *and* later? You have two choices: Put that little plant in a 6-inch (or 10-inch) pot and repot it to larger-size pots as it grows (we give you tips on repotting in the "Dividing and Repotting" section later in this chapter), or put it in a pot that can accommodate its ultimate size, and add annuals to fill the empty space for now. Make sure that the pot you decide to use is large enough to accommodate the ongoing root growth, and heavy and stable enough to remain topple-free as the plant matures.

Planting perennials in containers

At nurseries and garden centers, perennials are sold mostly in 4-inch and larger nursery pots. To plant these, follow the basic steps outlined in Chapter 5. Choose a potting mix that matches the perennial's normal soil requirements (if your plant's fussy about such things as acidity and alkalinity), and make sure that the mix contains plenty of sand or perlite to ensure that it drains quickly.

If you buy perennials by mail order, they may arrive as bare-root plants. The roots are exposed and devoid of any potting soil — a handy, lightweight way to ship perennials and a healthy way to start new plants. Again, refer to Chapter 5 for planting instructions.

Caring for Perennials in Containers

Perennials, like all good plants, expect their owners to satisfy their special requirements — but these guys, in truth, aren't terribly demanding. Keep in mind that the only plants that don't require some care are dead plants. The following sections cover some special care requirements that are specific to perennials.

Deadheading to keep the blooms coming

Flowering perennials share a common goal with all other plants — they live to make more plants. When you see a perennial whose flowers are fading, remember that you're seeing a natural process — after it flowers, the plant produces seeds. Your goal, on the other hand, is probably to enjoy the flowers.

 When the blooms fade, if the plant is still growing strong, you can encourage a new flush of flowers by *deadheading*. To deadhead, pinch or cut off the fading flowers right where the flowers attach to the stems (Figure 7-1 in Chapter 7 shows you where to pinch). After you deadhead, the plant doesn't have to put its energy into setting seed; instead, the plant can concentrate on making more flowers — just what you want. When you're removing spent flowers, take care not to damage nearby buds. On plants with multiple flowers on a single stem, like daylilies, it's easiest to wait until all the flowers on a stem have finished blooming before cutting the stem off at the base.

 Not all perennials require deadheading to continue blooming. And some plants stop blooming after a certain period no matter how religiously you deadhead; that's just the nature of perennials.

Cutting back for more growth

Some plants grow stronger and bloom better after you cut them back. If you cut back leggy stems as much as halfway, they usually come back fuller and bushier with more blooms. Some plants are best cut back in fall, others in spring. Recommendations for cutting back perennials in pots are the same as for perennials in the ground. Because there are many types of perennials and pruning techniques may vary by region, we don't have enough room to cover them all here. Check with a local nursery for advice on timing and how much to cut a particular plant back in your area.

Fertilizing for slow, steady growth

Because perennials and annuals grow differently, you need to fertilize them differently. Annuals grow quickly and bloom continually the entire growing season — they need a fertilizer that's available quickly and continually. Perennials grow more slowly and over a far longer period of time. Hence, they need a fertilizer that lasts longer. Starting with a potting mix that has been fortified with compost provides a good soil environment and some long-lasting nutrients. Mixing in some slow-release fertilizers before planting may provide enough nutrients for the first growing season.

In subsequent seasons, an annual application of a slow-release fertilizer in spring may be enough. Some gardeners like to feed weekly with a dilute solution. Aim for slow, steady growth. Too much fertilizer stimulates rapid but weak growth that can be susceptible to pest attack (see Chapter 18).

As a general rule for fertilizing perennials in containers, find out what specific varieties need in your area, and feed just a bit more than you'd deliver to the same plants in the ground. The extra food accounts for the loss of nutrients washed out during watering of container plants. For more details on fertilizing in general, see Chapter 16.

Whatever fertilizing method you choose, stop fertilizing by late summer to help signal plants to slow growth and begin entering dormancy.

Dividing and Repotting

Because perennials tend to grow larger — in some cases *much* larger — than annuals, you may find your plants outgrowing their pots. (A sure sign is roots that fill all available soil space or bulge out at the top. An even surer sign: roots bursting the sides of the container.) At times like these, you need to make some choices. You can repot them into larger containers, you can root-prune them and replant them in the same container, or you can divide them. Repotting and root pruning are covered in Chapter 17. Dividing is unique to herbaceous perennials, so we cover it here.

Some perennials, like coral bells and hostas, spread by underground roots. In pots, they can eventually grow so crowded that they no longer look good or grow well. When your plants enlarge to this size, think about dividing the clump. The ideal time to divide a plant depends on the type of plant and your locale. In general, in regions with mild to moderate winters you can divide plants in early spring or fall. In regions with very cold winters, most plants are best divided in early spring. In regions with very hot summers, divide plants in fall. Exceptions to these guidelines exist, so if you're unsure, do some research before digging in.

To divide a perennial:

1. **Ease the plant from the pot.**

2. **Wash off as much soil as possible — you need to be able to see the roots.**

3. **Using a trowel, garden knife, or whatever tool seems to work for you, gently tease apart the root mass into two or more clumps.**

   These clumps are called *divisions.* Be sure that each division has a healthy set of roots to support it.

Repot each clump into a new pot using the bare-root potting procedure described in Chapter 5. You can also plant some or all the clumps in the ground if you have the space and the right conditions. Or, share or swap divisions with your friends and neighbors.

The roots of some plants are such a tangled mass that it's impossible to tease them apart. In these cases, use a sharp knife or, for large plants, a sharpened spade to slice the plant in half, from top to bottom, so that the two remaining sections contain both top growth (or where the top growth was if the plant is dormant) and roots. Replant as you would a regular potted plant.

Choosing Perennials for Containers

The following popular perennials qualify as good candidates for container gardening. Everything on the list blooms for a fairly long season and is relatively easy to grow. Most of these plants can work alone in containers or can be combined with annuals or other perennials (as long as their sun/shade and soil moisture requirements are similar). Hardiness zones are noted for each plant (read more about hardiness zones in Chapter 2); however, keep in mind that the hardiness ratings are for plants growing in the ground and that plants growing in containers may need winter protection. (Tender perennials that are grown as annuals in most parts of the country are not listed here — we include them in Chapter 7.)

Don't be limited by the upcoming lists. Nearly any perennial can grow in a container if you're willing to work with it. If you're new to gardening, start with something easy. When you're ready to expand your plant horizons, visit garden centers and botanical gardens, talk to fellow gardeners, and consult regional gardening books and magazines for ideas.

Hardy perennials for sun

The following plants prefer full sun — at least 6 hours of direct sun each day. (In hot, sunny climates, some of these plants will thrive in part shade, too.) Most of these plants are hardy in zones 4 to 8; some are hardy even beyond that range.

- ✔ **Aster:** Wild asters grow as much as 6 feet tall, but cultivated varieties are much more compact, usually reaching about 18 inches tall. The plants grow unassumingly all summer, with attractive dark green foliage, then burst into bloom in late summer, with purple, pink, or white flowers blanketing the whole plant. Combine asters with spring and summer bloomers for a three-season flower show.

Most asters are hardy in zones 4 to 8 or 9 and thrive in areas with cool, moist summers. Plant in rich, moist soil in full sun. Pinch back shoots in spring and again in early summer to encourage bushiness and more flowers.

✔ **Blanketflower** *(Gaillardia):* These tough plants have a ruggedly handsome look with daisylike flowers in beautiful shades of yellow, orange, red, and burgundy in different patterns and combinations. Plants grow 2 to 4 feet tall, and spread into a dense mound of blooms.

Blanketflower is hardy in zones 3 to 9. Provide full sun, a fast-draining soil mix, and minimal water. When mature, plants can fill a container completely on their own — don't combine them with other plants in the same container. Cluster pots of blanketflower with other low-growing perennials, separate pots of annuals, or tall grasses.

✔ **Catmint** *(Nepeta):* Vigorous, drought-tolerant, and hardy, catmints are ideal for containers. If space is limited, look for compact varieties like Little Trudy and Kit Kat that grow just 12 to 18 inches tall. Walker's Low, the 2007 Perennial Plant of the Year, is larger, growing about 3 feet tall and wide. Most catmints, including these three varieties, have purple-blue flowers but there are a few varieties with pink or white blooms. Catmints provide a flush of spiky blooms in spring, followed by repeat blooming all summer long. The shrubby, gray-green, fragrant foliage is attractive on its own and is ideal for hiding yellowing bulb foliage.

Catmint is hardy in zones 4 to 8. Avoid overly wet soil and go lightly on the fertilizer, or you'll get more foliage than blooms.

✔ **Chrysanthemums:** Familiar autumn flowers make chrysanthemums a garden favorite. So-called florist's chrysanthemums are sold year-round at supermarkets and everywhere else — they're typically used for instant color and subsequently thrown away. But look beyond the florist version to hundreds of other varieties, typically in shades of yellow, white, bronze, and red, in sizes ranging from 6 inches to 4 feet tall. Choose compact varieties for containers. Use taller, more upright types in the center of large container plantings. Combine with spring- and summer-flowering plants for a long season of color.

Hardiness depends on variety. Provide full sun and regular water. Pinch back shoots in spring and again in early summer to encourage bushiness. Pick fading flowers to prolong the blooms. Divide clumps every few years.

✔ **Coreopsis:** A container of blooming coreopsis can look like a pot of golden sunshine on your patio. *Coreopsis grandiflora* grows to 2 feet high and 3 feet wide with 2- to 3-inch bright yellow flowers. *Coreopsis verticillata* has smaller flowers and delicate foliage (the common name is threadleaf coreopsis) and can stand on its own or complement any other plant.

Coreopsis is hardy in zones 3 to 9. Provide full sun and a fast-draining soil mix. Keep blooms coming by cutting off fading flowers. If a plant has too many faded blooms to cut individually, shear back all the stems at once — expect your reward to be another round of flowers.

✔ **Daylilies** *(Hemerocallis):* Choose from numerous varieties with flowers in yellow, orange, red, rust, burgundy, lilac, or purple — plus every imaginable color combination. Blooms rise regally above the leaves and face north, east, south, and west. Better yet, the daylily is an easy plant to grow almost everywhere. Varieties can be either deciduous (better for cold climates) or evergreen. The plants have long, strappy leaves that can grow 2 feet or taller. Dwarf daylilies — a nice choice for containers — typically grow to only 6 or 10 inches tall.

Daylilies are tough — they're hardy in zones 3 to 9. Provide full sun with a bit of shade in very hot summer areas. Make sure that you keep their soil moist during bloom time. To prolong the flowering season, snap off spent flowers. The plants spread by underground rhizomes and need to be divided every few years — dividing is easy. If you have a friend who grows daylilies that you admire, ask for a division next time he or she divides plants.

✔ **Delphinium:** Thumb through a gardening magazine, and you'll probably come across a picket-fence-enclosed garden planted with elegant, blue-flowering delphiniums — the classic, photogenic perennials. Delphiniums grow as tall as 6 feet with stalks of blue, lavender, white, pink, or yellow flowers, mostly in summer. More compact varieties — only 2 to 3 feet tall — work best in containers: Try to find Connecticut Yankee or Blue Fountains.

Delphiniums grow in zones 3 to 7 (up to zone 9 where night temperatures are cool). Plant in a rich, well-draining soil mix that's not too acidic. Provide full sun and fertilize regularly. You may need to stake tall flowers.

✔ **Echinacea:** Once limited to purplish-pink flowers, the last few years have seen dozens of new echinacea varieties in a rainbow of flower colors, making the common name, purple coneflower, obsolete. These tough, drought-tolerant, adaptable plants bloom from midsummer into fall and are magnets for butterflies. Flower colors now include yellow, orange, salmon, deep rose-red, and even green. Look for the Big Sky series, as well as Green Envy, Coral Reef, Pink Poodle, and Tiki Torch.

Echinacea is hardy in zones 3 to 8. Plant in full sun and well-drained soil, and go easy on the fertilizer. These prairie plants are adapted to lean conditions.

✔ **Hardy geranium:** Distinct from the large-flowered annual geranium (which is technically not a geranium at all but rather a pelargonium), hardy geraniums form low mounds of attractive, lobed leaves topped by delicate-looking, saucer-shaped flowers in shades of pink, blue, white, and purple. New varieties bloom all summer, including Rozanne, which was the 2008 Perennial Plant of the Year.

Geraniums are hardy in zones 5 to 8. Plant in full sun and moist but well-drained soil. Remove spent flowers to encourage reblooming.

✔ **Lavender *(Lavandula)*:** English, French, and Spanish lavender are just a few types of this fragrant, favorite perennial. Shrublike plants grow 1 to 3 feet tall with slender stalks of purplish flowers at the tips. Lavender is an outstanding container plant — mostly because portability lets you move your lavender plants where you can easily snatch a few leaves or flowers and appreciate the fragrance. Dwarf varieties — Compacta and others — work especially well in containers.

Lavender is hardy in zones 5 to 8, but varies by species. Lavender is evergreen in mild climates and dies back in cold places. If you live in a cold climate, you can overwinter your lavender plants or start with new ones each year. Provide full sun and well-drained, sandy soil. Let the soil dry out between waterings. Lavender works well by itself in pots — the perennial's preference for dry conditions makes it incompatible with most other plants. Cut plants way back (halfway or so) after the first bloom period.

✔ **Penstemon, or beard tongue:** Penstemons abound in all parts of the country. They're shrublike plants, 2 to 5 feet tall, with spikes of tubular flowers in shades of white to coral, pink to red, and purple. Hummingbirds love the flowers. Best bets for containers are *P. gloxinoides* hybrids, which sport bushy, compact growth. Combine them with lower-growing, broad-leafed perennials like lamb's ear.

Hardiness depends on variety. *P. gloxinoides* can grow year-round only in mild climates; elsewhere, treat it like an annual. *Penstemon digitalis* is hardy in zones 3 to 8; the variety Husker Red has unusual deep maroon foliage topped with white or pale pink flowers and was the 1996 Perennial Plant of the Year.

Provide full sun, unless you live in a very hot climate where plants may need a bit of shade in summer. Keep the soil mix very well-drained — too much water and soil that's too rich can be deadly. For a strong second bloom, cut off all dead flower spikes.

✔ **Pinks and carnations *(Dianthus)*:** This is a huge family, most of them carrying a familiar, wonderfully spicy fragrance — boutonniere-type carnations are the most familiar. For containers, consider compact types: cottage pinks, border carnations, and China pinks. Plants grow 8 to 16 inches tall and are covered with a profusion of fragrant flowers in white to pink to magenta.

Hardiness depends on variety; many are hardy in zones 3 or 4 to 9. Plant in light, well-drained soil. Provide part shade if summers are very hot in your area. Water well, but don't overwater. Cut or pinch fading flowers to prolong blooming.

✔ **Primroses:** Their long, crinkly leaves and clusters of flowers in bright shades of blue, yellow, magenta, lavender, and white make them the perfect cottage garden accent. At least 500 different species and varieties exist, but you can't go wrong with English primrose *(Primula polyantha);* it's easy to grow, and is one of the first plants to bloom in spring. In the garden, primroses are usually planted at the edge of borders to draw attention to their beautiful flowers. Use that same principle in mixed flower pots — plant primroses at the perimeter of large pots or fill containers with single colors.

English primroses are hardy in zones 3 to 7. Where winters are mild and summers long and hot (such as in California), primroses bloom from fall through early spring. Provide full sun in cool climates (or if grown to bloom in winter), part shade in warm climates. Make sure the soil mix is high in peat moss, and keep the soil moist.

✔ **Rudbeckia:** Commonly known as black-eyed Susans, rudbeckias, like echinaceas, are durable plants that thrive in a wide range of conditions. Most have yellow, daisylike flowers with dark centers. *Rudbeckia fulgida* Prairie Sun flowers have green centers. Goldsturm is a popular compact variety that grows up to 30 inches tall and is blanketed with blooms in late summer. It was the Perennial Plant of the Year in 1999.

Most *Rudbeckia fulgida* varieties are hardy in zones 3 to 9. *R. hirta* varieties, sometimes called gloriosa daisies, tend to be short-lived and are often grown as annuals. Plant rudbeckias in full sun and well-drained soil. Once established, they are relatively drought tolerant and need minimal supplemental fertilizer.

✔ **Sage *(Salvia):*** You may think of sage as a culinary herb, but the 900-plus types of ornamental sages are plants of tremendous beauty and usefulness in the garden. Perennial salvias tend to be shrublike, ranging from 12 inches to 6 feet tall. Flowers grow on spikes, in shades of pink, red, white, coral, blue, and purple. Some salvias stand tall and upright; others cascade.

Good choices for containers are mealy blue sage *(S. farinacea),* with foot-long spikes of blue flowers, and cherry sage *(S. greggii),* a low, bushy type. Both bloom from summer through fall and are hardy in zones 8 to 10. *Salvia nemorosa* is hardy in zones 4 to 8 and also blooms from summer to fall. One variety, May Night, has masses of deep blue flowers, and was the 1997 Perennial Plant of the Year.

Salvias like full sun. Pinch frequently, starting when plants are young, to produce bushy growth. Cut plants way back in spring.

✔ **Tall sedum:** This succulent plant's gray-green foliage provides a nice backdrop for spring- and summer-blooming plants. Come fall, it takes center stage with mounds of tiny flowers in shades of white, pink, red, and purple. Popular varieties include Autumn Joy and Brilliant. Black Jack has purple-black foliage and bright pink flowers.

Sedum is hardy in zones 3 to 9. Plant in full sun; good drainage is a must. Combine with other drought-tolerant plants in containers, and water and fertilize sparingly.

✔ **Yarrow** *(Achillea):* Available in many varieties, yarrows produce feathery leaves and tall stalks topped with flat clusters of flowers in various shades of yellow, pink, white, lavender, and red. Handsome foliage is green or gray-green, depending upon the variety. Yarrows' roots spread easily — a single plant quickly fills a 4-inch pot. Use low-growing, creeping varieties to fill blank spaces and spill over the edges of containers that include taller and bushier perennials. Use a taller variety (up to 3 feet) as the centerpiece of a mixed pot.

Yarrow is hardy in zones 3 to 8. Provide full sun and minimal water. Divide in spring when the clumps grow too large or too raggedy. Keep overwintering dormant plants on the dry side.

Hardy perennials for part shade and shade

The following plants thrive in part to full shade. Part shade includes areas that get morning sun or late afternoon sun, as well as areas under thin-canopied trees that provide dappled shade all day. In regions with hot summers, lean toward full shade locations; in regions with cool summers, go for part shade.

✔ **Astilbe:** Attractive mounds of glossy, fernlike foliage are topped with plumes of colorful flowers, making astilbes perfect for brightening up shady spots. Flower colors include pink, red, lavender, and white. The plant grows between 6 inches and 5 feet tall, depending on the variety.

Astilbe is hardy in zones 4 to 8. It does best in regions with cool summers, and it likes rich, moist soil. It thrives in dappled shade and is generally pest-free. The plant flowers in late spring and early summer, so combine it with summer- and fall-blooming plants that prefer part shade and moist soil.

✔ **Coral bells** *(Heuchera):* Flower clusters on stems as tall as 3 feet feature drooping, bell-shaped blooms in shades of red, deep pink, coral, and white. But the real star is the foliage. Plant breeders have introduced dozens of new varieties with foliage in every combination of silver, green, gold, orange, chartreuse, red, and purple, many with variegated leaves. Look for names like Caramel, Ginger Ale, Plum Pudding, Lime Rickey, and Marmalade — these describe the foliage color. Coral bells combine beautifully with annuals like pansies and other perennials such as hostas.

Coral bells are hardy in zones 4 to 8. Provide full sun in cool climates and part shade where it's hot. Plant groups of coral bells toward the rim of a large pot, next to taller and bushier plants that also require regular watering. Plants need to be divided every few years when they start to look woody.

✔ **Hellebore:** Valued for their glossy, evergreen foliage and nodding flowers, hellebores have seen a resurgence in popularity now that breeders have introduced varieties with larger, more colorful blooms. Use in planters set near windows and walkways so you can enjoy the early spring flowers. *Helleborus* x *hybridus* (a group of hybrids that includes many of the recent introductions) won the 2005 Perennial Plant of the Year award.

Hellebores are hardy in zones 4 to 9. They require fertile, moist soil and part to full shade. In zones 6 and warmer, the plants retain their evergreen foliage all winter. They have no serious insect or disease problems.

✔ **Foxglove *(Digitalis):*** Usually thought of as a towering background plant, consider the compact varieties for containers: Foxy, Excelsior, and Gloxiniiflora are in the 2- to 3-foot range. Flowers from late spring to early fall are tubular, in shades of purple, white, and yellow, with striped and speckled throats.

Foxglove is hardy in zones 4 to 8. Provide full sun or light shade and regular water. A single foxglove can fill a pot 18 inches in diameter. When the flower stalk fades, cut it at the base — you may get a second bloom. Most foxgloves are biennials and bloom only in their second growing season; however, one variety, Foxy, will bloom in its first growing season if planted early enough. A few foxglove species are perennial and will return year after year.

✔ **Hosta, or plantain lily:** This is a great plant for containers in the shade. Grow hosta for its big oval or heart-shaped leaves in deep green, chartreuse, and many other shades. The plants form mounds from 6 inches to 5 feet tall, depending upon species.

Hostas are hardy in zones 3 to 8. They prefer rich, moist soil and dappled shade. They're a favorite target for slugs and snails so keep an eye out for these pests; turn to Chapter 18 for techniques to deter them. Divide plants when they outgrow their containers.

Not-so-hardy perennials

This list includes plants that are hardy only to zones 8 or 9. They need careful overwintering in all but the warmest parts of the country.

✔ **Asparagus fern *(Asparagus densiflorus* syn *Protasparagus densiflorus):*** The overall effect of this plant is long, billowy clouds of green, sometimes studded with red berries. Arching stems 18 to 24 inches long have 1-inch long, flattened leaves that look a bit like needles. It's easy and fast-growing in containers — a great choice for baskets, either alone or with shade-loving companions.

Asparagus fern is hardy in zones 9 to 11. Provide full sun or part shade. Keep well-drained soil just barely moist. Overwinter in colder areas of the country. Trim out old dead branches, and repot overcrowded plants or divide old clumps. Asparagus fern is considered an invasive plant in parts of Florida.

✔ **Blue marguerite** *(Felicia):* Blue daisies with yellow centers are tiny but profuse. The plant's main bloom season is summer, but in frost-free areas, you can expect flowers in winter and early spring — especially if you remove faded flowers. Plants grow up to 2 feet tall, and are shrubby and a bit sprawly. This is a tender plant that's grown as an evergreen perennial in mild climates, but as an annual where winters are cold.

Blue marguerite is hardy in zones 9 to 11. Provide full sun. Constantly pinch, prune, and groom flowers to contain vigorous growth and control its tendency to become a bit raggedy.

✔ **Euryops:** This is a landscape and container mainstay in mild climates because it's long-blooming and very easy to grow. A shrubby daisy, it grows from 2 to 6 feet tall. It blooms heavily in late winter and early spring, then off and on throughout the rest of the year. *Euryops pectinatus* has gray-green leaves. *E. p.* Viridis has deep green leaves.

Euryops is hardy to zones 9 to 11. Provide full sun. Allow the soil to dry out a bit between waterings. After the main bloom period, cut the plant back by about one-third.

✔ **Ferns:** Many ferns do well in containers in shady spots — as striking single plants or combined with shade-loving annuals in mixed plantings. Most are not hardy and must be brought indoors in cold climates. Plant in a lightweight soil mix with plenty of organic matter. Keep the soil moist. Give foliage a misting whenever possible — especially when indoors. Here are a few among many great ferns for containers:

- *Big statuesque ferns:* Give these a good-sized container, up to 16 inches wide, and a prominent spot in the landscape. When the roots fill the container, transplant the fern into the garden. Tasmanian tree fern *(Dicksonia antarctica)* produces arching fronds as long as 6 feet and is hardy in zones 9 to 11. Australian tree fern *(Cyathea cooperi)* grows even larger but is dramatic in a container while young. It's hardy in zones 9 to 11.

- *Small ferns:* These combine nicely with other plants. Some are standouts in hanging baskets — alone or with other plants. All are on the tender side (zones 8 or 9 at best). Maidenhair ferns *(Adiantum)* are delicate, with wiry little stems and lacy fronds. Tuck maidenhair into a mixed hanging basket. Squirrel's foot fern *(Davallia)* gracefully fills a hanging basket by itself, creeping and clinging to the moss lining the basket. Sword ferns and Boston ferns *(Nephrolepis)* are classics indoors and out with dark green, feathery fronds.

✔ **Lily of the Nile** *(Agapanthus):* This South African native has long, strappy leaves that grow from 1 to 3 feet long. In spring and summer, the plants send out tall clusters of flowers in shades of blue-purple or white. A single plant easily fills a 24-inch pot and doesn't need to be divided for 5 or 6 years. The dwarf variety, Peter Pan, grows only to 12 inches tall, an ideal size for smaller containers.

Lily of the Nile is hardy in zones 8 to 11. Provide full sun or part shade. Keep the soil moist, but not wet. Divide when roots fill up the container.

✔ **Marguerite *(Chrysanthemum frutescens):*** If you're like many people, this may be the first perennial that you grow in a container — it's very easy, fast-growing, long-blooming, and abundant. White, yellow, cream, or pink daisies bloom continuously over the summer. Shrubby plants grow into a dense mass 4 feet tall.

Marguerite is hardy in zones 8 or 9 to 10 and can be grown as a summer annual everywhere else. Provide full sun. To control size and force more blooms, pinch the tips right from the beginning. In mild climates, cut back plants by at least one-fourth in early spring.

✔ **New Zealand flax *(Phormium tenax):*** Swordlike leaves form dramatic fans ranging in size from 18 inches to 6 feet or more. Leaves are bronze, red, purple, or green, often striped with another color. Plant this one alone in a large pot (18 inches or wider), or combine it with mounding perennials and annuals.

New Zealand flax is hardy in zones 8 or 9 to 10. Provide full sun or part shade. Let the soil dry out between waterings. This is not a fussy plant.

✔ **Peruvian lily *(Alstroemeria):*** Although not a true lily, it's just as beautiful and graceful. Intense hybridization has created a myriad of lilylike multicolored flowers in shades of white with pink, pink with white and yellow, lilac and purple, orange-yellow, and many more color combinations. Leafy stems range from 2 to 5 feet tall.

Alstroemeria is hardy in zones 8 to 10. In mild-winter areas, Peruvian lilies bloom much of the year. In colder-winter areas, bloom season may be May through summer. Provide full sun or part shade, depending upon variety, a high-quality soil mix, and moderate amounts of water. Roots are rather brittle; when you plant, set the root cluster fairly deep, with only the top showing. Roots prefer not to be disturbed, so plant in a container with plenty of room to grow.

✔ **Purple fountain grass *(Pennisetum setaceum Rubrum):*** Grasses are strikingly beautiful in pots. This is one of the more striking, forming graceful mounds of purplish-brown leaves up to 2 or even 4 feet tall. In summer, fuzzy pink or purplish flower spikes form. If you prefer to control the spread of grasses throughout your garden, cut off seed heads before they mature.

Purple fountain grass is hardy in zones 8 to 11, but you can grow fountain grass as an annual in colder climates. Provide full sun and almost any soil mix. Combine with other perennials that require little water.

Chapter 12

Sprucing Up Your Space with Trees, Shrubs, and Vines

. . . .

In This Chapter

▶ Using shrubs and trees creatively in your landscape

▶ Caring for your rich array

▶ Perusing the many planting possibilities

. . . .

You're most likely to appreciate growing shrubs, trees, and vines in containers if you have little or no ground space to grow them. These generously sized container plants can instantly transform a small, open space into an inviting, landscaped garden.

But any garden — old or new, large or small — can benefit from a handsome shrub or tree in a container. A container has a way of highlighting a plant that is otherwise pretty mundane. Mugho pine in a rugged terra-cotta pot evokes the sturdy dignity of the forest, while the same plant in the ground looks kind of like a green blob.

In this chapter, we lay out some benefits of growing trees and shrubs in containers, give you some reminders about planting and caring for them, and then give you all sorts of suggestions for what to plant.

 Reading a plant's description is one thing; seeing what a plant looks like is another thing. The best way to check out plants is in person: Visit your local public garden or arboretum, as well as nurseries and garden centers, to see what grows well in your region. Online nursery catalogs often have good photos, too, but you'll need to read plant descriptions carefully to find out what will thrive in your climate, as well as in the confines of a container.

Seeing What Shrubs and Trees Can Do for You

Shrubs, trees, and vines can perform big-time in containers. Here are just a few things they can do for you:

- **Create a sense of scale in a garden:** They can make a small terrace or balcony seem like a garden.

- **Produce seasonal displays:** They can provide spring blossoms, fall color, or winter berries. Woody plants with unusual branch structure or attractive bark provide year-round interest.

- **Look handsome or dramatic in their own right:** This is especially so if you prune them to emphasize their structure. When we refer to a *specimen plant* or *accent,* that's what we're talking about — a container plant that's attractive enough to stand alone and be admired.

- **Work hard in a landscape:** They can create a privacy screen, a divider, or shade. They can provide a dependable green background for seasonal container plants like annuals and bulbs.

- **Let you experiment:** Try plants that are dicey in your area because of cold weather or bad soil. For example, try growing hibiscus outdoors during the summer and indoors in the winter.

- **Attract wildlife:** Birds, especially, appreciate trees and shrubs for shelter. You'll probably get more birds at your feeder if you have a tree or shrub nearby.

Planting and Caring for Shrubs and Trees: The Basics

Permanent plants, including trees and shrubs, generally need less care than annuals or perennials, but they're not maintenance-free. You may not feel that bummed if you lose a pot of pansies that you forget to water, but it's a different matter when the casualty is a 7-year-old wisteria you just coaxed into bloom for the first time.

We describe special care requirements for different shrubs and trees in the later plant descriptions. Here are a few reminders that apply to most woody plants:

✔ **Planting:** The planting schedules for shrubs and trees in containers are the same as those for their in-ground counterparts. Generally, you plant in spring in cold climates, and in spring or fall in mild areas. The plants discussed here typically are available in gallon (or larger) cans, bare-root, or balled and burlapped. For more details about planting, see Chapter 5.

✔ **Soil:** Use soil mixes described in Chapter 4 or the special mixes we recommend for specific plants in the list that follows.

✔ **Container:** Pay special attention to container selection, because a permanent plant can live in the same container for a number of years. The basic rule applies: Start with a container that's 2 or 3 inches wider and deeper than the one in which the plant was grown. (Need some container ideas? Flip to Chapter 3.)

✔ **Feeding:** Permanent plants don't need the constant feeding that annuals do, but plan to feed them at least several times during the growing season. See Chapter 16 for details on fertilizing. For best results, incorporate compost and/or a slow-release fertilizer into the soil mix at planting time.

✔ **Watering:** No way around it, you have to water. Consider a drip irrigation system if you have a lot of containers. (Head to Chapter 15 for the specifics on watering.)

✔ **Pruning:** However flip it may seem, if you grow a lot of different shrubs and trees, the best advice may be to buy a pruning book. Pruning is a big subject, and you need to prune your container plants just as you do garden plants. Our plant descriptions later in this chapter give you some tips, and you can also check with the nursery where you buy your plants.

✔ **Repotting:** If you keep plants in the same containers for a few years, you can count on a round of repotting. Look for clues that it's time to replace your plant's happy home: when roots fill the pot or start to show at soil level, or the plant always seems dry. See the section on repotting in Chapter 17.

✔ **Pests and diseases:** Unfortunately, container shrubs and trees are susceptible to the same problems as their cousins in the ground. See Chapter 18 for some pointers.

Identifying Candidates for Containers

Shrubs and trees are lumped together because so many of them overlap in size and function, especially when grown in containers. To help you filter through the selections, we split them into two unscientific but useful categories:

> ✔ **Hardy:** Generally rated hardy to zones 5, 6, or 7, these plants will grow in most regions of the country and may or may not need winter protection, depending upon your winter climate.
>
> If you're not sure of your hardiness zone, check out the USDA's Hardiness Zone Map in Chapter 2, or ask at your local nursery.
>
> ✔ **Not-so-hardy:** Rated to zones 8, 9, or 10, these plants will grow outdoors in summer everywhere but need careful winter protection in all but the mildest climates.

Within each of the two preceding categories, you'll see two subcategories: deciduous (plants that drop leaves in the dormant season) and evergreen.

Hardy trees and shrubs

Below is a sampling from among the many hardy trees and shrubs suitable for container growing. Remember that the hardiness zones given are for plants growing in the ground, and that plants growing in containers may need protection from extreme cold. (Review Chapter 10 for overwintering techniques.)

Deciduous

These plants drop their leaves in fall, go dormant in the winter, and begin growing again in spring.

> ✔ **Cotoneaster:** Among the many kinds of cotoneaster, several are container standouts. Creeping cotoneaster *(C. adpressus)* and bearberry *(C. dammeri)* can spill from pots and hanging baskets, producing bright berries. They're small (less than a foot tall) and easy to grow. Provide full sun. Most are hardy in zones 6 to 9.
>
> ✔ **Crape myrtle *(Lagerstroemia indica):*** Take your pick — crape myrtle can serve as a handsome small tree or a hanging basket trailer. Not many plants can fill both these roles. Plant full-size varieties in large containers to grow as single-trunk or multitrunk trees, 8 or 10 feet tall. The bark develops an interesting combination of scaliness and smoothness, and summer flowers come in rich pinks, reds, and purples. A favorite tree for shopping centers and business parks, crape myrtle is always handsome. Miniature varieties really can go into hanging baskets: They bloom nicely and have trailing branches.
>
> Provide full sun. Watch for mildew, which probably means your climate is too cool. Crape myrtle is hardy in zones 7 to 9.
>
> ✔ **Flowering cherry, crabapple, or plum trees:** These trees aren't for beginners, but their beautiful spring blossoms may tempt you to give growing them a try. Some produce fruit, and some don't. Our advice in a nutshell: Get a big container (like a half barrel), choose small varieties,

and prune after spring bloom to keep the trees small. Hardiness varies. Flip to Chapter 13 for information on growing other fruit trees.

✔ **Harry Lauder's walking stick** *(Corylus avellana Contorta):* This plant is a genuine conversation piece in a container (you may have suspected as much from the name). Its contorted branches and shiny brown bark are shown off best when the plant is leafless in winter. In a container, expect a height of about 4 to 6 feet. Put it where you can enjoy its fascinating shape and bark up close.

Provide full sun or part shade. Make sure the soil mix drains quickly. In spring, prune branches that interfere with the shape you want. Harry Lauder's walking stick is hardy in zones 4 to 9.

✔ **Hydrangea:** Huge flowers and bold foliage make *Hydrangea macrophylla* a summer show-off in 18-inch or bigger containers. Flowers in clusters a foot or more wide come in blue, pink, red, or white. Plants grow 4 feet tall and larger.

Hydrangea macrophylla is hardy in zones 6 to 9 (some other hydrangea species are hardier). Overwinter plants in cold climates, or look for new varieties, like Endless Summer, that bloom reliably and repeatedly in cold climates. Provide sun or part shade, and protect plants from hot summer sun. Use a soil mix with plenty of organic matter. Hydrangeas are water hogs, but they're good about drooping and telling you when they need water.

Apply aluminum sulfate to the soil before the bloom season to make pink-flowering varieties turn blue.

✔ **Japanese maple** *(Acer palmatum):* You may want to put Japanese maples at the top of your container plantings list (provided you live in an appropriate climate). Why? Japanese maple is just plain beautiful — in both form and leaf color, whether spring green or fall red. Some say its bare branches in winter are so handsome that they don't need leaves to look great. And they're the right scale for patio container plants. A typical Japanese maple can grow 15 feet or more in the ground, but it's much shorter in a container. Compact varieties work best in containers: Dissectum and Crimson Queen are just two. Look for varieties with bright fall colors or even colorful bark (Sango Kaku has coral bark).

Japanese maples are hardy in zones 5 to 9. They don't do well in hot, dry climates. Provide afternoon shade in most climates. Plant in a soil mix containing lots of organic matter, and keep the soil most (Japanese maples are sensitive to alkaline soil and too little water, causing the leaves to turn brown at the tips). Shelter from dry winds. In spring, prune lightly to remove dead wood or to shape growth.

Japanese maple grows fairly quickly: Plan to repot it in progressively larger containers or to root-prune frequently to keep it in the same container. Start with a gallon-size plant in a 12-inch pot; put a 5-gallon-size in a 16-inch pot or tub.

✔ **Rose:** There are thousands of roses, and theoretically you can grow all of them in containers. But some varieties are much better suited to container life than others. If you want to grow a particular rose just because you like the flower (most likely, it's a hybrid tea type — that's what florists sell), feel free, but be aware that the plant may not produce many flowers, it may not look that great, and it may quickly outgrow its container. We suggest the smaller, more compact roses that are categorized as miniatures, polyanthas, floribundas, and some shrub roses. They grow from less than 2 to 5 feet, and their bloom season is long (from spring through early fall) and prolific (especially for floribundas and polyanthas). Here are our favorites for containers:

- **Betty Prior:** Pink floribunda
- **Bonica:** Pink shrub
- **Brass Band:** Apricot-yellow floribunda
- **Carefree Delight:** Pink shrub
- **Carefree Wonder:** Pink and white shrub
- **China Doll:** Pink polyantha
- **Europeana:** Red floribunda
- **The Fairy:** Pink polyantha
- **Flower Carpet:** Several colors, shrub
- **Iceberg:** White floribunda
- **Knockout:** A series of long-blooming, disease-resistant varieties
- **Margaret Merrill:** White floribunda
- **Margo Koster:** Coral floribunda
- **Regensberg:** White and pink floribunda
- **Sarabande:** Orange-red floribunda
- **Sun Flare:** Yellow floribunda
- **Watermelon Ice:** Pink shrub

Provide full sun and typical soil mix (nothing special). Give miniatures and other small roses at least a 12-inch-diameter container. For larger varieties, use a 14-inch pot or a half barrel (especially if you combine a rose with annuals or perennials). Select containers that are at least 16 inches deep to provide room for vigorous root growth. Make sure the soil never dries out.

Rose hardiness depends on variety. The best advice we can give you is to check locally for climate adaptability. Much is involved in growing first-rate roses, and some people take extreme measures to create special conditions for roses. That's why whole books have been written on the subject. We recommend *Roses For Dummies,* 2nd Edition, by Lance Walheim and the editors of the National Gardening Association (Wiley) for more advice on pruning, feeding, pest control, and choosing varieties.

Evergreen

These hardy trees and shrubs hang onto their foliage year-round, making them good candidates for background plantings, for privacy screens, or to shield an unsightly view. Some make striking specimen plants — worth showing off individually — especially as they grow older and are pruned to expose more of the trunks and branches.

Prune evergreens — especially needle-bearing types — with care. Some take well to shearing; others don't, leaving you with lots of dead stubs.

- **Aucuba:** *Aucuba japonica* is grown for its bright red berries in fall and big, shiny leaves (dark green or splotched with yellow variegation). Aucuba also gets big enough — up to 6 feet tall — to create a privacy screen or a backdrop for smaller container plants. Oh, one more thing: Aucuba does well in shady spots where few other plants can thrive.

  Provide part or full shade and ordinary soil mix. Soil can stay on the dry side. Prune back tips of new growth to encourage bushiness. Aucuba is hardy in zones 7 to 10.

- **Azaleas and rhododendrons:** Consider yourself lucky if you live in an area where you can grow these magnificent, spring-flowering shrubs — happily, containers can improve your odds. Rhododendrons and azaleas are closely related, and literally thousands of varieties exist: Check with local nurseries for varieties that do well in your area. Following are a couple recommendations:

  - **Evergreen azaleas:** Usually grown as small shrubs, these are the most reliable for containers. Read plant tags carefully because some are hardy only to zones 8 or 9. Also, keep in mind that some types of azaleas are deciduous — another reason to read the tags carefully! Plant gallon-size azaleas in 14-inch pots.

  - **Rhododendrons:** Try to find small, compact types, which grow 4 to 6 feet tall in containers. Ironclads do well in containers and are hardier than most (to zone 5). Rhododendrons are usually sold in larger sizes than azaleas, and eventually they require a big container, usually a redwood box 16 to 24 inches in diameter.

  Rhododendrons and azaleas share some rather demanding needs — an acid-type soil mix and just the right amount of sunlight. Containers allow you to move the plants around and experiment a bit. These plants are difficult to grow in hot, dry climates, especially where water is alkaline. In cool, overcast climates, grow the plants in full or nearly full sun. Elsewhere, plant them in part shade.

Make sure the soil mix is on the acidic side and fast draining (see Chapter 4): Nurseries sell mixes specifically for rhododendrons and azaleas. Don't plant too deep — level the top of the root ball with the top of the soil mix or even a fraction of an inch higher. Start fertilizing when the blooming season ends: Use an acid-type food (choose one labeled for rhododendrons and azaleas) at the frequency recommended on the label or monthly through the growing season. After bloom, cut off dead flowers right away. Watch for brown leaf tips that indicate salt burn. Flush salts every few months with a couple of extra heavy waterings. Never let the soil dry out.

Rhododendrons and azaleas need a lot of pampering, but you'll be rewarded with gorgeous blooms (and lots of compliments!). Move them out of the way when not in bloom, and put them in your most prominent spot when they're flowering.

✔ **Boxwood:** The first word in formality, boxwood is a shiny, dark green evergreen that lends itself to shearing in geometric shapes: globes, rectangles, and so on. Grow in urns, glazed pots, or other formal containers. Picture boxwood sheared into round balls, growing in matching containers, flanking a front entry. Provide full sun or part shade. Roots are shallow. Don't let soil dry out. Boxwood is hardy in zones 6 to 8.

✔ **Camellia:** Here's a wonderful choice for containers if you live in a favorable climate, primarily the southern and western United States. Grow camellias for their glossy, evergreen leaves and their beautiful flowers — white, pink, and red — in late winter and early spring. Plants are handsome year-round, and in containers can grow slowly to 5 or 6 — or even 12 — feet.

Thousands of varieties exist — check out nurseries and choose plants with appealing flowers. *Camellia japonica,* the most familiar species, makes a fine container plant. Also consider *C. reticulata* varieties with spectacular flowers on rangy plants. *C. sasanqua* varieties can spill from containers or stand upright, and the flowers come at a most welcome time — early fall.

Pay special attention to planting and care. Camellias aren't fussy, but they do need special conditions for best growth. Put gallon-size plants in 12-inch tubs and larger plants in 16-inch containers. Plant on the high side, with the top of the root ball above soil level. Provide part shade or full sun in cool climates, and move plants to a protected spot during cold weather in marginal climates. Use a soil mix that's fast-draining and acidic — if you want, just choose a mix labeled for camellias and other acid-loving plants — and make sure the soil is constantly moist. Pick up dead flowers to stop spread of petal blight. Start feeding after bloom with camellia or acid food.

Camellias are hardy in zones 7 to 9; some new varieties are hardy in zone 6.

✔ **Conifers:** Conifers are some of the most beautiful and striking plants for growing in containers, and they're available in a remarkable array of colors, forms, and sizes. Foliage may be green, blue-green, gray-green, chartreuse, gold, or silvery blue, depending on the species and variety. Some conifers have sharp, spiky needles; the needles on others are soft and draping. Size and shape vary widely, too. Some grow in tall columns; others are low and spreading. A grouping of different conifers in similar pots makes an elegant display. Look for dwarf or small-statured varieties and check hardiness ratings.

Some needle-bearing conifers, like spruces and firs, can make nice living Christmas trees — indoors for a few weeks and outdoors the rest of the year.

✔ **Daphne *(Daphne burkwoodii):*** This evergreen shrub is a garden workhorse, easy to grow and reliable. Growing 3- or 4-feet tall, it produces sweet flowers in spring. Place containers where you can enjoy the fragrance — near a door or walk.

Provide part shade in most climates, full sun in cool areas. Take care not to disturb roots when planting. This plant can stay in the same container for a long time without repotting. Daphne is hardy in zones 5 to 8.

✔ **English laurel *(Prunus laurocerasus):*** Often used in hedges, English laurel in a container makes a dense, glossy evergreen screen or backdrop for shady spots. Plants typically grow up to 6 feet tall, but compact types, such as Zabeliana, stay lower.

Provide sun or shade. This plant is easy to grow. Shape by pruning rather than shearing. Move to a protected spot in cold areas. English laurel is hardy in zones 6 or 7 to 9.

✔ **Heavenly bamboo *(Nandina domestica):*** Not a real bamboo, nandina is a graceful, erect-growing evergreen shrub that performs solidly in all seasons. It's easy to grow in a container. Clusters of small, white flowers bloom in spring and summer; red berries and crimson foliage follow in fall and winter. Expect mature plants to grow 5 feet tall or more in a container. Dwarfs are much more compact (Nana is only about a foot tall, and lacks the grace of the taller types).

Provide sun or part shade. This plant can live in the same container for several years without repotting. In cold climates, you can move heavenly bamboo indoors for the winter. It's hardy in zones 6 or 7 to 9.

✔ **Holly:** Picture a pair of glossy, spiny-leafed hollies covered with red berries in matching containers flanking your front door for the Christmas holidays. How possible is it? Well, hollies can grow well in containers — if they're suited to your climate, you satisfy their rather demanding needs, and have enough patience to grow the plants for at least several years. Also, for berry development, you have to grow both a male and female plant (they're sold labeled by sex). If you want two berry-bearing (female) plants by your front door, you'll need a third male plant nearby.

English holly (*Ilex aquifolium*) is the traditional type; it grows to 6 to 10 feet in a large container. Chinese holly (*I. cornuta*) is easier to grow, especially in hot climates. Yaupon holly is native to the southeast United States and is the most reliable choice for that region.

Provide full sun or part shade in hot climates. The soil mix must be high in organic matter and drain quickly. Shear young plants to encourage bushiness, and prune as needed to keep the spiny leaves from scratching passersby. Hardiness varies. In the United States, English holly is really reliable only in the Pacific Northwest and northern California.

✔ **India hawthorn (*Rhaphiolepis*):** This dependable, versatile landscape plant also is — surprise — a dependable, versatile container plant. It provides glossy leaves year-round and bright pink flowers in spring. Plants form rounded mounds up to 4 feet tall. Nurseries sell India hawthorn trained as small trees (standards) with globelike tops on 3- or 4-foot trunks.

Provide full sun or part shade. Don't worry about providing any special care. Plant in a 12-inch pot, and keep plants small and bushy by regular pinching starting when they're young. India hawthorn is hardy in zones 7 or 8 to 10.

✔ **Lily of the valley shrub (*Pieris japonica*):** This shrub is so understated that you may not guess that it's a rhododendron relative. Lily of the valley shrubs always look nice. Their foliage is handsome year-round, tinged with red in spring. Little bell-shaped, white flowers are charming in spring. Expect a height of 8 feet in the ground, lower in a container.

Provide part shade or full sun in cool, overcast climates. Use an acid soil mix suggested for azaleas and rhododendrons. Lily of the valley is hardy in zones 6 to 8.

Not-so-hardy trees and shrubs

The plants in this list are less hardy than the ones above; most are hardy only to zones 7 or 8. They're good options for warm climates and for gardeners in cold-winter climates that are willing to provide winter protection.

Deciduous

These plants drop their leaves, leaving the branches bare for anywhere from a few weeks to a few months depending on the species and locale, then resprout.

✔ **Chinese paperbush (*Edgeworthia chrysantha*):** This multistemmed shrub or small tree grows to a height of about 6 feet with attractive bark and oblong, bluish green leaves. In early winter, it drops its leaves to reveal silvery flower buds. A month or two later, the fragrant, tubular flowers begin opening, before the new leaves emerge. Chinese paperbush is hardy in zones 7 or 8 to 10.

✔ **Fuchsia:** If you're climate-blessed, you can grow fuchsias as permanent plants. They're terrific in baskets (trailing types) or pots (upright types up to 6 feet tall). Their flowers are spectacular: intricately flared and dangling, richly colored in white, pink, purple, and many other colors.

Fuchsias are demanding, but worth the effort. Provide part shade. Use containers from 6 to 12 inches in diameter. Make sure the soil mix is high in organic matter and drains quickly. Keep the soil moist, and increase humidity in dry climates by misting daily. Start pinching new growth early in spring. Fertilize every two weeks during the growing season. Keep an eye out for mites.

Fuchsias are hardy to zone 9 or 10 to 11 — frost will do them in. Grow them as annuals in cold climates.

✔ **Lantana:** This shrubby plant's bright flower colors suggest sunny, tropical places — clusters of flowers bloom over a long season in white, gold, pink, orange, red, and white. Use trailing lantana *(L. montevidensis)* in hanging baskets for sunny, dry spots; expect it to sprawl gracefully over the sides of the basket. Common lantana *(L. camara)* is good in a big container, growing to 4 feet tall and spreading about as wide. It's also available trained as a small tree (standard).

Provide full sun. Keep the soil on the dry side. Prune off dead wood in spring. Lantana is hardy in zones 7 or 8 to 11.

Evergreen

These plants stay green year-round, making them ideal for adding winter interest in warm climates. In regions with cold winters, be prepared to protect them during the winter.

✔ **Fatsia, or Japanese aralia** *(Fatsia japonica):* This plant's bold leaves add drama to shady spots. An evergreen shrub, it can grow to 6 feet tall or more, making it suitable for use as a specimen plant in an entry or dark corner. This is a favorite plant to bring indoors for the winter; it can also serve as a permanent houseplant.

Provide part shade or full shade. Plant in a large container. Don't let soil dry out. And don't be afraid to prune back stems, which otherwise become leggy. Fatsia is hardy in zones 8 to 10.

✔ **Gardenia:** A prima donna — but at least you stand a better chance of giving gardenia the conditions it needs when you plant it in a container. No other plant can match the romance of its legendary fragrance. While they're alive, the plants are handsome too, with glossy, deep green leaves. Mystery (what a perfect name for a plant you may never figure out!) grows 4 or 5 feet tall. Veitchii is a compact 3 feet.

Provide part shade in hot climates and full sun in cool places. Use a fast-draining, acid-type soil mix. Plant so that the top of the root ball is just above soil level. Make sure the soil stays moist. Fertilize frequently with acid food (azalea fertilizer) during the growing season. Good luck! Gardenia is hardy in zones 8 to 10.

✔ **Hawaiian hibiscus:** The symbol of Hawaii, of course this shrub is tender. But cold-climate gardeners are tempted every year by nursery plants sporting huge (up to 6-inch) blossoms in bright reds, yellows, and other vivid shades. The solution is easy: Transplant hibiscus into a 12-inch or so container, put it in a warm spot, grow it for the summer, and then get rid of it — in other words, treat it like a petunia or other annual. You can also bring it indoors for the winter in cold regions, but you'll probably already have gotten your money's worth with summer blooms. In containers, plants grow quickly to as tall as 6 feet; leaves are bright green and glossy.

Provide full sun (reflected light, too, if you have it). Make sure the soil stays damp. Feed at least once a month during warm weather. Pinch young shoots for bushy growth. Hawaiian hibiscus is hardy to zones 9 or 10 in protected spots.

✔ **Myrtle:** Shear these little evergreens into topiaries or other formal shapes. For containers, look for dwarf myrtle varieties like Compacta and Microphylla, which reach 2 or 3 feet tall.

Provide full sun, and make sure the soil stays moist. Myrtle is hardy in zones 8 to 11.

✔ **Norfolk Island pine *(Araucaria heterophylla):*** You may not know it by name, but this is a popular and highly recognizable tree for containers. Its unusual growth habit displays feathery foliage in horizontal tiers. Slender and tall, it grows up to 10 or 12 feet. Another outstanding quality: Norfolk Island pine can live indoors for the winter (it has to in cold climates) — or even all the time. Use it as a living Christmas tree.

Provide full sun or part shade. No special care is necessary. This is not a true pine — it comes from the South Pacific. Norfolk pine is hardy to zone 9.

✔ **Oleander:** Resiliant and easy to grow, oleander is another one of those basic landscape plants that takes on a whole new personality in a container. Use it as a specimen in a big pot, or create a privacy screen with a row of plants in containers. Oleander can also be trained as a small tree. Its summer flowers are white, pink, red, or yellow. Plants grow to 6 feet or more. Best choices for containers are dwarf varieties ("Petite" in the name is a good clue).

Provide full sun. You can keep soil on the dry side, but oleander can also take frequent watering. Give the plant a big enough container: at least 14 inches for best growth. Prune hard in spring to control size. Oleander is hardy in zones 8 to 10.

All parts of the oleander are poisonous.

✔ **Pineapple guava *(Feijoa):*** This subtropical can produce edible green fruit while in a container, and it makes a handsome specimen plant for a patio or deck. Expect it to grow 5 or 6 feet tall; pruning keeps it more compact.

Provide full sun. A large container (14 inches and up) encourages the best growth. Don't let the soil dry out. Pineapple guava is hardy in zones 8 to 10.

✔ **Pittosporum:** Several kinds of pittosporum that are used as evergreen landscape plants also excel in containers. Not particularly showy, they're just solid-citizen types, with dense, shiny foliage that can be sheared into formal shapes. Use several to create a portable hedge or privacy screen. *P. tobira* Wheeler's Dwarf is very compact; Variegata has cream and light green foliage that lights up in shade. Cape pittosporum (*P. viridiflorum*) can make a multitrunk small tree in a large container.

Provide full sun or part shade. No special care is needed. Pittosporum is hardy in zones 8 to 10.

✔ **Podocarpus:** Dependable and evergreen, podocarpus grows slowly and can live in a container for a long time. It's useful where you want something tall and slender — to block a view or accent a corner. Podocarpus lends itself to growing along an eave, or you can train it to grow flat against a support like a wall. Fern pine (*P. gracilior*) has thin, gray-green leaves. Yew pine (*P. macrophyllus*) has broader, dark green leaves. Neither is a true pine.

Provide full sun or part shade. Podocarpus is hardy in zones 8 to 10.

✔ **Pomegranate:** An unlikely choice for a container, pomegranate has much to offer. The orange-red flowers are pretty, and the fruit is fun (and tasty). The full-sized variety can turn into a rambunctious handful (that means a tangled, oversized mess) in a container. Try Nana, a more compact type growing to 3 feet. Its flowers are abundant, but the fruit is small and not worth eating. Deciduous foliage turns a nice yellow in the fall.

Pomegranate thrives in hot climates. Provide full sun, and keep the soil on the dry side. Prune in spring by cutting back long shoots and removing tangled branches. Pomegranate is hardy in zones 8 to 11.

✔ **Strawberry tree *(Arbutus unedo):*** This can make a handsome miniature tree or shrub in a container. It has attractive bark, small white flowers, and beautiful red berries (the "strawberry" in the name). Compact varieties like Compacta work best in containers: Expect a maximum height of 5 or 6 feet.

Provide full sun or part shade. The strawberry tree is a favorite West Coast landscape plant. It can stay in a 12-inch container for a number of years. It's hardy in zones 8 to 10.

✔ **Sweet bay *(Laurus nobilis):*** A cook's dream is to have sweet bay in a container right outside the back door. This evergreen is the source of bay leaves used in the kitchen and in wreaths for the home and head (in ancient Greece). This plant grows to 6 feet tall but can be sheared to stay smaller and to create more formal shapes like cones and globes.

Provide full sun or part shade. The container needs to be 12 to 14 inches or larger. In cold climates, bring sweet bay indoors for the winter. It's hardy in zones 8 to 10.

✔ **Sweet olive *(Osmanthus fragrans):*** This nondescript evergreen shrub shows the value of container planting: Keep it in the background most of the year and then move it near the front porch in fall when its barely noticeable flowers produce a truly delicious fragrance. This plant generally grows 5 or 6 feet tall in containers.

Provide full sun or part shade. No special care is needed. Prune to shape growth. Sweet olive is hardy in zones 8 or 9 to 10.

Selecting Six Vines for Containers

Growing vines on trellises and other supports is a good way to add height to container plantings. A vine-covered arbor makes a lovely garden entryway, and vines growing on lattice can shield a porch from hot summer sun — and from your neighbors. Many perennial vines get too big too quickly to make them practical for containers; below we list a few that are more manageable.

If you want to grow climbing vines that you know will need winter protection, you have a few options for overwintering:

✔ You can place the trellis right in the pot, so you can move the whole thing into a sheltered spot.

✔ Depending on the climate and type of plant, you may be able to leave the plant where it is and insulate the pot with a thick layer of straw or other mulch.

✔ You can cut the plant off the trellis at the end of the growing season and move the pot to its sheltered spot. Most vines will resume vigorous growth in spring.

For colorful blooms or year-round greenery, the following vines are well worth a try.

Bougainvillea

The sight of bougainvillea sprawling along a lush roadside in Hawaii or engulfing a building in Puerto Vallarta hardly suggests that the plant can thrive in a container. Actually, bougainvillea's a great choice — if you select the right variety and put it in the right place. It seems perfectly at home in a terra-cotta pot near a swimming pool. The papery flowers have a tropical vividness in shades of red, orange, purple, white, and other colors. Look for dwarf varieties (La Jolla is a good one) for containers — they spill nicely over the sides. Trailing types (Crimson Jewel) are best for hanging baskets. Tall varieties can be tied up as a vine.

Provide full sun except in the hottest climates. Keep the soil on the dry side; drainage must be perfect. When planting, take pains not to disturb the roots at all. In spring, prune off any cold-damaged wood or crossing branches. During the growing season, prune off branches growing where you don't want them to go.

Bougainvillea is hardy in zones 9 to 11 (some varieties are hardier than others). Yes, bougainvillea is tender and can be grown outdoors in only the mildest climates. But in cold places, you can grow it as a summer-only container plant, and bring it indoors for the winter; give it your sunniest spot near a window.

Clematis

Fortunately, the most spectacular clematis are also the best suited to containers. These are the deciduous hybrids with the beautiful, huge, six-petaled flowers in blue, purple, red, and many other shades. The vines can climb as high as 20 feet. Use one in a container with a trellis or train the vine up and over an entryway. Choose from many varieties at your local nursery or in mail-order catalogs.

Provide full sun or part shade. Conventional wisdom says to put the plant in a place where the container is in shade and the uppermost growth is in the sun if you can find such a location: The idea is to keep the roots cool and the flower buds exposed to light. The roots need plenty of room; make sure the container's at least 16 inches deep. The soil mix must drain quickly; don't let it dry out. For top flower production, proper pruning is critical and depends on variety; consult with local experts.

Most are hardy in zones 4 to 9. You may need to move clematis into a protected spot for the winter. Sweet autumn clematis *(C. terniflora)* is classified as an invasive plant in some parts of the country.

English ivy (Hedera helix)

English ivy is easy to train and, in a container, easy to bring indoors. Let English ivy drape from a hanging basket filled with shade-loving annual flowers. Train it into topiary shapes. Use it in a container where it can climb up a trellis or wall, like in an entry or on a patio. Choose from among hundreds of varieties: with leaves of different shapes, sizes, variegations, and so on.

Provide part or full shade, or even full sun in cool climates. Keep the soil moist. Pinch young plants to encourage bushy growth. English ivy is hardy in zones 5 or 6 to 9. Bring plants indoors during the winter in cold regions. English ivy is considered an invasive plant in some parts of the country.

Mandevilla

You can find this tropical vine sold almost everywhere during the warm months. Buy it in bloom, move it into a 12-inch-wide container or hanging basket, and enjoy it for the summer. Flowers of *Mandevilla amabilis* Alice du Pont are big pink trumpets, up to 4 inches wide.

Provide full sun or part shade. Keep the soil moist. Feed at least monthly.

Mandevilla is hardy in zones 10 and 11. Frost kills the plant. Try bringing it indoors and growing it in a sunny window for the winter.

Star jasmine (Trachelospermum jasminoides)

With its glossy evergreen foliage and wonderfully sweet white flowers in summer, star jasmine deserves a spot in any garden where it can grow. In a container, train star jasmine up a trellis or espalier and tie it to a nearby wall — wherever you can appreciate its fragrance.

Provide full sun or part shade in hot climates. The soil should be kept moist for best growth, although plants can withstand dry conditions. Pinch branch tips of young plants to encourage bushy growth. Shear older plants after bloom to shape growth. This plant is easy to grow, and is hardy in zones 8 to 10. Star jasmine can be moved indoors for the winter in colder climates.

Wisteria

Chinese wisteria *(W. sinensis)* and Japanese wisteria *(W. floribunda)* are probably the ones that come to mind with their thick, woody vines dripping with fragrant blossoms. Both grow into enormous plants and are classified as invasive in many regions. Instead, consider the more manageable and well-behaved native species, American wisteria *(W. frutescens)*. Train it on a trellis or frame, or prune it into a small, single-trunk tree over a number of years. The plant produces the familiar clusters of purple-blue or white blossoms.

Provide full sun and a strong support. Wisteria is hardy in zones 6 to 9.

Checking Out a Few Hard-to-Classify Plants

The following plants don't fall neatly into any of the above categories — at least not to a botanist. Although they can be used in similar garden situations (to add height and provide privacy, for example) they aren't true woody plants. So in the spirit of botanical correctness we've created a separate category for them.

Bamboo

Statuesque in a container, bamboo actually is a giant grass. One reason to grow it in containers is to confine the running types that can take over a garden if let loose in the ground. Bamboo looks great as a single plant or combined with small pines or azaleas. Or plant several to create a privacy screen.

Many kinds are available. Golden bamboo, a notorious spreader, is easy; black bamboo is striking. Both grow to 8 feet tall. Provide full sun or part shade. Plant bamboo in a container at least 15 inches in diameter. Treat it like a grass — don't let it dry out. You can bring bamboo indoors for the winter — just make sure to provide lots of light. Hardiness varies by species.

Palms

Indoors and outdoors, palms are proven winners as traditional potted plants. Actually, most kinds benefit from an arrangement that keeps them outdoors for the warm months and indoors when frost threatens. (Flip to Chapter 14 for details on indoor container gardening.) In the mildest climates, palms can live outdoors all the time. They make striking container plants for decks, patios, and doorways. Consider the following varieties:

- ✔ **Kentia palm** *(Howea belmoreana)* is up to 7 feet, with a pretty, feathery look. Lady palm *(Rhapis excelsa)* reaches 10 or 12 feet. This is a terrific indoor plant, tolerating low light. Slender stems grow in clusters like bamboo.

- ✔ **Mediterranean fan palm** *(Chamaerops humilis)* can take a few degrees of frost. It's great in containers when young and small. Growth is clumpy, with fan-shaped leaves.

- ✔ **Parlor palm** *(Chamaedorea elegans)* is a classic. It grows just 3 or 4 feet tall, with a single trunk and feathery leaves. Fit three or four plants in one container to create a grove effect.

- ✔ **Pygmy date palm** *(Phoenix roebelenii)* reaches 6 feet — very slowly. It develops a single trunk and a dense, feathery-leafed top.

Outdoors, grow palms in part shade or even full shade, protected from wind, which can tatter fronds. Indoors, palms get along on average light conditions. Plant in a container just a bit larger than the nursery container. Keep the soil moist. Fertilize as often as once a month during growing season. Watch for spider mites (see Chapter 18), and hose off palms every few weeks to wash away dust and insects.

Sago palm *(Cycas revoluta)*

Botanists tell us that this is not a true palm, but rather a cycad. It may fool you, too. Regardless, it's a bold container plant, with slow-growing, spiky fronds arising from a central core that take years to grow taller than 2 or 3 feet. Provide part or full shade. Water and fertilize lightly. Sago palm is hardy in zones 9 or 10 to 11. Bring it indoors during cold weather.

Chapter 13

Nurturing Fruits and Berries

. . . .

In This Chapter

▶ Getting a quick course in fruit and berry biology

▶ Discovering the characteristics of winning candidates for containers

▶ Finding out what fruit producers need

▶ Looking at the plants you have to pick from

. . . .

*W*hile growing flowers and vegetables in containers can be a snap, growing fruit trees and berries takes a little more forethought. You need to become familiar with such things as rootstocks, pollination, and climate adaptation. You may need to prune and thin. We get to all those details in this chapter, but first, the good news.

Growing your own fruit is tremendously rewarding. Nothing, and we mean nothing, tastes better than homegrown fruit harvested at peak ripeness. Imagine the pleasure of adding a handful of blueberries or strawberries to your cereal in the morning or serving an apple pie made with home-grown fruit from the tree on your deck. And fruiting plants can also be quite good-looking — many have colorful, fragrant flowers, attractive foliage, and, of course, beautiful fruit.

Many types of fruits and berries adapt nicely to growing in containers. And plant breeders continue to develop compact varieties especially suited to container growing. Growing fruit in containers has advantages, as well. Most noteworthy is the mobility that containers provide. If frost threatens, you can move your fruit trees under cover for protection. So although container fruit growing takes a little more effort than growing flowers or vegetables, the pay-offs are well worth it. In the second half of this chapter, we list berry plants and fruit trees that are easy to grow in containers, and we give you some tips for each one to help make your efforts fruitful (pun intended!).

A Bowl of Fruit Facts

Before you can set off on your growing adventure, you need to pack in a few fruit-gardening terms and concepts that come up again and again in this chapter. We concentrate on deciduous fruit trees (apples, peaches, and so on) because they're the most complex and also the most rewarding. The following sections explain the biology of how trees come to bear fruit and how normally large fruit trees are cultivated to be suitable for container gardening.

Pollinating: It's the bee's knees

You probably remember from Biology 101 all about how pollen moves from the male part of the flower to the female part, fertilizing it, and causing a fruit to grow. Some fruit trees, like peaches, have compatible male and female flower parts on the same plant — this kind of plant is called *self-fruitful*. You can grow one peach tree — or other self-fruitful plant — by itself, and it will produce fruit.

Other fruits, including some apples and blueberries, produce more and better quality fruit if they're *cross-pollinated,* which means that they receive pollen from another variety. You can grow one apple or one blueberry plant and probably get some fruit, but you'll get much better production if you have a second, different variety growing nearby. For example, if you plant one or two Bluecrop blueberries, you'll get some fruit, but if you plant one each of Bluecrop and Earliblue varieties of blueberry, you'll get a bigger, better harvest.

For some fruits, such as plums, you need a specific variety (usually one that blooms at the same time) for proper cross-pollination.

So now that you know about pollen, what about pollinators? Pollinators carry pollen from flower to flower, or even from one part of a flower to another part. Pollinators are usually bees, flies, or other insects, and you probably have plenty of those in your garden. Even city dwellers will have bees and flies buzzing around, especially if they plant flowers nearby.

Planting a combination of flowers, veggies, and fruits makes your container garden a one-stop shopping place for our pollinating friends.

Downsizing fruit trees for containers

Most fruit trees have two parts: the rootstock and the scion. The *rootstock* is the below-ground portion of the plant. The *scion* is the above-ground, fruiting part of the plant. The point at which a scion joins the rootstock is called the *graft union* or *bud union.* The graft union (as we choose to call it) is usually indicated by a swollen or curved part of the trunk a few inches above the soil level. Below the graft union is the rootstock; above is the scion.

Why are there two parts? We figured you'd ask. In simple terms, when nurseries grow fruit trees, they *bud* or *graft* (methods of fusing or joining two closely related plants) the scion variety onto the rootstock to take advantage of the best attributes of each plant.

Obviously, the scion produces great tasting fruit — that's a considerable attribute. But a good rootstock can contribute qualities like adaptation to specific soil types, hardiness, or size control. Size control? Yes, size control. And that's why we brought up this whole rootstock-scion business in the first place.

If grown on their own roots, most fruit trees get huge — way too big to grow in containers. But if grown on rootstocks that keep them smaller, called *dwarfing rootstocks,* these same fruit trees become ideal for containers. Apples perfectly demonstrate the value of dwarfing rootstocks. A normal apple tree can grow up to 40 feet high. But the same variety grown on a dwarfing apple rootstock can be reduced in size by over 75 percent, reaching just 10 feet tall.

Not every type of fruit is available as a dwarfing rootstock. But luckily, another type of elfish fruit tree exists — a *genetic dwarf.* The genetic dwarf fruit tree is naturally smaller. For example, a standard (normal size) peach tree may reach 25 feet high. A genetic dwarf peach rarely gets over 6 feet high — perfect for containers. The number of genetic dwarf fruit tree varieties available is growing. Unfortunately, their fruit isn't always as good as that of standard varieties, but it's certainly better than store-bought fruit!

If you have a favorite variety of fruit, look for it on a dwarfing rootstock first. If you can't find one, check to see whether it's available as a genetic dwarf.

Semi-dwarfing rootstocks dwarf the trees about 25 to 50 percent. Depending upon the type of fruit tree and variety, these may also be good choices for large containers.

Selecting Plants for Their Container-Friendly Traits

Certain characteristics make some fruits better than others for growing in containers. But first and foremost, grow what you like to eat! If you love fresh strawberries on your cereal, by all means give them a go. If blueberries are your morning fruit of choice, plant those. And if you live in Minnesota but still dream of having a lemon tree, containers make it possible.

One of the great things about growing in containers is that you can modify soil mixes and move plants as necessary to provide the best conditions, so don't be afraid to experiment. Fruits that wouldn't thrive out in your garden may adapt well to growing in containers. The following sections indicate some other considerations when choosing fruit plants for containers.

Small size

Some fruiting plants are just smaller than others and, consequently, make easy container subjects. Strawberries, for example, grow on tiny, clumpy plants that are perfect for pots.

Even within fruit types, some varieties can be better for containers than others. Meyer lemons, for instance, are compact plants that easily stay below 6 feet in a large container. Eureka lemons, on the other hand, get huge — upward of 20 feet — not a good container choice.

You can keep some fruit trees smaller with vigorous pruning, but the roots still eventually outgrow the container. In that case, you may want to try root pruning (see Chapter 17).

Climate adaptation

Not all fruits can be grown everywhere. Fruit trees have varying degrees of hardiness to winter cold temperatures. Many also need a certain amount of winter cold (called chilling hours) before they bloom and set fruit; types that set fruit in mild winters are called low-chill. Some, like peaches, grow best where summers are hot and dry. Others, like raspberries, prefer cool summers. Remarkable differences in adaptation even exist among different varieties of the same fruit type. The point is, if you want to grow quality fruit, select types and varieties that are well adapted to your area. To find out for sure, ask your local nursery person or Cooperative Extension agent.

Fruits grown in containers are less winter-hardy than those grown in the ground. Even hardy trees and shrubs, such as apples and blueberries, need winter protection in cold climates. Move evergreen citrus and other semitropicals into a greenhouse or indoors in winter. Chapter 10 provides details on overwintering container-grown plants.

Basic Planting and Maintenance

Most good potting soils work fine for growing fruit and berries (see Chapter 4). Blueberries are an exception — they require a very acidic soil, which can be created by mixing any good potting mix with 50 percent peat moss.

In general, the bigger the container the better, as demonstrated in Figure 13-1. For most fruit, you need at least a 15-gallon size container or one with at least an 18- to 24-inch-wide diameter. Half barrels work well. Strawberries and some dwarf blueberries can be grown in smaller pots. (For more on containers, see Chapter 3.)

Figure 13-1:
When it comes to fruit, the bigger the pot, the better.

Fruit and berries can be purchased bare-root (without any soil around their roots) during the dormant season or already growing in containers at other times of year. We cover planting techniques in Chapter 5.

Fruits and berries need full sun and regular water and fertilizer. Skimp on any of these, and you'll get reduced yields and poorer fruit quality. For more specific cultural requirements, see the fruit descriptions in the upcoming sections.

Pruning techniques vary for each type of fruit. To get the full scoop, you'd need a book dedicated to growing fruit. However, some basic techniques apply to most types:

- ✔ Remove criss-crossing, diseased, or dead branches.
- ✔ Prune out some of the inward-facing branches to allow light to penetrate the canopy and to increase air circulation.
- ✔ Try to keep branches evenly spaced around the plant so it doesn't become lopsided.
- ✔ Remove old or unproductive branches. Allow young, vigorous branches to take their places.
- ✔ In general, prune peaches and nectarines more severely than other fruit trees.

Some fruit trees produce so much fruit that, if you don't remove some, you end up with nothing but small fruit at harvest time. Removing fruit before they reach maturity is called *thinning*. Apples, peaches, nectarines, and plums all have to be thinned by hand, or the fruit will turn out small. The best time to thin is in early spring, when the fruit is about the size of a quarter. Simply pinch off the small fruit so that you have one remaining fruit per cluster and about 6 to 8 inches between fruit. Thinning can be a bit painful, especially with genetic dwarf trees, where you may have to remove more than 75 percent of the young fruit to achieve the proper spacing. But if you don't do it, you'll later regret your restraint.

The day will come when you want to move your plant from one side of the deck to the other, or you'll need to move it indoors for the winter. If you need some pointers on how to best move a heavy, soil-filled pot and plant without doing too much harm to the plant, pot, or yourself, flip to Chapter 17 where we offer some useful moving strategies.

Cherry-Picking Fruits and Berries for Containers

With persistence and constant care, almost any fruit or berry can be grown in a container, but some are much easier than others. In the following sections, we describe the less-demanding possibilities and give you tips for growing each type. We also tell you about some of the different varieties that are available, and offer insights into which ones are best adapted to various climates.

Small fruits

These are perfect for first-time fruit-growers. Blueberries and strawberries are easy to grow, produce fruit relatively quickly, and are forgiving if you make a minor mistake. Also, they don't take up too much space. And they're yummy!

Blueberries

Blueberries adapt well to growing in containers as long as you give them the acidic soil they require. You can choose from low, half-high, and high bush varieties. The plants are very attractive, with pretty spring flowers and handsome foliage that turns bright red before dropping in fall.

- **Growing tips:** Purchase a special potting mix formulated for blueberries and other acid-loving plants, or create your own by mixing equal parts standard potting soil and peat moss. Plant at least two different varieties to ensure cross-pollination (you can plant three in one large container). Mix early-, mid-, and late-season varieties for a long harvest season. Prune regularly to renew fruiting wood. In hot summer areas, grow in part shade. Don't let plants dry out. Fertilize with an acidic plant food like one formulated for azaleas and rhododendrons.

- **Adaptation:** Most blueberries prefer areas with cool summers and cold winters, but different types demonstrate varying adaptation. Lowbush blueberries, such as Tophat, reach about 2 feet high and are grown mostly in northern climates. Half-high blueberries, such as North Country and Northsky, are very hardy and grow only 18 to 24 inches high. They can be grown in smaller pots. Highbush blueberries are the familiar supermarket type. They reach up to 6 feet high and need a large container to produce their best crop. There are varieties adapted to southern regions (for example Misty and Sharpblue) and northern regions (Earliblue and Blueray). Rabbiteye blueberries, such as Tifblue, grow better in hot-summer climates, like the southeastern United States.

Feed the birds . . . not!

Most gardeners welcome birds into their landscapes — except when fruit is ripening. A few birds can devour or damage every strawberry or blueberry in short order, sometimes just minutes before you head out to harvest. If you're growing fruits, assume that birds will find the plants and protect them before they start ripening. Cover plantings with chicken wire or bird netting, securing it to the container so birds can't find their way underneath, and propping up the covering so birds can't reach through the holes to get at the fruit.

Strawberries

Few edible plants are as well adapted to container life as strawberries. Their neat, compact habit fits perfectly into even small containers. Strawberries can also be grown in hanging baskets and even have a pot named after them — see Chapter 5 for information about planting a strawberry jar. In larger containers, like a half barrel, you can put in enough strawberry plants to provide a pretty substantial harvest — a large raised bed of strawberries can feed the neighborhood. And the plants are really attractive — they exhibit dark green, lobed leaves; lovely white flowers; and pure poetry in the way the fruit dangles over the edge of a pot.

There are three types of strawberries. June-bearing varieties, such as Earliglow and Jewel, produce one big crop in late spring or early summer. Everbearing varieties, such as Tribute and Tristar, produce a more prolonged harvest over the entire summer — you don't get as much fruit all at once, but you get fruit for a longer period. Alpine strawberries, such as Mignonette, produce small, sweet fruit all summer long. They don't produce *runners* (stringlike arms that set out roots), so they're great for smaller containers.

✔ **Growing tips:** You can start with bare-root plants in winter or plant from six-packs any time. Strawberries are self-fruitful, and the fruit doesn't need to be thinned. However, if you pinch off the first flowers that form on newly planted strawberries, the plants have a better chance to get established and give you more fruit later. Strawberry plants reproduce themselves by sending out new plants (babies) at the end of runners. Wherever the runners land, they set roots and grow. If you let all the babies take hold, your container will become overcrowded and start to decline in production. To prevent this, thin out the plants occasionally, removing the oldest ones.

Strawberry plants begin producing poorly when they're about 3 years old, so plan to get rid of them then. You can clip off the runners and replant the babies, or purchase new plants and start over.

✔ **Adaptation:** Strawberries can be grown almost anywhere as long as you choose locally adapted varieties, and you can find many of these. Check with your local nursery for the best varieties for your area. Everbearing varieties can be grown as annuals: Plant in early spring for a late summer harvest.

Brambles

The term brambles refers to plants in the genus *Rubus*. The plants produce long, usually thorny stems called canes and small, juicy aggregate fruit (made up of individual little drupelets, in case you want to know). Brambles are some of the easiest fruits to grow in the garden, but can be challenging in containers because of their rampant growth.

Blackberries

Most blackberries are too vigorous, thorny, and rangy to grow in containers easily. They really need more room and a trellis to do the job right. But a few varieties of thornless blackberries, like Arapaho and Navaho, are easier to handle and can be grown without a trellis in a large container.

✔ **Growing tips:** Plant three to five plants in a half barrel or similar-size container. Let the canes grow about 4 feet tall during the first summer; then pinch the tips to force lateral branches. The following spring, pinch the laterals back to 2 feet long; fruit will appear soon after. The following winter, remove the canes that have borne fruit, and repeat the process with the new canes that grow from the base of the old ones.

✔ **Adaptation:** Blackberries are one of the more widely adapted berries, growing well almost anywhere they're planted.

Raspberries

Unlike their close cousins, the blackberries, raspberries can be grown relatively easily in containers if you choose the right varieties and handle them properly — and if you live in the right area (see the following "Adaptation" bullet).

✔ **Growing tips:** Raspberries are self-fruitful and don't require fruit thinning. Plant three to five plants per half barrel or similar size container.

Try everbearing varieties like Heritage, Fall Gold, or Fall Red, all of which normally produce two crops when grown in the ground (one in early summer and one in fall). Prune the summer-bearing canes after they finish fruiting. The new growth will produce a crop in fall and again the next summer. If you want to focus on just a fall crop, cut all the canes to the ground in late fall or winter. The new growth that emerges the following spring will produce a crop in fall only. You'll sacrifice the summer crop, but get a larger fall crop.

✔ **Adaptation:** Raspberries grow best where summers are relatively cool and winters are cold. Bababerry is one variety that grows better in mild-winter, hot-summer areas.

Tree fruits

Apples, peaches, and other tree fruits are ideal candidates for containers. Beautiful spring flowers followed by luscious fruit — what's not to love? Fruit trees do require a bit more care than other fruits, especially when it comes to managing insects and diseases. (Chapter 18 provides lots of tips to help you out.) The results are well worth the extra effort.

If you want full-sized fruit on your apple, peach, plum, or nectarine tree you have to remove some of the fruit by hand, called *thinning,* which lets the tree focus its energy on the remaining fruit. When the fruit is about the size of a quarter, pinch off all but one fruit per cluster, leaving the remaining fruit are 6 to 8 inches apart. Don't feel bad about removing so many developing fruit; you'll be rewarded come harvest time.

Apples

Most apple varieties are available grown on a nice selection of dwarfing root-stocks that allow you to choose almost any size tree. The rootstocks are usu-ally labeled Mark, EMLA, or MM plus a number. One of many good rootstocks for containers is EMLA 27, which usually gives you a 5- to 7-foot-high tree.

To find the best selection of apple trees grown on dwarfing rootstocks, browse the mail-order catalogs listed in the appendix. Some genetic dwarfs are also available (sometimes called *spur* varieties, like spur Gold Delicious) which are smaller than standard varieties. If space is really at a premium, look for *colonnade* apple trees, which grow just 8 feet high and 2 feet wide. Northpole and Golden Sentinel are two good varieties to try.

✔ **Growing tips:** Most apples need cross-pollination to produce a good crop, so you may need to plant more than one variety. Trees need regu-lar pruning to remain productive. The fruit must be thinned if you want large apples.

✔ **Adaptation:** If you choose the right varieties, apples can be grown almost anywhere temperatures don't fall below –20 degrees Fahrenheit. Varieties like Red Astrachan, Haralson, and Honeycrisp are particularly hardy. In mild-winter areas, choose low-chill varieties like Anna and Dorsett Golden.

Apricots

Apricot trees generally get too big (about 15 feet) to grow in containers for any prolonged period. However, some catalogs sell varieties on dwarfing rootstocks, which may reduce their size by 25 to 50 percent. The smaller trees, such as Moorpark, are the best choice for containers.

> ✔ **Growing tips:** Some varieties need cross-pollination to produce fruit; others are self-fruitful. Trees require annual pruning to remain healthy and fruitful. The fruit must be thinned to reach full size.

> ✔ **Adaptation:** Apricots have a rather limited range of adaptation, preferring areas with long, dry summers. In other areas, they're prone to disease. Trees also bloom very early, making the blossoms subject to frost damage. In areas where apricots don't grow well, try Flavor Delight aprium, a plum-apricot hybrid with wider adaptation and an apricot-like flavor. For pollination, plant it near a Flavor Supreme pluot *(plew-ott),* a similar hybrid with fruit more like a plum.

Citrus

Where winter temperatures don't fall much below 26 degrees Fahrenheit, many varieties of citrus make excellent container plants year-round. In other areas, trees can be brought indoors (only a well-lit, cool spot with ample light and humidity can keep the tree healthy) or into heated greenhouses for protection during winter. Plants have deep green, evergreen foliage, fragrant spring flowers, and very colorful fruit — all in all, they make very handsome container subjects.

Some of the naturally smaller citrus that can thrive in containers for years include Meyer lemon, Bearss lime, and the hardier Nagami kumquat and Satsuma mandarins. Otherwise, grow just about any variety grafted on Flying Dragon dwarf rootstock for the perfect 6- to 8-foot-high container tree.

> ✔ **Growing tips:** Most varieties are self-fruitful and don't need to be pruned to remain productive. Feed with fertilizers that contain zinc, iron, and manganese to avoid micronutrient deficiencies (see Chapter 16 for more information).

> ✔ **Adaptation:** Varieties vary by cold hardiness and the amount of summer heat that they need to ripen fruit. In very cool summer areas, grow acidic fruit like lemons and limes.

Cherries

Normally quite large trees (upwards of 35 feet), most sweet cherries are not well-adapted to growing in containers. Dwarfing rootstocks, like Giessen, result in a tree half the size — still pretty large to stay in a container for very long. There are bush cherries available, such as Jan and Joel, that get 4 feet tall and wide. You need two varieties for cross-pollination.

✔ **Growing tips:** Most varieties must be matched carefully with another to ensure cross-pollination. Some, like Dwarf Northstar, are self-fruitful. Prune annually to keep trees healthy and productive.

✔ **Adaptation:** Local variety adaptation is very important. Cherries are best grown in areas with mild, dry summers. In other areas diseases can run rampant.

Figs

With beautiful, large, lobed, tropical-looking leaves, figs are really eye-catching in containers. Although they're normally quite large trees (up to 40 feet high), severe pruning can keep them more pot-size — and they still bear fruit. Figs are only hardy to about 15 degrees Fahrenheit, but they can be brought into a cool garage to get them through cold winters.

✔ **Growing tips:** Figs are pretty much carefree — just keep plants watered, fertilized, and if necessary, protected in winter. Some good varieties to try are Brown Turkey and Petite Negri.

✔ **Adaptation:** Other than the sensitivity to cold temperatures we mention earlier, figs are widely adapted.

Peaches and nectarines

Peaches and nectarines are closely related plants. In fact, a nectarine is just a fuzzless peach.

Both types of fruit are available in genetic dwarf varieties, like El Dorado, Garden Gold, and Stark Sensation peaches and the nectarine, Nectarcrest. All are perfectly suited to container growing. They're attractive trees with a compact, muscular-looking appearance. They reach about 4 to 6 feet high in a container and are self-fruitful.

✔ **Growing tips:** Prune the trees annually to keep the center open. Thin heavily to ensure large fruit at harvest time.

✔ **Adaptation:** Peaches and nectarines are best adapted to areas with hot, dry summers. They can be grown in other areas, but diseases are more troublesome.

Pears

Pears are available on dwarfing rootstocks, but the result is still a tree that can reach 10 to 15 feet high, pretty big for all but the biggest container. However, pears are quite attractive trees with glossy foliage, nice fall color, and white spring flowers — they may be worth a try.

- ✓ **Growing tips:** Fruit thinning usually isn't necessary. Some varieties need cross-pollination. Otherwise, pears are pretty easy to care for.

- ✓ **Adaptation:** European varieties like Bartlett, Bosc, and Comice are best adapted to dry summer areas that have fairly cold winters. Hybrid pears, like Kieffer, often have lower chilling requirements. Asian pears, which are hard like an apple (they're often called pear apples), are widely adapted.

Plums

Plums are generally too large to remain healthy in anything but the largest container for more than a few years. Some varieties are available on dwarfing rootstocks, but even these can get over 10 feet high.

- ✓ **Growing tips:** Prune regularly to keep them healthy and productive. Thin to maintain fruit size. Japanese plums, the type you see in supermarkets, require another variety nearby for cross-pollination. European plums, or prunes, are self-fruitful.

- ✓ **Adaptation:** Plum trees are widely adapted but subject to diseases in areas with warm, wet summers. Japanese plums bloom early and are subject to frost damage.

And just a few more

Many other, less common fruiting plants can be grown in containers. In mild winter areas, you may want to try tropical plants, like bananas and guavas, or slightly hardier plants, like pomegranate, loquat, and pineapple guava *(Feijoa)*. In colder areas, experiment with currants, elderberries, and gooseberries.

Chapter 14

Indoor Container Gardening

In This Chapter
▶ Finding the right fit with indoor plants
▶ Selecting containers and soil
▶ Getting the caretaking specifics for some indoor possibilities

Do you live in a high-rise, ten stories up, with no garden or even a balcony? Does your house or apartment lack that certain something, despite all the effort you've put into decorating and artwork? To us, an apartment or house without any indoor plants lacks a sense of life and always benefits from an infusion of nature. Not everyone is up to owning a conservatory filled with exotic trees, vines, and shrubs, but anyone can grow at least a few indoor plants.

Plus, indoor gardening offers benefits beyond decor — many plants are known to improve air quality. Spider plant, ivy, mother-in-law's tongue, and bamboo plant are among those found to absorb toxins from the air. In addition, plants use up carbon dioxide while releasing oxygen during photosynthesis. So take a deep, refreshing breath, and read on for details on how to nurture your indoor garden. We focus here on plants that are reasonably easy to grow indoors, along with a few special plants that require a bit of extra care but are worth it. Finally, we look at a few edibles you can grow indoors.

Matching a Plant's Needs to Your Home

From small African violets to towering ficus trees, the indoor plant possibilities are as limitless as your budget, patience, and imagination. Most plants sold as houseplants are native to the tropics, and these are usually the easiest to care for. That's because most people keep their homes at a relatively constant, warm temperature year-round, mimicking a tropical climate. A few require more temperature variation and other exacting conditions to perform their best, making them a bit more challenging.

When choosing plants, keep three things in mind: the light level where you'll keep the plant, the plant's shape and size, and, for lack of a better word, its fussiness — how challenging it is to keep it happy and healthy. Later in the chapter you find a list of plants that includes this information. But first, here's an overview of these factors.

Some indoor plants are toxic if ingested, so if you have pets that tend to nibble now and then, stick to nontoxic plants. The American Society for the Prevention of Cruelty to Animals (ASPCA) lists toxic plants at `www.aspca. org/pet-care/poison-control/plants/`.

Assessing the amount of light

Like outdoor plants, houseplant species vary widely in their light prefer-ences. Some need a sunny window to thrive; others suffer leaf scorch in direct sun and prefer lower light levels. A few plants will even survive in a corner that receives little light.

One rule of thumb is that if it's too dark to read a book, it's probably too dark for any plant to thrive.

If you're buying a new plant to fill a particular spot, take the time to evalu-ate the amount of light that area receives. Does the spot get any direct sun? Plants in curtainless, south-facing windows will get the most sun (unless a tree, balcony, eave, or building blocks the light). Look for plants labeled for high-light levels for these spots. East-facing windows get morning sun, and west-facing windows get afternoon sun. These areas are good for medium-light plants. North-facing windows get bright light but no direct sun and are fine for medium- to low-light plants. Plants that aren't near windows are gen-erally in low-light areas.

Keep in mind that sheer curtains block some light, and that drawn shades and heavy curtains turn a bright-light area into a low-light one.

Selecting a plant for its size and shape

As you would with outdoor plants, match the shape and size of indoor plants to the location. Houseplants grow relatively slowly, and most can be kept in bounds with regular pruning and occasional root pruning (refer to Chapter 17 for details), but it just makes sense to buy a plant that suits the spot right off the bat.

Tall, narrow plants, like some dracaenas, fit neatly into a corner. Palms, on the other hand, need room for their arching fronds — they look silly squished against a wall. Some indoor plants have sharp-edged leaves,

Petunias have covered these moss-lined wire baskets, creating a striking display. For tips on planting hanging baskets, turn to Chapter 5.

Placing containers near water doubles their impact, as the reflection of this mum-and-croton-filled planter attests.

Fill raised beds with top-quality soil, and you can grow vegetables. Turn to Chapter 4 for details on soil mixes.

Railing planters, like this one brimming with petunias, make it easy to dress up your deck. Head to Chapter 5 for pointers on planting these types of containers.

Dwarf citrus trees are ideal for growing in containers; you can move them to a sheltered spot during cold weather. Chapter 17 explains how to move large containers.

This "three sisters garden" includes corn, beans, and squash, and is planted in compost-filled fabric tubes made by Filtrexx. Check out Chapter 8 for more on planting edibles in containers.

This wall-mounted planter containing impatiens and ivy displays plants at eye level; the small figurine adds a whimsical touch.

The urns flanking this front door create a somewhat formal but still inviting entrance. The right combination of plants and container can create a specific mood.

The blue pot adds another facet to this eye-catching display that includes coleus, petunia, and calibrachoa plants. Chapter 19 has details on design elements.

Upside-down planters are popular for growing tomatoes, but they're perfect for peppers, too. Read about these planters in Chapter 3.

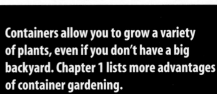

Containers allow you to grow a variety of plants, even if you don't have a big backyard. Chapter 1 lists more advantages of container gardening.

This leaf-patterned clay pot filled with chrysanthemums fits in perfectly with the stone, water, and sculpture in its surroundings.

If you're looking for a challenging but rewarding hobby, try bonsai. Chapter 20 can get you started.

Combining plants with different shapes and growth habits is a recipe for container success. For a variety of planting recipes, look at Chapter 19.

Yes, there is a container underneath all these plants, meaning this display has received regular watering and fertilizing. Those topics are the focus of Chapters 15 and 16, respectively.

Create a Lilliputian landscape with miniature plants in a small dish garden. Chapter 14 contains details on indoor container gardening.

The tree, annual flowers, and ferns complement each other in this patio display. You can swap containers in an arrangement like this one as the seasons change.

These tabletop-style planters allow wheelchair-bound gardeners to enjoy their hobby. Chapter 21 offers ideas on making gardening accessible to everyone.

Sometimes keeping it simple is best. Here, a terra-cotta planter with red cordyline makes a striking statement on its own.

Anything that holds soil can become a planter! Peas are right at home in this antique bathtub. Let Chapter 3 inspire your container choice.

Silver foliage plants complement any color scheme but are especially attractive with cool colors like blue and purple. Read about color considerations in Chapter 19.

Be sure you have a solid structure to hang a planter from. The combination of soil, plant, and water, as in this hanging plastic pocket planter featuring mums, can get heavy.

This clay pot contains yellow-flowered bidens, orange-flowered thunbergia, and red-flowered mandevilla vines. The trellis is secured in the ground behind the container. Read more about vines in Chapter 12.

These clever fabric planting bags are lightweight, easy to transport, and perfect for small plants like herbs. Find out more about fabric pots in Chapter 3.

so place these where they won't harm passersby. Some houseplants are vines that can drape down or be trained to grow up on a trellis or around a window frame.

Getting a feel for a plant's fussiness

Next time you're at the mall or doctor's office, look at the indoor plants. (And rest assured — there will be plants!) Most likely, the plants you'll see will be among the most reliable and the easiest to care for.

Building a terrarium

For a really self-sufficient indoor garden, try a terrarium (see the accompanying figure). Closed up in a large jar or aquarium, this kind of garden creates its own atmosphere and moisture. A terrarium needs only a good start in life, an occasional breath of fresh air, and, if necessary, the removal or addition of a plant here and there. Just follow these steps:

1. **Start with a clear glass or plastic bottle, dish, or aquarium.**

   A cover is optional.

2. **Add a layer of aquarium gravel (up to 2 inches), cover with a thin layer of charcoal, and top with material to serve as a screen.**

   Plastic or a layer of sheet moss or landscape cloth will do the trick.

3. **Add soil, and start planting.**

   Create your own little world by incorporating rocks, driftwood, tiny dinosaurs, or whatever accessories appeal to your imagination.

Some indoor plants (especially those growing in low light levels) need very little to keep them going. A bit of water (perhaps as rarely as once a month) plus one or two fertilizer applications per year and an occasional pruning or removal of dead leaves are all these plants need. They thrive on neglect — you can actually kill by paying too much attention to them — and they're at the low end of the fussiness scale.

At the other end are plants that require daily nurturing — misting to increase humidity or moving from room to room to provide just the right light levels and temperatures. If you like challenges, by all means give them a try. But don't take it personally if they drop leaves, won't produce flowers, or kick the bucket entirely. In the list of individual plants later in this chapter, we comment on how easy or challenging the plants are to maintain.

Indoor plants high on the fussiness scale include azaleas, cyclamen, gardenia, gerber daisies, maidenhair fern, and poinsettia. Consider them short-term plants and enjoy them while they last. If you can keep them healthy, give yourself a pat on the back.

Presenting a Pretty Plant

When you purchase a plant, it'll most likely be in a cheap plastic pot — not the most attractive look to display in your home. So you may want to transplant the plant into a pretty pot. For that, you'll need a container and some soil. The next sections give you some guidance on what to use. (See Chapter 5 for help on replanting in a new container.)

Choosing containers

Considering the wide array of available container styles, you can safely let interior design or personal taste guide your selection when choosing a pot for an indoor plant. The only requirement, as always, is to make sure the bottom of the container has a drainage hole. Don't despair if your choice is a gorgeous copper pot with no hole: Just set the plant in a plastic pot, set the pot in a saucer, and put both in the copper pot. Keep in mind that you need to be able to drain any excess water from the saucer.

Before choosing a decorative container, remove the plant from its plastic nursery pot and examine the roots. If the plant is root-bound — with a tight, tangled root ball or roots circling the inside of the pot — then choose a decorative pot that's an inch or two larger in diameter and depth than the current pot. Otherwise, you can repot in a similarly sized container.

Refer to Chapter 3 for tips on selecting containers: The same general principles apply indoors and out. Remember that you need something waterproof under plants to keep them from damaging furniture and other surfaces. It helps to put heavy plants on a dolly, so you can roll them out of the way to clean underneath them.

Getting the right soil mix

If you decide to repot your plant into a container that's larger than its current home, you need some soil to fill the extra space. A general indoor potting mix is adequate for most plants. Exceptions are orchids and cactuses, and you can find commercial specialty mixes clearly labeled for both types (if you want more information about growing cactuses, head to Chapter 20). Most indoor plants need generally well-draining soil, but there are always exceptions. The orchids that we discuss later in the chapter are *epiphytes,* accustomed to growing on the trunks of trees: When grown indoors, they need to grow in a medium containing little soil and a lot of bark. (See Chapter 4 for more on soil mixes.)

Keeping Your Plants Alive

Providing the right conditions and maintenance are the secrets to success with indoor plants. Here's a rundown of what you need to know.

Providing the right amount of water

Some folks are overzealous and drown the poor things, while others let their plants dry up past redemption before noticing that it may be time to water. Find out how much water your plants require, and, if you have a difficult time remembering to check plants, use refrigerator notes, a calendar, or whatever works to jog your memory.

Unfortunately, there's no easy formula to calculate how much water a plant needs. A range of factors influence how much water a particular plant needs, including its type and size, the amount of light it receives, the air temperature and humidity level, the size of the container and the material the container is made from, how vigorously the plant is growing, and whether the plant is root-bound. (Refer to Chapter 15 for more information on factors that influence water needs.)

As a general rule, it's best to water the plants thoroughly so that the entire root ball is moistened. Let excess water drain, and then empty the saucer. Wait to water again until the soil has dried out slightly. Small plants in porous clay pots in a sunny window may need daily watering. A plant in a large, plastic container in a low-light corner may need watering as little as once a month.

Here's a low-tech way to tell whether a plant needs watering: Stick your finger into the soil. If it's dry, water it. There are exceptions to this rule, so pay attention to phrases like *keep soil evenly moist* and *allow to dry out between waterings* in plant descriptions.

Many plants grow more slowly in winter when days are shorter (there's less daylight) than in summer, so water needs may drop. On the other hand, central heating often dries the air, so some plants may need more frequent watering as moisture evaporates more quickly from the soil.

For many indoor plants, providing humidity is just as important as watering. Some require high humidity, making them a good choice for a bathroom window. You can also increase humidity by placing gravel in a tray or saucer, adding water, and setting the pot on top of the gravel so that the pot doesn't actually sit in the water, but above it. Daily misting can briefly raise humidity, but it can also promote leaf diseases.

Tending to temperature

For most plants, ideal temperatures range between 55 and 75 degrees Fahrenheit — plants that come with descriptions such as *cool, average,* or *high* all fit into that range. Just like in their native habitats, plants indoors generally prefer cooler temperatures at night and in the winter. Most foliage plants are relatively adaptable. Some flowering plants, on the other hand, have strict requirements for day and/or night temperatures before they'll set flower buds. Orchids, in particular, are fussy about temperatures, but they're fussy about everything. You may need to move plants in winter to keep them away from cold drafts and heating vents. Don't let plant foliage touch cold windows.

In cold-winter regions, take extra care to make sure plants stay warm during transit. When you buy a plant in cold weather, have the sales clerk wrap it in paper or plastic and take it right out into a heated car. Then take it directly home. A houseplant may suffer damage if temperatures drop into the 40s and may die if exposed to freezing temperatures. Don't leave it in a cold car while you're at a movie or dining out.

Maintaining adequate light levels

Keep an eye on light levels. A plant in front of a window may be shaded in midsummer when the sun is high in the sky, but receive direct sun the rest of the year when the sun is lower in the sky. Plants that thrive in summer in an out-of-the-way corner may do better if they're moved closer to a window in winter, to take advantage of the limited daylight.

Some plants give you clues that they're receiving too little or too much light. With too little light, stems may become elongated (with wider spaces between leaves), the leaves may be smaller than normal, and the colors of variegated plants may fade. In contrast, plants that prefer low light levels may show browned, burned leaf edges and splotches when placed in direct sunlight.

Because leaves turn toward light — trying to make the most of photosynthesis — you may eventually find many of your plants leaning toward the windows. If you want a more symmetrical look, turn pots every week or so. You may not want to bother with that 8-foot rubber tree in the corner — no one sees the other side anyway.

Nourishing with fertilizer

Just how big do you want that philodendron to be? Overfertilization can result in lush growth, requiring more frequent repotting and offering a dinner invitation to any stray insect pest that prefers soft new growth. On the other hand, underfertilizing results in plants that just look wan or worse.

Helping plants get acclimated

Houseplants are usually grown in climate-controlled greenhouses where their every need is met. Bring them home and they almost always suffer some degree of shock, which often manifests itself with dropped or yellowing leaves. As long as you put the plant in the appropriate light level, it should recover.

If you move plants outdoors for the summer, take time to acclimate them to the harsher outdoor conditions. Be sure that the weather has really warmed up before moving them outdoors.

Then acclimate them slowly over the course of a few weeks by gradually exposing them to more and more sun and wind. Do the same thing in reverse in fall as the weather starts to cool. Place them in a shadier spot for a week or so to get them used to lower indoor light levels. And before you bring plants back inside, be sure to check for any hitchhiking pests. Look on the undersides of leaves, on the stems, on the soil surface, and on the bottom of the pot.

A happy medium for most indoor plants is to use a soluble fertilizer three times during spring and summer, when most plants do the majority of their growing. Exceptions to this are noted in the plant descriptions — as always, some plants are more demanding than others.

Fending off pests and diseases

Unfortunately, pest and disease problems do make their way indoors. As with outdoor plants, cultural factors come into play. If you put the right plant in the right place (meeting its requirements for light, water, humidity, and temperature), you're much less likely to have a problem. The most common houseplant pests include scale, spider mites, mealybugs, and aphids, all of which can be controlled by washing them off or using sprays of insecticidal soap or horticultural oil. Quarantine affected plants to keep the pest from spreading to healthy plants. See Chapter 18 for more on pest and disease control.

Maintaining shape by pruning

Regularly snip off spent flowers, dead leaves, and stems. Cut leggy vines back to a node (where a leaf meets the stem); the plant will send out new shoots from there. (Occasionally cut a few of the longest vines right back to the leaf nearest the soil — the new sprouts will keep the pot looking full and lush.) Trees like ficus may need regular pruning to keep them in bounds.

Cleaning for well-being

Just like your furniture, houseplants benefit from regular dusting. Not only does it help them look their best, it also maximizes their ability to photosynthesize by removing the dust accumulation that blocks light from reaching the leaves. You can wash most plants in the sink or shower, spraying the tops and bottoms of leaves with water to rinse off dust buildup (and any small insects that may be lurking). This is a good way to clean plants with lots of small leaves, like ivies and palms. Washing plants like this invariably saturates the soil, so let any excess water drain thoroughly. Another way to clean plants with large, smooth leaves, like dracaenas and crotons, is to wipe the tops and undersides of the leaves with a damp cloth. Don't wash plants with fuzzy leaves, like African violets and begonias, because moisture on their leaves invite disease. Instead, use a soft brush to gently remove dust. Use leaf-shine products sparingly, if at all (and only on smooth-leaved plants) because they can clog the plants' pores.

Selecting Plants for Different Light Levels

Because light level is the most important factor in choosing indoor plants, in the sections that follow, plants are grouped according to the amount of light they need for optimum growth. We also give you a brief description of the size and shape of the plant, how fussy it is, and specifics on the temperature, humidity, watering, and fertilizing requirements of those plants that need special care (the inevitable exceptions to the rules we provide in the previous sections).

Plants that get along in low light

Place plants that adapt well to low light in east or north windows, foyers, stair landings — anywhere that receives little or no direct sun. But remember, if it's too dark for you to read a book, it's too dark for a plant to grow there. The following plants fall into this category:

- **Cast-iron plant** *(Aspidistra elatior):* Dark green, elongated leaves grow vertically, reaching a height of up to 3 feet. Place this plant in an area with a cool to average temperature. Expect it to grow slowly. Let the soil dry out between waterings, and fertilize infrequently. The cast-iron plant is one of the easiest and most reliable houseplants.

- **Chinese evergreen** *(Aglaonema):* Some Chinese evergreens have dark green leaves marked across with white (Maria); others have yellow-green leaves with darker splotches (Silver Queen). Both types grow into lush, leafy mounds. Height varies, so read plant labels. They thrive in average temperatures as long as they're not exposed to cold drafts. Let the soil dry out between waterings. Cut back older canes to promote new growth from the base. Chinese evergreens are very easy to grow.

- **Dracaena:** Many species are available, and most are slow-growing. The most familiar species include Madagascar dragon tree *(D. marginata),* with long, thin leaves coming out like a fountain; corn plant *(D. massangeana),* common in office buildings, with tall canes sprouting wide leaves at the top; and *D. warneckii,* a large, shrubby plant with green-and-white-striped leaves. Place these plants in an area with an average temperature and medium humidity. Let the soil dry out between waterings, and fertilize infrequently. Leaf tips and margins may turn brown and crispy if the plants are overwatered. Dracaenas are easy to grow.

- **Mother-in-law's tongue** *(Sansevieria trifasciata):* This has been a houseplant since Neanderthal times, which explains the politically incorrect name. Its familiar vertical blades grow slowly to 18 inches. These plants thrive in cool to hot temperatures. Fertilize infrequently. Mother-in-law's tongue is very easy to grow.

✔ **Peace lily** *(Spathiphyllum):* Here's the ubiquitous mall plant, and for good reason — its dark, glossy foliage, on 1- to 4-foot plants, looks sharp without too much attention. Peace lilies occasionally sport white flowers. They can tolerate low humidity. Let the soil dry out slightly between waterings. If the soil dries too much, the plant will wilt dramatically; however, it will usually recover an hour or two after watering. Peace lilies are easy to grow.

Plants that grow in medium light

Some direct light is fine for plants that prefer medium light, but for the most part, they need bright but indirect light. Place them near a west or southeast window where they receive bright daylight but no direct sun, or in a window with sheer curtains. The following are well-suited for medium-light locations:

✔ **African violet** *(Saintpaulia):* A classic indoor plant, the African violet seems to bloom like crazy for a few owners and hardly at all for others. The fuzzy leaves on this 4- to 6-inch-tall plant form a rosette, with flowers that come in white, pink, lavender, and purple. Provide an average to warm temperature and medium to high humidity. Keep the soil evenly moist. Avoid getting water on the leaves, which causes spots and rot. One good way to feed is to use a diluted fertilizer with every watering — you can choose from many foods developed especially for African violets. These plants are easy to grow, but getting them to flower can be challenging.

✔ **Begonia:** With colorful and varied foliage plus showy flowers, begonias have it all. The type of begonias that have large, gorgeous flowers (called tuberous or Rieger begonias) are considered disposable. Enjoy them as long as they last, knowing that they're unlikely to endure. Longer-lasting begonias include angel wing (sporting spotted leaves and insignificant flowers); rex begonias (with foliage that's variegated with gray, purple, or magenta); and *B. schmidtiana* (featuring dark green crinkled leaves with reddish undersides). Keep the soil evenly moist, and avoid getting water on foliage. Fertilize lightly and regularly during the growing season. Repot annually. Begonias get a medium fussiness rating.

If you grow bedding (wax) begonias outdoors during the summer, bring them in their containers indoors for the winter. Move them inside before the first frost, cut back leggy stems, and keep the plants in a sunny window.

✔ **Bird's nest fern** *(Asplenium nidus):* This fern's apple-green fronds unfurl to 3 feet. It thrives in areas with an average temperature and high humidity — a great plant for close proximity to the shower. Keep the soil evenly moist. Bird's nest ferns are easy to grow.

✔ **Boston fern** *(Nephrolepis exaltata* **Bostoniensis***):* Don't overlook this fern just because it's so popular. The look is tropical, full, and lush when well kept — but scraggly when untended. Dallas fern (*N. exaltata* Dallas) is short and dense; Fluffy Ruffles has frilly fronds. Keep the soil evenly moist. Boston ferns are easy to grow, but can be annoying because they tend to shed leaves. Shake them out occasionally to minimize daily sweeping up.

✔ **Bromeliad:** Sporting rosettes of sharp-edged, leathery leaves that are covered with grayish, waxy scales, the "flowers" of bromeliads are colorful bracts that remain showy for weeks. In their native habitat, these are epiphytes that grow on tree branches. The plant's foliage creates a vase that you can fill with water. Allow the soil to dry slightly between waterings. Bromeliads are easy to grow.

✔ **Christmas cactus** *(Schlumbergera):* Its name comes from the plant's bloom time, which results in abundant flowers that are pink, salmon, or red with bent-back petals. Related species are known as Thanksgiving and Easter cactus, depending on when they bloom. The fleshy, segmented leaves grow in arches to form a 12-inch mound. The flowers and buds of Christmas cactuses knock off easily, so keep them away from traffic. Christmas cactuses require an extended period of cool (50-degree-Fahrenheit) temperatures and 12 to 14 hours of total darkness at night to be coaxed into blooming. At other times, provide average to warm temperatures. Let the soil dry out between waterings, and give them less water in winter. They get a fussiness rating of medium.

✔ **Coleus:** Traditionally used outdoors in shady summer beds, its colorful foliage in reds, yellows, and oranges can brighten up your indoor space as well. Place in an area with high humidity. Keep the soil evenly moist during the growing season, and barely moist in winter. In spring, cut well back and repot plants. Pinch tips to keep growth bushy.

✔ **Croton** *(Codiaeum variegatum):* A striking plant — the colorful orange, yellow, or red midribs of the croton's shiny leaves make it look like it was dipped in paint. Provide a medium to warm temperature, high humidity, and moist soil. Crotons are easy to grow.

✔ **Dumb cane** *(Dieffenbachia):* This is another easygoing indoor favorite, with white and green variegated leaves on 3-foot-tall canes. Provide an average temperature and medium to high humidity. Let the soil dry out between waterings. When older canes become bare except for top leaves, you can cut them back to 3 inches. Occasionally, take a deep breath and cut the tallest, leggiest dumb cane stem down to 3 inches so that shorter stems may take over. Dumb canes are easy to grow.

The plant's name comes from the numbing effect that the sap has if ingested. Avoid this plant if there's a chance that a pet or child may chew on it.

✔ **Ivy:** English ivy *(Helix hedera)* and related species are easy to grow and reliable. You can keep them pruned to a compact shape, let the vines trail down, or train them up and over a window. There are variegated as well as plain green types. Keep the soil evenly moist and watch out for spider mites. Ivy is easy to grow.

✔ **Moon Valley pilea *(Pilea):*** The leaves of this plant have dark veins and look finely quilted. Count on it to grow quickly. It thrives in cool to warm temperatures, but prefers high humidity. Let the soil dry out between waterings. Pinch plants back to keep them bushy. These plants are easy to grow.

✔ **Moth orchid *(Phaleanopsis):*** This is the easiest orchid, which isn't saying much. Like other orchids, it can be fussy about blooming. Many varieties come in flower shades of pink and white. One blooming stem can last 18 months, which makes all the effort worthwhile. They prefer warm days and cool nights. Avoid overwatering, and fertilize once a month year-round with an orchid formula.

✔ **Norfolk Island pine *(Araucaria heterophylla):*** This is a charming small tree (indoors at least), 4 to 6 feet tall, with branches in tiers — a good candidate for an indoor Christmas tree. Provide a cool to warm temperature — hot, dry conditions can cause the needles to drop. Keep the soil evenly moist. The Norfolk Island pine gets a medium fussiness rating.

✔ **Palm:** When it comes to houseplants, palms come in all sorts of shapes and sizes, from neanthe bella, which fits neatly on a tabletop, to date palm, which can reach 60 feet tall growing outdoors. In between are areca palm, fishtail palm, kentia palm, ponytail palm, and sago palm, among others. (Not all plants with *palm* in the common name are true palms, but we won't worry about that.) Some palms are graceful and sway in the breeze; others have more rigid fronds and look almost prehistoric. Because palms vary in mature size, light and water requirements, and other characteristics, read plant labels carefully before you buy. Most palms are a little temperamental and are frequently attacked by spider mites, so they get a fussiness rating of medium.

✔ **Peperomia:** Widely available, peperomia forms a dense mound of pleated leaves. Red Ripple has deep red stems. Water when the soil is dry. Peperomias are easy to grow.

✔ **Philodendron:** Choose from a wide variety of plants to suit any taste — cutleaf, purplestem, and elephant ear are a few possibilities. These plants become vines unless you pinch them back. They're popular houseplants for good reason: They're among the easiest to grow and most reliable.

✔ **Pothos *(Epipremnum):*** This vining plant grows and grows, making it the plant of choice for training up and over your windows or anything else that will stay still. It can also be kept shrubby with frequent pruning.

The leaves are usually variegated with splashes of creamy yellow. Let the soil dry out between waterings. Pothos is very easy to grow.

✔ **Spider plant _(Chlorophytum comosum):_** The spider plant is a fine choice for a hanging basket. Vittatum, with variegated foliage, is the most common. Provide cool to average temperatures. Let the soil dry out between waterings. Repot when roots fill the pot. You can grow more plants by rooting spiderlets (the miniature plants extending off the mother plant) in soil or water. Note that fluoride in tap water can cause the leaf tips to turn brown.

✔ **Umbrella plant _(Schefflera actinophylla):_** An imposing 6 to 8 feet at maturity, the umbrella plant is a good choice for a big, empty corner. Keep the soil evenly moist (drier in winter). Repot every two years.

Plants that need lots of light

To stay in top condition, sun-lovers need a south or west window exposure and direct light much of the day. Plants that require a lot of light include

✔ **Aloe vera _(Aloe barbadensis):_** Long, succulent spikes grow from the center of the plant. The gel inside the leaves is used to relieve minor skin irritations. Aloe vera is slow-growing, but undemanding with regard to temperature and water. Allow soil to dry out between waterings. Divide offsets, and pot them up for new plants.

✔ **Ficus:** A large class of plants that includes fig trees, rubber plants, fiddle-leaved figs, and creeping figs, ficus plants are similar in that they all have a milky sap that can be irritating to skin. Plant in regular potting soil and keep the soil slightly moist — avoid overwatering. Most types do best in bright, indirect light, warm temperatures, and medium humidity. Ficus is easy to grow.

✔ **Hibiscus:** These tropical plants are known for their shiny foliage and huge, saucer-shaped flowers. Left on their own, they'll grow into a shrubby tree. You can keep them small with regular pruning, or train them to a _standard_ (single-trunk tree). Provide rich, moist soil and bright, indirect light. Because they can be temperamental when it comes to flowering and are often attacked by aphids and whiteflies, they get a medium rating for fussiness.

✔ **Meyer's lemon:** In addition to fruit (which is far from a sure thing indoors), this small tree produces glossy leaves and fragrant flowers. Put the plant outside in summer. Indoors, provide average to cool temperatures. The tree may need supplemental light in winter. Keep the soil evenly moist. Growth is slow; don't repot too often. Lemon trees are prone to scale insect pests, need consistent fertilizing, and may require hand-pollination for fruit set, making them a medium on the fussiness scale.

✔ **Polka-dot plant** *(Hypoestes phyllostachya):* This plant is best described as perky, with dark green leaves speckled with pink. It grows quickly. Keep the soil evenly moist. Cut plants back to keep them small and bushy. Polka-dot plants are easy to grow.

Growing Edibles Indoors

If you have a sunny windowsill, you can grow a few herbs and perhaps a lettuce plant or two. Edible plants like these that are grown for their foliage are the easiest to grow indoors. Purchase small plants or start them from seed. Refer to Chapter 5 for step-by-step planting instructions and Chapter 8 for more on growing lettuce and herbs.

If you want to venture further into the edible plant kingdom, you probably need to provide supplemental light, especially in winter. Plants grown for their fruit, like tomatoes and peppers (yes, these are, botanically speaking, fruits), require full sun, or the artificial equivalent, to produce flowers and set fruit.

When it comes to providing indoor supplemental lighting, incandescent light bulbs (the bulbs typically used in households) emit too much heat to be very useful. The light tends to be too much on the red end of the spectrum for healthy plant growth. You have a couple options:

✔ **Fluorescent lights:** Cooler and more efficient than incandescent lights, these are commonly used for seed-starting. Regular "cool white" fluorescent lights, which produce light on the blue end of the spectrum, are fine if you're growing plants for their foliage. If you want to grow plants that produce flowers and fruits, look for full-spectrum lights, which provide a balance of light across the spectrum. However, even full-spectrum fluorescent lights aren't bright enough to grow healthy, vigorous fruiting plants. But you may be able to harvest a tomato or two.

✔ **HID (High Intensity Discharge) lights:** These are the most efficient when it comes to converting electricity into light and they are the lights of choice for professional growers and serious hobbyists. The bulbs are very bright and draw a lot of electricity, which can tax home electrical systems. HID bulbs are expensive, but they also last longer than fluorescents. If you want to grow tomatoes and other fruiting plants indoors in winter, they may be worth the investment.

You can also purchase self-contained growing systems that include lights suspended over special containers, and hydroponic units in which plants are constantly bathed in a nutrient solution. These systems are expensive for the amount of food you're likely to grow, but if you want to garden year-round, they may be worth it to you.

Part IV
Keeping Your Plants Healthy

The 5th Wave   By Rich Tennant

"Plenty of sunshine, organic matter, and the right soil will keep them bright and colorful. And what that won't do, a box of fluorescent felt tip markers will take care of."

In this part . . .

Without water, nutrients, periodic transport to a bigger place of residence, maybe a haircut now and then, and, okay, an occasional debugging, the plants that you love so much can become dried-up brown shadows of their former selves. Give them what they need, and they'll reward you with healthy growth, beautiful flowers, and the tastiest and most nutritious fruits and vegetables. Dig in for details.

Chapter 15

Quenching Your Plants' Thirst

· ·

In This Chapter

▶ Finding out what impacts the amount of water needed

▶ Determining how often to water and how much water to use

▶ Exploring watering methods and timesaving tricks

▶ Conserving the precious resource of water

· ·

*P*lants growing in containers are at your mercy when it comes to getting the right amount of water. Unlike plants growing in the ground that can rely on deep roots to get them through dry spells, container-grown plants have limited soil from which to draw. When they dry out, they really dry out. On the other hand, if container-grown plants are left to sit too long in saucers full of water, the roots can die from lack of oxygen. The repercussions of becoming parched or waterlogged are usually more severe and permanent than if the plants were in the ground.

It comes down to this: If you want to be successful growing plants in containers, that is, if you want your flowers to bloom well and your fruits, herbs, and vegetables to produce a bountiful harvest, you have to be an attentive and efficient waterer. In this chapter, we show you how.

Accounting for Various Factors in the Watering Equation

Beginning gardeners often ask, "How often should I water my plants?" Unfortunately, there's no simple answer. How often container plants need water and how much they need at any given time depend on several factors. We address these in the following sections.

When you choose plants and containers for different sites, consider the effect they'll have on your watering chores. Do you really want to lug a 2-gallon watering can to the far edge of your backyard to water a porous container filled with moisture-loving plants? Place higher-maintenance plants closer to water sources, and you'll be more likely to tend to them properly.

Considering location

Just because a plant lives outside doesn't mean it benefits from Mother Nature's rain showers. Plants growing under eaves or beneath a dense tree canopy may be deprived of rain. Stand next to the container and look up. Can you see the sky? If not, plants in that container will get little or no water from Mother Nature, so you'll need to quench their thirst. Obviously, plants growing on a covered porch or beneath an awning must receive all their water from you because they're not out in the rain.

Containers placed in full sun almost always need more frequent watering than those in shady areas. That's pretty obvious, but other contributing factors are more subtle. For example, containers situated on a hot surface like a concrete patio are likely to dry out faster than those on a wood deck, which tends to stay cooler. Plants near a light-colored, south-facing wall, which reflects light and heat, dry out faster than those farther away.

Contemplating climate and weather

Climate is determined by the average weather where you live on a season-to-season, year-to-year basis. If you live in an area like Seattle, Washington, or Biloxi, Mississippi, where the air is humid and rainfall is regular and reliable, watering isn't a constant chore, except in prolonged dry spells or periods of drought. In drier, hotter areas like Los Angeles, California, and Phoenix, Arizona, you may need to squeeze watering container plants into your schedule on a daily, or even twice-daily, basis.

Weather is what's happening outside right now, and it's up to you to pay attention. Hot winds on a cloudless day can dry out a plant growing in a hanging basket or a clay pot in a matter of minutes. Heavy rains saturate plants and fill the saucers underneath them.

Table 15-1 tells you in a nutshell how to adjust watering according to weather conditions. You may also find it helpful to think about how you feel — and how much water you're inclined to drink — in different weather conditions. If you're frequently thirsty, chances are your plants are, too.

Table 15-1	Watering According to Weather
Water Less	*Water More*
Cooler temperatures	Warmer temperatures
Cloudy or overcast	Bright sunshine
Low wind	High wind
High humidity	Low humidity
Rain	No rain

Evaluating pot type and color

The porosity of a container influences how much water evaporates through its sides — and that can be a lot. At one extreme are hanging baskets lined with sphagnum moss, which seem to dry out as soon as you turn your back on them in hot weather. At the other end of the spectrum are plastic pots, glazed ceramic, metal, and thick concrete containers that hardly lose any moisture through their sides. In the middle are unglazed clay pots, which are pretty porous and dry out quickly, and wooden containers, which dry out slower but may lose water through their sides.

The container's color also affects how quickly plants dry out. Lighter-colored containers reflect more sunlight and dry out more slowly than darker-colored ones, which absorb heat.

Seeing the impact of soil variations

Most potting soils used in containers are formulated for good drainage, which means they dry out fairly quickly. But some dry out faster than others. For example, potting soils that are higher in organic materials like peat moss or compost can hold more water than those that contain a higher percentage of mineral components like sand or perlite. You can find out more about potting soils in Chapter 4.

Regarding root-boundedness

Is that a word? Even if it isn't, the term means a lot to anyone who grows plants in pots. As a plant grows in a container, the roots become more and more crowded, which affects how much water the plant needs.

At first, the roots of a recent transplant may not even fill the pot, so the plant's drinking system may not be able to absorb all the water in the soil. At this stage it's easy to overwater plants. Over time, roots grow throughout the potting mix and are able to use the reservoir of water it contains.

Eventually, as plant roots continue to grow and the organic matter in the potting mix begins to break down, the pot contains more roots than soil. When this happens, the plant is root-bound and the root ball (roots and soil) can be difficult to keep moist. You can either vow to be extra attentive to the plant's water needs, or transplant it into a larger pot. For help doing that, see Chapter 17.

Observing genetic disposition

Different species of plants are adapted to different growing environments — picture the Brazilian rainforest and the Mohave Desert. Most of the plants we commonly grow in containers need consistently moist soil to thrive, but some plants thrive in drier conditions than others. For example, if you let a pot full of lettuce go dry, the leaves will lose moisture and probably won't ever completely recover — you may as well replant. Cactuses and succulents, on the other hand, tolerate dry spells quite well; in fact, most prefer to be on the dry side. If they get too much water, many cactuses and succulents rot.

Xeriscaping is a term used to describe gardening with water-thrifty plants. If water is expensive or scarce in your region, or you just want to minimize your watering chores, choose plants listed as good for xeriscaping for your container gardens. However, even these plants will still need watering.

Water Ways: Methods for Watering Container Plants

You can always use a good, old-fashioned watering can to water your plants. However, there are tools and techniques that make the job easier. For example, if you have lots of containers or aren't always available to water daily, timesaving techniques take on greater importance. If you live in a region where water is scarce, every drop is precious — and expensive — so water conservation is a focus. If plant diseases are common in your area, keeping water off the plant leaves and applying it only to the soil is key. (If a disease does strike your plants, flip to Chapter 18 for help in dealing with it.) The following sections describe different tools and techniques you can use to apply water to containers, including their benefits and drawbacks.

Watering by hand

Probably the most commonly used method, hand watering allows you to easily adjust how much water each pot gets according to its size and specific needs. For indoor watering, using one of the many handheld watering cans on the market is generally easiest, but little hose setups that can be hooked to the sink faucet are also available. Outdoors, most gardeners simply drag hoses around to water their pots.

Many excellent types of hose-end attachments let you turn the water on and off without going all the way back to the faucet. Bubbler attachments soften the output of the water, which can prevent washing soil mix out of the container. You can even purchase extensions that make it easier to water hanging pots (see Figure 15-1).

Whatever you do, don't let the hose run so forcefully into the container that it washes out soil; soften the water stream with your hand, at least.

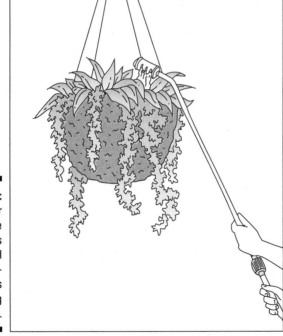

Figure 15-1:
A bubbler on a hose extender is a neat tool for watering plants in hanging baskets.

Setting up sprinklers

Although lawn sprinklers are available in a variety of styles, they're not very efficient for watering containers — too much water is wasted. In a pinch, you may set up a sprinkler to water a raised bed or a grouping of containers, but if you find this becomes a habit, you're better off putting in a drip system, as we describe in the next section.

One problem with overhead watering, whether from a hose, watering can, or sprinkler, is that it can encourage the spread of disease. Most plant diseases are caused by fungi, which need a film of water in order to spread. Wet foliage provides an ideal breeding ground, especially in humid climates where leaf surfaces dry slowly. In such areas, either install a drip system or apply water directly to the soil to avoid moistening foliage or flowers.

Installing drip irrigation

Drip irrigation is a very effective and efficient way to water containers. A drip system provides water slowly through holes, or *emitters,* in a black plastic pipe. You connect the pipe to a water supply, install a filter and often a pressure regulator, and then place emitters in each container. When you turn on the water, it drips slowly from the emitters, as shown in Figure 15-2.

Emitters differ in terms of how much water they put out per minute: ½ gallon per hour, 1 gallon per hour, and so on. Drip systems usually have to run at least several hours to wet a large area, such as a raised bed. In smaller pots, emitters may only need to be run for an hour, depending on their output. Larger pots may need more than one emitter. Watch your system carefully the first few times that you water. Poke around in the soil to see how long you need to water to wet a container, or how long it takes before water runs out the drainage holes. Then make adjustments accordingly.

Drip irrigation systems hooked to automatic timers can really relieve the chore of watering a lot of containers. And although you may be hard-pressed to imagine weaving plastic pipe all over your porch or patio without creating a messy nightmare, rest assured that all it takes is a little creative thinking. You can bury some piping or run piping above your plants, along eaves.

If you live in an area where the soil freezes, don't leave your drip system outside in winter. Your pipes may burst. Instead, drain out the water, roll up the piping, and store it in the garage.

Figure 15-2:
A drip
irrigation
system.

Drip irrigation systems are sold in many garden centers and big box stores. You can also purchase them through the mail (see the appendix). Pressure-compensating emitters apply water consistently from one end of the line to the other, regardless of pressure changes due to uneven ground.

Cousins of drip irrigation, soaker hoses are porous and release water along their entire length. However, they can release it unevenly, with less and less water released as you get farther from the spigot. Also, if the soil surface on which soaker hoses lay is uneven, the hoses apply water unevenly. But they can still be useful in level, raised beds.

Relying on self-watering pots

Self-watering pots include a water reservoir, usually in the walls or base of the container, which is connected to the root ball of the plant through a small wick (like those you see in Tiki torches). As the root ball dries out, the wick sucks up water from the reservoir and supplies it to the root ball, keeping it nice and moist. Flip back to Chapter 3 for an illustration of a self-watering pot.

Be careful with self-watering pots. In hot weather the reservoir can run dry in a day or two. Self-watering pots can also keep some plants too wet, causing them to rot and die. And because there's no way to leach the salts from a self-watering pot, salt burn can develop. For information on curing salt burn (which isn't easy), see Chapter 18.

Figuring Out How Often to Water

Plants' water needs vary with the weather and the seasons — plants need less water in cool weather, more in warm weather, and so on. Thus, even an automated system requires adjustment so that it waters less in spring and more in summer. Because we can't come to your house and give you a precise watering schedule for your specific situation, we advise you to practice your powers of observation and make watering adjustments accordingly.

You can also take advantage of these other ways to tell when your plants need water or when containers are getting dry:

- **Pay attention to what your plants tell you.** That's right, plants can communicate with you. When plants start to dry out, the leaves droop and wilt. The plant may also lose its bright, glossy, green color and start to look a little drab. Make it your goal to water before a plant reaches that point (consider it a cry for help).

- **Dig in the ground.** Stick your finger an inch or two into the soil in the top of a pot. If the soil feels dry, it may be time to water. For small containers, you can carefully slip the root ball out of the pot to see whether it's moist.

- **Lift the pot.** As soil dries out, it gets lighter. Compare how heavy a pot is right after watering thoroughly with how it feels a few days later. By simply tilting a pot on its edge and judging its weight, you eventually figure out how to tell when it's dry or getting close to it.

- **Use a moisture sensor.** Nurseries sell various devices for reading soil moisture. Most have a long, needlelike rod connected to a meter. You push the rod into the soil, and the meter tells you how wet the soil is. These sensors can be pretty handy, but don't trust them too much right off the bat. Some can be thrown off by salts in the soil. To start, see how their readings compare to what you discover by feeling the soil and lifting the pot. Then make any necessary adjustments.

By taking these various factors into consideration, you'll eventually get a sense of how often each container needs water.

Not Too Much, Not Too Little: Applying Just the Right Amount of H$_2$O

When you water a container plant, the goal is to moisten the entire root ball and apply just enough water so that some drains out the bottom. Now, if the container is properly planted, a space exists between the top of the soil and the container's rim that you can fill with water. It may be anywhere from 1 inch in small containers to 4 or 5 inches in larger ones. But whatever the case, you have to fill it more than once to get enough water to wet the root ball. That means filling the pot once, letting the water soak in, and then repeating the process until the whole root ball is moist.

This whole soaking process is a bit tricky for one reason. As the root ball in a container dries, it shrinks, usually pulling away from the edges of the pot. So when you water the first time, the water drains down the edges without reaching the root ball at all. This phenomenon explains why you need to make several passes with the hose or watering can — so that the root ball swells up a bit and seals the edges of the container, at which point the water can soak in. This is also why you can never judge how wet a root ball is by the amount of water that comes out the drainage hole. You may be fooled every time. Check water penetration by lifting the edge of the pot or poking in a finger, as we describe earlier.

The fact that drainage holes may fool you doesn't mean you should do away with them. Without them, the plant drowns. Periodically check the drainage when you water. Even if your containers have holes in the bottom, they may fill up with roots, preventing proper drainage. Cut the holes open with a knife if necessary.

You can wet shrunken root balls or plants that are really root-bound in a few other ways:

- **Water from the bottom.** If you place small trays or saucers underneath your pots to catch excess water, that water is gradually reabsorbed by a dry root ball. You're basically watering from the bottom, at a pace dictated by the plant.

  It's not a good idea to have a container sitting in water for a long time. The root ball becomes too wet and eventually the plant drowns. But submerging a pot partially, or even completely, for just a little while doesn't hurt, and it's a great way to wet a really dry root ball. In fact, if your plants get too dry, set them in a container filled with several inches of warm water — use the kitchen sink, a 5-gallon bucket, or your child's swimming pool, whatever's easiest. Let the pots bathe for an hour or so; then remove the plants and let the excess water drain off.

- **Use drip irrigation.** Drip emitters apply water at a slow, steady rate and do a great job of thoroughly wetting the root ball.

Water plants deeply and thoroughly; then allow them to dry out a bit before watering again. Avoid frequent light sprinklings, which encourage roots to form near the soil surface where they're prone to drying out. Deep but less frequent watering encourages healthy, deep roots.

Being Water Wise: Strategies to Save Water

Water shortages are a reality in almost any climate or region at one time or another, and container plants use a lot of water — more than the same plants in the ground. Here are a few things you can do when water is scarce or limited, when you want to conserve the precious resource of fresh water, or when you just want to ease your watering chores:

- ✔ **Install drip irrigation.** It applies water slowly without runoff. Drip irrigation is definitely the most frugal watering system that you can use.

- ✔ **Double-pot.** If you take a small pot and put it in a bigger pot, you reduce the amount of sunlight that hits the sides of the smaller pot, which helps cool the soil. Cooler soil means less water is needed.

- ✔ **Use soil polymers.** Soil polymers are weird, gelatin-like materials that hold hundreds of times their weight in water. If you mix them dry with your soil before you plant, you can stretch the time between waterings. Follow the label directions carefully, because a little goes a long way.

- ✔ **Transplant.** Moving a root-bound plant into a bigger container, where it has more soil to draw water from, can greatly reduce your watering chores. Better yet, if a container plant is really too much trouble to water, maybe you're better off planting it in the ground.

- ✔ **Move pots into the shade.** If the weather gets really hot, move your pots into the shade to cool them down and reduce water usage. A few days of less sun won't hurt them. Some sun-loving plants thrive on getting only morning sun in the hottest part of summer.

- ✔ **Group pots.** If you put pots close together, they can shade each other and the amount of sun that hits their sides is reduced.

- ✔ **Bury the pots.** Huh? That's right, just dig a hole and bury the pots just deep enough so that the rims are covered. Or, you can build a wooden box, put the pots in it, and fill it in around the edges with potting soil or organic material like peat moss or ground bark. You still have to water, but you use a lot less, especially if you also wet the soil around the pots. This method is drastic, but if water is really tight or you're going out of town for a while, it works.

✔ **Mulch.** A mulch is a layer of organic matter that's spread over the soil surface around a plant. Several inches of heavy mulch, like large pieces of bark (so that they don't float away when you water) or other material, can cool the soil and reduce evaporation, thus saving water.

✔ **Pull weeds.** Weeds steal water meant for container plants, so keep them pulled.

✔ **Water efficiently.** Do as we suggest earlier in this chapter, and wet the entire root ball. You'll have happier and healthier plants, and use less water in the long run.

✔ **Use rainwater.** Put a barrel or other collector where the drain pipes from your roof empty. Then use that water on your flowers.

✔ **Measure rainfall.** Keep track of how much rain you get. An inch is usually enough to let you skip a watering for plants that are out in the open. You can buy fancy rain gauges, or just set out an empty tuna fish can. If it overflows, you've received more than an inch of rain.

✔ **Choose plants that aren't very thirsty.** Some cactuses and succulents can get by on little water, even when grown in containers. Look for plants described as drought-tolerant or good for xeriscaping. These plants will still need regular watering but not as much or as often as thirstier species.

Seeing that Your Plants Get Water When You're Away

So you're going on vacation and can't find anyone to water your plants. What are you going to do? Start by considering some of the water-saving methods described in the preceding section, especially burying the pots or setting up a drip system with an automatic timer. The following sections provide a couple other solutions.

Wicking water

Choosing to wick water is kind of like building your own self-watering pot (see the section "Relying on self-watering pots" earlier in this chapter) and works best on smaller containers, especially houseplants. Go to a hardware store and buy some long wicks like those used for Tiki torches (for really small pots, you can use thick cotton string). Wet the wick and use a pencil to push it a few inches into the wet root ball of the plant. Stick the other end in a bowl or glass of water. As the root ball dries, it sucks water from the bowl through the wick, keeping it wet.

Don't try this the day you're getting ready to leave. Set it up a week in advance to make sure it works and to see how much of a water reservoir you need. If you use a big bucket to hold the water, you can water several plants at once.

Using soil polymers

Buy some soil polymers (see the section "Being Water Wise: Strategies to Save Water") at your local nursery, put some in a small plastic cup, and add water to turn them to gelatin. Turn the cup upside down on top of the soil in your pot. Over time, the polymers slowly release their moisture to water the plant. As with water wicks, don't wait until the day you leave to try this method. Test it a week or so before you go away to see how fast the water is released and how much polymer you need to use.

You may be able to buy a product that already has ready-to-use, hydrated polymers in a cup. You just flip it over on top of the soil in your pot. See whether your nursery has it in stock.

Implementing ingenious devices

You've probably seen them advertised on television — those funny, elongated glass bulbs that you fill with water, turn upside down, and plunge into the soil. They drain water slowly as the plant needs it, so you don't have to water as often. These Aqua Globes are handy for all types of containers, not just houseplants. Use several of them in larger containers to provide water while you're out of town.

You can create your own self-watering device by filling a 1-liter plastic soda bottle with water, then poking a few holes in the cap and replacing it. Place the bottle upside-down in the container, burying the top of the bottle in the soil so the water can drain slowly through the holes. It isn't as pretty as a fancy glass bulb, but it gets the job done.

Chapter 16

Food for Thought: Fertilizing Your Plants

. . . .

In This Chapter

▶ Nourishing your plants for healthy growth

▶ Scoring comprehension in chemistry

▶ Shopping smart with fertilizer lingo

▶ Growing with organic fertilizers

. . . .

Thinking of your container plants as pets is understandable — after all, plants and pets are living things that provide you with amusement, companionship, and even an occasional gift of shedding (fortunately, hairballs aren't important to this discussion). In return for what your pets/plants do for you, you have certain obligations, with feeding right near the top. Your plants depend on you in much the same way that your border collie Max does. Generations ago, Max lost the ability to go out and forage for himself. Likewise, container plants can't send roots down deep and outward in the ground the way garden plants can. Plants grown in the cushy but confined environment that you create for them must search for nutrients within their own boundaries.

In this chapter, you find out why plants need nutrients along with general information on how you can fill those requirements. For details specific to certain types of plants (annuals, perennials, and so on), refer to the chapters in Parts II and III.

Knowing Your Plants' Nutritional Needs

Although fun, drawing an analogy between feeding your plants and feeding your pets isn't quite accurate. Through photosynthesis, plants manufacture their own food (we've never seen a dog do that). In fact, all life on earth relies on this phenomenon by which plants, using the energy of the sun, convert water and air into sugars — the "food" they burn for energy to live and grow. In the process, they consume carbon dioxide and release oxygen. (Every once in a while, take a deep breath and give thanks to plants across the globe for providing us with oxygen and sugar. And chocolate. And coffee. And even prime rib, because cattle eat plants.) So when you say you're feeding your plants, that's not exactly what you're doing; rather, you're *fertilizing* them — supplying them with certain nutrients they need to thrive. Think of fertilizer as akin to the vitamins we take.

Plants absorb most of their nutrients from the soil — specifically, the *soil solution,* which is the moisture contained in the spaces between soil particles. If any nutrients are lacking or are present only in forms that plants can't absorb, plants won't grow to their full potential. Plants growing in the ground have far-ranging roots that seek out what the plants need. Plants whose roots are confined to containers rely on you to provide a consistent supply of nutrients. (Refer to Chapter 4 for details about how soil supports plant growth.)

For healthy growth, plants need 16 different elements. Carbon, hydrogen, and oxygen — the foundation blocks for photosynthesis — are required in large quantities. Plants get these from air and water. Plants also need relatively large amounts of nitrogen, phosphorus, and potassium. These elements are called primary nutrients, and they form the basis for most fertilizers. Table 16-1 gives you a rundown of the roles they play, as well as signs that a plant is lacking a particular nutrient.

Table 16-1	Primary Plant Nutrients		
Nutrient (and Abbreviation)	**Role**	**Symptoms of Deficiency**	**Notes**
Nitrogen (N)	Key part of plant proteins and chlorophyll; the green pigment that plays a vital role in photosynthesis	Yellowing of older leaves first; general slowdown in growth	Mobile in soil — easily washed away during watering
Phosphorus (P)	Healthy root growth, plus flower, fruit, and seed production	Stunted plants with dark green or purplish foliage and stems	Immobile in soil; may be present but unavailable to plants due to improper pH or cool soil
Potassium (K) (also known as potash)	Vigorous growth, disease resistance, and fruiting	Yellowing along leaf edges and between veins; poorly developed fruit	Avoid over-fertilizing with potassium, as it can make other nutrients unavailable to plants

Secondary nutrients — calcium, magnesium, and sulfur — are required in smaller quantities. While they're usually present in sufficient quantities in garden soil, they may be lacking in soil-less mixes, especially those that contain few ingredients.

The micronutrients — you guessed it — are needed in even smaller amounts. They include iron, manganese, copper, boron, molybdenum, chlorine, and zinc, and perhaps others — researchers are still studying the nuances of plant nutrition. Like secondary nutrients, micronutrients may be lacking in soil-less mixes.

Figuring Out the Finer Points of Fertilizer

At first glance, a nursery shelf lined with fertilizers is a bewildering sight. But confusion doesn't have to crowd your senses. When you know what nutrients your plants need and what type of fertilizer you prefer, you can choose the fertilizer that's best for you.

A fertilizer's *guaranteed analysis* (the amount of nitrogen, phosphate, and potassium) is one of the most important guidelines for choosing the right fertilizer, but there are other considerations, too. For example, do you want all-natural fertilizer, or are you willing to use a fertilizer that was made synthetically? Should the nutrients be released quickly or over a longer period of time? And would you rather apply it in liquid form or solid form? The following sections give you insights into these choices.

Decoding the numbers on the label

When you buy a commercial fertilizer, the guaranteed analysis is listed on the label with three numbers. These three numbers tell you how much of each of the primary nutrients is in the fertilizer. The first number indicates the percentage of nitrogen; the second, the percentage of phosphate; and the third, the percentage of potassium, also known as potash. A 10-5-5 fertilizer is 10 percent nitrogen, 5 percent phosphate, and 5 percent potash by weight.

Do the math, and you find that a 100-pound bag of 10-5-5 fertilizer contains 10 pounds of nitrogen, 5 pounds of phosphorus, and 5 pounds of potash — a total of 20 pounds of usable nutrients. Although the remaining 80 pounds contain some useful nutrients (also listed on the label), most of the balance is either filler or carrier left over from manufacturing.

Debating organic versus synthetic

Most organic fertilizers derive their nutrients from plants, animals, or minerals. Synthetic or chemical fertilizers are manufactured from mineral salts. Is one better than the other? That question is the subject of countless debates and philosophical face-offs. Some gardeners believe organic is better — for their health and the health of the planet. Others say, hey, the plants don't know where their nitrogen is coming from. Here we (briefly) give you an overview on each, and leave the philosophical wrangling up to you.

Organic fertilizers usually contain familiar-sounding materials, such as fish emulsion and kelp (seaweed). They may also contain various composted animal manures, including cow, poultry, and horse manure, as well as slaughterhouse by-products such as bone, blood, and feather meal. Some fertilizers even contain added beneficial microbes. Individual ingredients may contain limited nutrients; for example, fish emulsion contains mostly nitrogen; bone meal mostly phosphorus. But many organic fertilizer formulas contain a wide range of nutrients, especially the micronutrients that may be lacking in synthetic formulas.

If you want to be sure you're using a product appropriate for organic growing, look for the term *OMRI-Listed* on the label. The Organic Materials Review Institute (OMRI) is a nonprofit that evaluates products to see whether or not they conform to the standards established by the National Organic Program. If the label says OMRI-Listed, the product has been approved for use in certified organic farming.

Synthetic or chemical fertilizers are manufactured from mineral salts and usually have higher N-P-K ratings than organic ones. Sold as ready-to-apply or in concentrates requiring dilution, they are sterile and provide a precise dose of nutrients. They're usually relatively inexpensive.

Table 16-2 provides a rundown of some benefits and drawbacks to organic and synthetic fertilizers.

Table 16-2	Organic versus Synthetic Fertilizers
Organic Fertilizers	*Synthetic Fertilizers*
Often contain a wide range of nutrients, including secondary and micronutrients	Contain only what's on the label; often just N, P, and K
Actual nutrient content can vary from batch to batch	Nutrient content is precise
Often more expensive than synthetic fertilizers	Usually relatively inexpensive

Organic Fertilizers	Synthetic Fertilizers
Nutrients contained in complex molecules; less likely to be leached from soil	Nutrients in soluble form can be washed away during watering
Unlikely to burn plant roots	Improperly diluted soluble fertilizers can "burn" plant roots due to high salt concentrations

Using fast-release versus slow-release

The nutrients in some fertilizers are ready for plants to use immediately after you apply them. These fertilizers are dubbed *fast-release*. In other fertilizers, the nutrients are released slowly over time, earning the descriptor *slow-release* (creative, we know).

If plants are in need of a quick pick-me-up, a fast-release formula may be in order. Fast-release synthetic fertilizers, such as Miracle-Gro, are used by plants right away; however, any fertilizer not used may be washed away in the next watering.

Most fast-release synthetic fertilizers must be mixed with water before using. Improperly diluted, they can "burn" plants, because they're derived from mineral salts that can leach moisture from plant roots, harming or even killing them. Diluting and applying fertilizers according to the directions on the label is critical.

Slow-release fertilizers provide nutrients to plants over time under particular conditions and are often best added to the soil mix at planting time. For example, Osmocote, a synthetic fertilizer formulated into small beads, releases nutrients in response to soil moisture. Different forms of these slow-release synthetic fertilizers are often added to commercial soil mixes. Check out Chapter 4 for more on soil mixes.

Overall, organic fertilizers tend to be relatively slow-release because the nutrients are bound up in complex molecules that break down slowly into plant nutrients. However, some act faster than others. For example, a fish-emulsion/seaweed mix provides some nutrients right away.

Container-grown plants often fare best with a combination of the two types of fertilizer. Even if you've added a slow-release product to the soil mix, watch your container plants carefully. If plants grow slowly or are a bit yellowish even on a diet of slow-release fertilizer, give them a boost with an application of a fast-release formula, especially one containing nitrogen, such as soluble 10-10-10 or fish emulsion.

Organic growing in containers versus in the ground

As more people turn to organic growing in their gardens, it's natural that they want to do so for their container plants, too. However, there are some important differences between growing organically in the ground and doing so in containers.

Organic gardeners "feed the soil, so the soil can feed the plants." In the garden, adding lots of organic matter like compost promotes a healthy soil ecosystem filled with beneficial microbes, insects, and earthworms. This soil life breaks down organic matter slowly, releasing it to plants as they need it. If their soil is rich

and healthy, organic gardeners may not need to apply additional fertilizer during the growing season.

However, soil in the confines of a container can't support such a diverse ecosystem. So even if you start off with a mix containing lots of organic matter, you'll likely need to apply additional nutrients throughout the growing season. However, you can still grow plants organically if you use organic fertilizers. (You can find information about how organic matter improves soil structure and nutrient levels in Chapter 4.)

Understanding fertilizer formulations

Most fertilizers are sold either in granular or liquid form.

- ✔ **Granular fertilizers** are available in bags or boxes. Slow-release types are usually best added to the growing mix prior to planting, although some can be scattered on the soil surface to dissolve slowly. Fast-release types are usually mixed with water and applied when you irrigate. Follow label directions for application rates and methods.

- ✔ **Liquid fertilizers** are available in bottles or jugs. On a per-nutrient basis, most liquid fertilizers are more expensive than granular ones. Most liquid fertilizers need to be diluted in water before you apply them, but some are ready to use. Liquid fertilizers are applied when you water and can be injected into irrigation systems, which is the reason many professional growers prefer them. Some liquid fertilizers are sold in hose-end applicators that eliminate the need for mixing.

Liquids are particularly well-suited for plants grown in containers.

Becoming familiar with fertilizer lingo

Before you venture off to ring up your newfound fertilizer knowledge, consider a few more fertilizer phrases that may come in handy:

- **Complete fertilizers** contain all three primary nutrients — nitrogen (N), phosphorus (P), and potassium (K). The term "complete" is linked more to fertilizer industry laws and regulations than to satisfaction of the plant's actual requirements for nutrients.

- **An incomplete fertilizer** is missing one or more of the major nutrients, usually the P or the K. Fish emulsion, which usually has a guaranteed analysis of 5-0-0, is an incomplete fertilizer. Incomplete is not necessarily bad. In fact, less is sometimes good enough. Incomplete fertilizers are usually less expensive; if your soil has plenty of P and K, why apply more? Too much can harm your plants.

- **Chelated micronutrients** are in a form that allows them to be absorbed into a plant quicker than the more commonly available sulfated forms. If your plants just won't green up (they stay mottled yellow and green, or just plain yellow), no matter how much nitrogen you apply, you probably have a micronutrient deficiency of iron, zinc, or manganese. Chelated micronutrients are the quickest fix, although you may also have a soil pH problem that's preventing the nutrients from being absorbed by the plant (see Chapter 4 for more information on pH).

- **Foliar fertilizers** are applied to the leaves of plants rather than to the roots. Leaves aren't as effective as roots at taking up nutrients, but they do absorb quickly — so foliar feeding is a good, fast feed. Most liquid fertilizers, including seaweed/fish emulsion, can be used as foliar fertilizers, but make sure that the label instructs you accordingly. Don't apply fertilizers in hot weather because they may burn the leaves.

- **Specialty fertilizers** are supposedly formulated for specific types of plants. For example, you may find a fertilizer labeled *flower food* with an analysis of 0-10-10. The logic behind such a fertilizer is that a blooming plant needs more P and K than it does N. That's because the P and K are important in the formation of flowers, and the N promotes leaves. And you want flowers, right? Well, not so fast. Remember that P and K don't move into the soil as well as N does. So you can apply all the P and K you want, and these major nutrients may not get to the roots. Besides, if you're using a good potting mix, your plants probably have plenty of P and K already.

Truth be told, we think specialty fertilizers are more marketing strategy than high-tech solution — and more expense than can be expected with other fertilizers.

Preparing a Balanced Fertilizing Plan

If you've read this far, you really know your fertilizers now. The next step is to formulate a plan for fertilizing your container plants.

Plants growing in containers need more water than those growing in the ground. The more you water, the more you flush nutrients from the soil, and the more often you have to fertilize.

You can offset some of this constant loss of nutrients by mixing slow-release fertilizers into the soil mix before planting. But some gardeners prefer the less-food-more-often approach. In other words, plants are given a little liquid fertilizer every time, or every other time, that they're watered. Cut the recommended rates on the bottle of fertilizer in half or into quarters.

If frequent feeding poses too much hassle for you, use a water-soluble fertilizer once every week or two. Follow the rates recommended on the label. Your container plants can still respond well.

Overfertilizing can be much worse than not applying enough nutrients. Excess nitrogen, for example, can burn the edges of leaves and even kill a plant. Besides that, if you apply too much, fertilizer can leach from containers and run off into storm sewers and groundwater, and then you're a nasty polluter. Always follow label instructions to the letter.

Also, don't apply fertilizer to dry plants or during extremely hot or windy weather conditions, because doing so can burn your container garden. Fertilize only actively growing plants. Adding fertilizer to a dead-looking stick of a plant won't miraculously cause it to come back to life. The fertilizer will just get washed away with the next watering.

Chapter 17

Repotting Plants and Caring for the Containers They Call Home

. . . .

In This Chapter

▶ Repotting and pruning: Tips and techniques

▶ Hefting heavy containers

▶ Cleaning, painting, and preserving containers

▶ Sparing your containers an untimely demise

▶ Getting organized: Storing your planting supplies

. . . .

A number of odd jobs concerning containers don't quite fall into any particular category, and while they're not necessarily essential, they are noteworthy. In this chapter we take you through the basics of these various odd jobs because, in the long run, they help you grow beautiful and healthy container gardens.

In this chapter we show you when and how to repot plants, as well as how to clean, paint, and repair containers. We shore up everything from wire to wood to metal so that your containers are shiny and shipshape when you plant. You find out how to move heavy planters and store all your gardening supplies efficiently. All of these tasks are intended to make your gardening activities easier and more successful.

All About Repotting

Sooner or later when you're container gardening, you'll have to repot a plant or three. There are two reasons to repot:

✔ When plants have outgrown their containers and they need more space to allow for additional growth

✔ When you want to slow the growth of plants so they can stay happy and healthy in the same size container

Repotting is no big deal. With a few basic tips, you can quickly become an expert at recognizing what needs to be repotted and when the time is right for repotting so you can minimize trauma to your plants. In the following sections, you also find out how to select a new pot and get some pointers on moving plants from one container to another.

Knowing what to repot and when to do it

When does a plant need repotting? Any time its roots are overcrowded in the container. The following clues tell you it's time to repot:

- ✔ You see lots of roots coming through the drain hole.
- ✔ You find matted roots near the soil surface.
- ✔ You slip the plant from its container and you see more roots than soil.

Don't wait for outward signs that a plant needs repotting: poor flowering, quickly dried out soil, stunted leaves and stems, and even leaf drop and *die-back* (parts of the plant turn brown and die). These are signs of distress. Plants give these signals because they're not able to draw enough nutrients and moisture from their current root situation. Check container plants regularly, if possible, slipping them out of their pots to examine the roots for crowding.

Annual flowers and vegetables that you've started from seed in small containers need frequent repotting into progressively larger containers, perhaps as often as every month, until they're ready for their season-long home, which should be a container chosen to accommodate their mature size. Ditto for young transplants that you purchase.

Permanent plants, such as trees, shrubs, and perennial flowers, may need repotting every few years. Permanent plants are best repotted when growth is slow or when they're dormant, either before or after flowering. With this schedule, plants have a chance to recover from the root disturbance that invariably occurs during repotting, no matter how careful you are. Repot spring-blooming permanent plants in fall and evergreens in spring or fall.

Choosing a new container

If you want to increase growth, you need to give plants more room for their roots by transplanting them into larger pots. How much larger? It's best to move plants to larger pots incrementally, choosing a pot that's just a few inches larger than the current one. Choose a similarly shaped pot so you won't have to reshape the root ball to fit the new container. (For more pointers on selecting containers, flip to Chapter 3.)

If you want to control growth and keep the plant from getting too big, you need to trim the roots (head to the "Pruning roots: A little off the ends, please" section later in this chapter for the ins and outs of trimming roots) and return the plant to the same pot or one of similar size.

When the plant is going back into the same pot, take the time first to thoroughly wash the pot using hot, soapy water or a 5 to 10 percent bleach solution to remove potentially disease-causing fungi and bacteria. See the "Cleaning up containers" section for more details about cleaning pots.

Repotting techniques

In general, you can follow the same basic techniques as you do for regular planting: Refer to Chapter 5 for step-by-step instructions.

Your biggest challenge may be getting the plant out of its current container. This may be easy, or it may take some effort if the root ball is a tangled mess. For small to medium plants, turn the container upside down, tap the rim, and slide the plant out. For larger, heavier plants, tip the container on its side and roll it around gently. You may need to use a rubber mallet to tap the sides if the root mass is stubborn.

Protect large ceramic and clay pots from chipping or cracking by wrapping an old towel or piece of carpeting around the outside before you tilt them and tap the sides.

Try to slip the container off the plant, rather than yanking on the plant to pull it from the pot. In some cases, you may have to trim off large roots poking through the drain hole to release the plant from its pot.

With large containers, let the roots dry out a bit first because this tends to shrink them, making them easier to extract from the pot.

Next, examine the roots. For plants going into larger containers, gently loosen and pull apart tangled or circling roots. If you're repotting into the same-sized pot to slow growth or to maintain the plant's current size, you'll want to root prune it; see the following section on root pruning for details.

Add an inch-deep layer of fresh, moist soil mix to the new container. (Refer to Chapter 4 for details on selecting soil mixes.) Place the root ball in the new container, adjusting the depth of the fresh soil as necessary so that the top of the root ball sits a few inches below the rim of the pot. Begin filling in the gaps around the edges with fresh soil mix, tamping it down gently as you go.

If you don't have time for a complete repotting job, a temporary solution is to remove the top few inches of potting soil and replace it with fresh potting mix with a little added fertilizer.

Pruning roots: A little off the ends, please

Root pruning is just what it implies — using shears to cut away root growth — and you do it to container-grown trees and shrubs once they've reached their desired size. Root pruning controls growth and stimulates the plant to produce lots of the young roots it needs to take up water and nutrients.

The goal in root pruning is to remove about one quarter of the root ball. After removing the plant from its pot, gently untangle the edges of the root mass and use shears to cut away roots, especially the largest, woodiest ones, until you've cut off about a quarter of the root ball. For tight root balls that are difficult to untangle, use shears or a garden knife to cut off about one quarter of the root mass, slicing down the sides as shown in Figure 17-1. Then make vertical cuts, from top to bottom, an inch or so deep in several places. And, please, do this without flinching. Snipping away at a living organism may seem harsh, but in the long run you're helping the plant and new roots to grow. Really, you are!

Figure 17-1:
Prune tightly
packed root
balls by
slicing off
the sides.

Moving Large Containers to a New Location

Consider carefully where you want large pots, planters, and barrels to go before you move them into place. If it's practical, move heavy containers into place before you plant them because they're lighter without the added weight of the soil and plant. If you have to move large pots later on, here are a few tips to keep in mind.

For relocating large pots, tubs, and some barrels, you can buy wooden rolling plant dollies or plastic saucers with wheels. (Check out Figure 17-2 to see these and other methods in action.) These are ideal for many planters, but you need to be sure they can hold the weight of the planted, watered container. And if you can plan ahead, hold off on watering to lighten the load.

To move other large, heavy containers like planter boxes and concrete or stone pots, try using an old piece of carpeting or a throw rug. With a helper, tip the container and slide the end of a long carpet strip underneath. Slide the container so that it rests completely on the carpet; then you can tug it along as your assistant steadies it. Cardboard, blankets, and large sacks can work this way, too.

The tugging, lifting, and pushing associated with moving heavy objects like these can put enormous strain on your back. Planters that tip unexpectedly can crush toes. Be sure you have enough help, and consider hiring out big jobs.

Sometimes an ordinary hand truck or furniture dolly can be useful. Take care to move long plant stems away from the sides as you balance the container on the foot of the dolly. A hand truck can work for long rectangular containers as long as you can balance them.

If you have to go up or down stairs, use a pair of long wooden planks to form a ramp and tie the container to a rope. With a helper, pull up or gently lower the container slowly and securely. Err on the side of safety, and call in as many helpers as you need.

Figure 17-2:
There are
many ways
to move
large pots.

Keeping Your Containers in Tip-Top Condition

Your containers are more than a pot to hold soil and plants. They're your plants' living quarters, and they decorate your home and landscape as well. That's why you need to make sure your containers are in good shape. Dirty containers (yes, we know that sounds contradictory) can affect plant health, and faded or drab-looking pots distract from the appearance of your arrangement. Read on for advice on how to keep your containers in great shape.

Cleaning up containers

They're outside, they get wet, they hold dirt — so why should you bother to clean containers? The answer is easy. Plants grow better in a clean and sterile environment, and you lower the chances of having pests and diseases hanging around to harm your plants. While you're cleaning your containers, be sure to clean any stakes or plant supports that have seen duty in previously planted pots. Here are some quick and easy steps for keeping containers clean:

1. **Get rid of potting soil and debris by brushing the inside and outside of the container thoroughly.**

   Use a stiff plastic or wire brush for the job.

2. **Wash small containers in a basin (or a bucket for larger containers) filled with hot, soapy water.**

   For added security or with especially dirty pots, add a few drops of liquid household bleach to the water (wear rubber gloves for this job). Be sure to scrub both inside and out.

3. **Rinse the container well, and allow it to air dry overnight before replanting.**

   Remember to use fresh soil mix, too, to minimize insect and disease problems. If you're starting seeds, use a sterile seed-starting mix.

Maintaining metal or wire items

Awesome flowers in shabby containers or pretty pots on chipped and peeling plant stands don't provide the good looks that we bet you're going for. Naturally, containers exposed to the elements invariably fall into disrepair.

Here's a quick and painless course on the how-tos of refurbishing metal or wire plant stands, brackets, and hanging baskets:

1. **Inspect these items at the start of the season and look for any signs of rust or chipped or cracked paint.**

   If a metal surface is exposed, expect it to sustain damage under outdoor conditions.

2. **Wash off any dirt and debris, and let items dry thoroughly.**

3. **Select new paint, choosing a rust-free type that's designed for exterior applications.**

   Check out new "textured" paints that leave a stonelike finish. Read the instructions before you begin.

4. **On a dry, warm day, find a covered or protected spot outdoors for painting.**

   As inviting as it may seem on a sunny day, avoid doing the painting under a tree, especially if it's breezy, or you're likely to get all sorts of twigs and leaf bits embedded in the paint. If you must work indoors, choose a well-ventilated garage or toolshed.

5. **Protect surrounding surfaces with a drop-cloth or newspapers, especially if you're using spray paint or spraying on a sealer.**

6. **Sand all surfaces to remove rust or mineral deposits and to smooth the metal so the paint adheres adequately.**

   Use steel wool or sandpaper in a medium to fine grade.

7. **Spray or paint on a light coat, and let it dry.**

   Sand lightly between coats with a very fine grade of steel wool. Repeat this process one to three times. Several thin layers give good protection.

8. **Finish with a coating of clear protectant designed for outdoor use.**

   Marine varnish offers excellent protection. Choose between glossy or matte finish and, again, go for a couple of applications.

Preserving wood containers

You can save work in the long run if you make sure that wooden containers are ready to withstand the elements before you begin planting. Choosing rot-resistant materials in the first place is a wise decision; redwood and cedar are your best bets. These materials survive for years without any additional help.

Prolong the life of wooden containers — especially those made of soft woods, like pine — with a wood preservative safe for plants. Many nontoxic products can do the job. Check label directions and cautions before you buy to be sure the preservative you choose isn't harmful to plants. Treating the inside helps the container last; treating the outside preserves its looks. Using preservative on the outside of cedar and redwood containers helps retain their natural wood color. Otherwise they weather to gray, which actually can be attractive, too.

Another option is to paint or stain your containers — a good route to go with window boxes, because you can match them to your house. These surface treatments give wood longer life and allow you other decorating angles as well. You can follow the refurbishing tips in the previous section (ignoring the directions that are specific to metal pieces, of course), although there are a few key points to keep in mind when you're painting or staining wooden containers:

✔ **Make sure to use exterior-grade paint or stain.** This is critical, unless you particularly like the whole process of refinishing wood — over and over.

✔ **Don't skimp on preparing the surface.** Sand. Sand. Sand. Smooth surfaces are much easier to paint or stain evenly. Follow directions for what to do between coats, and use a tacky cloth to pick up any fine particles or sawdust.

✔ **Consider penetrating oils.** They're as easy to apply as stain, and they repel water very well. Some even come in different colors.

✔ **Test your paint, stain, or oil on the underside of the container first to avoid unwelcome surprises after application.** The pictures on brochures and paint-can labels aren't always what they seem.

✔ **For planters, boxes, and barrels that have quite a coat of grunge from mold, mildew, and water stains, consider using a chemical wash first.** Usually designed to clean decks or siding, these products can be found in home centers and hardware stores. Generously spray or paint the wash liquid on, let it work for several minutes, and wash it off. For very grungy surfaces, you may have to scrub with a wire brush or repeat the process. After treatment, your container is all set for painting, staining, or oiling.

Some gardeners like to line the inside of wood containers with 4- to 6-mil black plastic. Lining does help keep moisture away from the wood surfaces, but it only works for the sides because you need to poke holes in the bottom for drainage. Be sure to trim the plastic at the top of the soil level so it doesn't show.

Humpty-Dumpty Duty — Repairing Broken Containers

It had to happen. That wayward pass ended up in the pansies and the football found your favorite pot, which took a tumble and is now in pieces. All is not lost. If the damage isn't too bad, you can repair the pot and return the world to peace and harmony. If the pieces still fit tightly and you use the right adhesive, these tricks can help you successfully mend your wounded containers:

✔ Choose an epoxy glue. You mix the two components — one part glue, one part hardener — before you cement the pieces. Read the package directions for mixing, then apply the mending goo to both parts before joining them.

✔ Fit the pieces together and tie the pot so that it's securely held in place, as shown in Figure 17-3. Use cord or rope for large pots; try easy-to-remove painter's tape for small ones.

✔ Wipe off any glue that spills out of the cracks when you fit the pieces together. You can use sandpaper after the glue is dry to remove any residue.

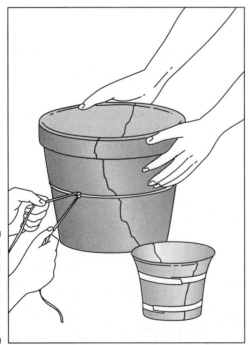

Figure 17-3:
Using rope or tape can help you repair a broken pot.

The time may come, too, when you need to repair wooden containers. While the damage may not be as earth-shattering as broken pottery, wooden boxes, tubs, and barrels still require care to stay in good working order. Constant moisture and the natural breakdown of materials may leave you with loose boards and poorly fitted joints. Here are a few things to look out for and a few ways to mend any wear and tear that you find:

- **Prevent — or at least reduce — the chance of rot with wooden containers by raising them off the ground.** Bricks, pavers, or even wooden blocks placed underneath the containers can give them just the lift they need. Raising the container allows the wood to dry between waterings. Use enough supports so that the box or tub is stable and level.

- **Watch for new or widening gaps where pieces join.** Check planters, window boxes, wooden troughs, and barrels often — at least every couple of months.

- **If containers suddenly show signs of excessive drainage and you see water pouring out, check to see whether some part has come loose or started to rot away.** Make these repairs without delay.

- **Look for exposed nails, staples, or screws.** Sometimes manufacturers assemble wooden containers with staples, and over time these can pull away. Small gaps only become larger under the weight and pressure of soil and plants.

- **Rejoin boards using galvanized wood screws.** The screws should be long enough to penetrate each piece by an inch or more. You get the best hold over the long run.

- **Reinforce wooden sections that may be starting to rot by adding new pieces on the inside of the container.** Use redwood or cedar blocks on corner or end joints, and insert screws through the original wood and well into the new piece.

- **With barrels, you may need to reposition and reattach staves (the metal bands that hold them together) that are beginning to slip.** Slide the stave up into its original spot, and use small nails with large heads to secure it in several places around the container.

Stashing Your Plant Paraphernalia

We know that you're organized. You know exactly where to find your 2004 tax return if anyone asks (we won't), and you can quickly locate the ½-inch socket wrench in your garage. So why not extend this high level of efficiency to your containers and supplies? Then you'll be able to find important ingredients in your container gardening pursuit more easily. Plus, you can expect many containers and other materials to hold up longer if they're stored properly. Here are some quick storage ideas for you to consider (someday, at least!):

✔ Make a place for all your movable pots and materials, including soil, fertilizer, stakes, tools, and so on. Your reward arrives when you're ready to plant.

✔ A storage shed is ideal. But if you don't have one, designate a place in the garage for your gardening essentials. A generous cabinet may do the trick. Safe storage is especially important with chemical and toxic materials that need to be locked away from curious eyes, hands, and mouths.

✔ Make it a practice to wash containers before you store them. Brush them down inside and out and use a bit of soapy bleach water if you see or suspect mold and mildew. Let them air-dry completely before storing.

✔ Invert pots, planters, and barrels if you must store them outside, so that moisture, debris, and rainwater don't collect inside. Cover everything with a waterproof tarp if you don't have any other shelter available.

✔ Look through chemicals — fertilizers, insecticides, and herbicides — at the end of the growing season to check effective dates. Dispose of outdated chemicals properly. Check with local authorities to discover proper methods and sites for disposal. Store the ones you're keeping in a safe (child- and pet-proof), dry place. Check the label for any storage temperature restrictions; some products should not be allowed to freeze and must be brought indoors in cold weather.

Chapter 18

When Bad Things Happen: Pests and Diseases

Many beginner gardeners are surprised by just how many pest and disease problems can affect plants. And many are equally surprised by how many problems they can manage with nontoxic methods. Gone are the days of weekly pesticide sprays to annihilate all potential pests. Our health — and the health of the planet — require us to take a more reasonable approach.

The key to this approach is knowledge. The more you know about the plants you grow and the pests and diseases that affect them, the better able you'll be to identify problems and manage them in an environmentally sound way.

One benefit of growing plants in containers is that you can provide them with optimum growing conditions and sometimes even locate them where they're less susceptible to pests and diseases, preventing problems before they start. Growing in containers doesn't eliminate problems, but it can help minimize them.

In this chapter we give you a slew of techniques for preventing pests and diseases. Sooner or later, however, chances are you'll encounter problems on even the most carefully tended plants. We show you the least toxic ways to manage different types of pests and diseases safely and effectively.

Maybe you'll never encounter a pest on your plants. And maybe we'll win the lottery. They're both possible, but the odds are against us. But fear not, help is right here. Read on!

Warding Off Pests and Diseases from the Get-Go

Keeping on top of pest and disease control in your container plants is often easier than in those growing in the garden. Here are a few reasons why:

- ✔ Containers are where you are — on the patio, on the porch, on the deck — rather than out in the garden where most pests lurk. And if a problem does develop, you usually see it right away so you can tackle it before it gets out of hand.

- ✔ You can provide individual plants with just the right amount of shade, soil moisture, and fertilizer to keep them healthy and growing vigorously. This strong growth helps plants endure and recover from diseases and pest attacks, and, ironically, many insect pests attack weak plants before going after healthy ones.

- ✔ Because container growing often makes use of sterile soil mixes that start out free of insects and diseases, soil-borne problems rarely occur, especially if you start with fresh soil mix each time you plant.

Despite the lower risk, it pays to be diligent about checking plants and controlling pests and diseases. Container plants are often on display, and you don't want to surround yourself with struggling, bug-infested plants. Also, you probably have fewer plants in containers than you would in a sprawling backyard garden, so you want to make sure that each one performs at its best.

A word about weeds

Just because you're growing plants in a container in potting mix doesn't mean weeds can't find them. Granted, they won't be as plentiful as in the garden, but weed seeds carried on the wind will sprout in your container as readily as they would in the garden. Pull weeds as soon as you see them so they don't compete with your plants for the limited supply of water and nutrients.

Starting with Integrated Pest Management

Experts have coined the term *integrated pest management,* or IPM, to describe a common-sense approach to managing pests. IPM consists of a series of steps, the first of which is to try to prevent problems. However, even with the best prevention techniques many plants will be affected by insect pests or diseases at some point in their lives. Rather than jumping for the pesticide spray at the first sign of trouble, IPM asks you to first consider whether or not control is even necessary. If it is, then you start with the least-toxic controls first — those that target the pest and cause the least harm to other organisms. If these don't manage the pest adequately, stronger controls may be warranted; however, controls are always chosen with an eye toward protecting benign and beneficial organisms and the environment as a whole.

Preventing pests

Pest management is as much about prevention as it is about control. If you do the right things for your plants, they're better equipped to fend off insect attacks. Here's a list of common-sense pest prevention measures:

- **Choose resistant plants:** If you know a certain pest is common in your area, choose plants that resist it. Read plant labels — if a variety is resistant to a common pest, you can be sure the label will tell you. You can find plants resistant to various diseases, insects, and even animal pests like deer, so do your homework before planting.

- **Grow healthy plants:** You can't hear it enough times. Healthy plants are less likely to have problems. Start with a good soil mix as recommended in Chapter 4. Put plants in the right location. Pests take advantage of plants weakened by less-than-ideal growing conditions. Water and fertilize plants as needed so they grow strong.

- **Keep your garden clean:** Practice good garden sanitation. Remove spent plants, diseased foliage, dead branches, and other garden debris to eliminate hiding places for pests. Clean pots well before using them, and don't reuse old potting soil. If you're treating a container of plants for an insect problem, move it away from other plants until you have the problem under control. Clean tools regularly.

- **Grow a diversity of plants:** If you grow ten pots of geraniums and one of them gets geranium budworm, you can bet that all the plants will eventually be affected. Growing a variety of different plants reduces the chances that one pest will damage all your plants. And a diversity of plants encourages a diversity of insects, many of which are beneficial and will help control the pests.

✔ **Attract insects that prey on the insects that damage your plants:**
Garden pests like aphids are food for ladybugs and many other insects.
These beneficial insects can do a remarkable job of managing pest outbreaks, so it just makes sense to invite them into your landscape. See
the "Enlisting the help of beneficial insects" section later in this chapter
for more details.

Monitoring plants

It's important to know what a healthy specimen looks like so you're able
to recognize problems. Observe plants frequently, looking under, over,
between, and around the leaves, stems, and flowers for signs of problems.
It can be challenging for beginner gardeners — and experienced gardeners growing unfamiliar plants — to know what's normal for a specific plant
and what symptoms indicate a problem. One helpful technique is to keep a
garden journal with plant names and varieties (or keep plant tags in a scrap-
book) so you can research what your plant should look like. Are those spots
on the leaves normal for this variety or do they indicate a problem? You can
look up the plants online or in gardening books and compare your plant with
the photos of healthy specimens.

Identifying the culprit

If you see a problem, determine what's causing the damage. Sometimes the
damage is caused not by insects or diseases, but by heavy rain, wind, heat,
or cold. Find out how to identify the most common pests affecting the plants
you're growing, including the damage they cause. For a start, consult our list
of common pests and diseases coming up later in this chapter. If you need
more help, contact reference books and Web sites, garden center personnel,
or gardening neighbors.

Your local Master Gardeners' group may have workshops and hotlines to help
you identify pests. For a map with links to state Master Gardener programs, go
to this American Horticultural Society Web page: www.ahs.org/master_
gardeners.

Establishing damage thresholds

Decide how much damage you're willing to tolerate. (And yes, you have to be
willing to tolerate some.) Don't grab a spray can if you see the nibblings of a
few pests or if the pests show up late in the season when plants are winding
down anyway. But if you find masses of crawling insects or rapidly spreading
diseases, you'll want to take action.

Most proponents of IPM avoid using words like annihilate, destroy, eradicate, exterminate, obliterate, and other words of warfare. Contrary to what some pesticide advertisements might have you believe, most garden pests are simply living their lives as part of the garden ecosystem. They're not the enemy; they provide food for birds and other garden denizens, and some are larvae of the butterflies we enjoy and try to attract. Keep the word *manage* in mind — the goal is to manage pests so you can enjoy your garden while causing the least disturbance to the ecology of your landscape.

Enlisting the help of beneficial insects

Gardens typically are populated by huge numbers of different insects, most neither good nor bad. The critters are just hanging out at no expense to the plants. But some insects are beneficial and prey on pest insects. (Well, they're beneficial to *us*, if not to their prey.)

These good bugs are no fools. They hang out in gardens that offer the most reliable menu. Ladybugs, for example, feed on aphids. If you eliminate every last aphid with frequent pesticide sprays, ladybug passersby will take one look, see that the diner is closed, and move on. If they find a few aphids here and there, they'll settle in for a snack and hang around to keep the aphid population in check.

To encourage beneficial insects to take up residence, maintain a diverse garden with many kinds and sizes of plants. Doing so gives the beneficial insects places to hide and reproduce. Variety can also provide an alternative food source, because many beneficial insects eat pollen and flower nectar, too. Some plants that attract beneficial insects include Queen Anne's lace, parsley (especially if you let the flower develop), sweet alyssum, dill, fennel, and yarrow.

Following are some beneficial insects to invite into your landscape:

- ✔ **Green lacewings:** Their voracious larvae feed on aphids, mites, thrips, and various insect eggs. These insects are among the more effective pest control forces.

- ✔ **Lady beetles (also known as ladybugs):** Both the adult and the alligator-like larvae are especially good at feeding on small insects like aphids and thrips.

- ✔ **Spiders:** Yes, we know it's unpleasant to walk into webs or come face-to-face with a particularly creepy specimen, but spiders are important allies in preventing insect pest outbreaks.

- ✔ **Syrphid and tachinid flies:** Syrphid fly larvae prey on aphids and thrips; tachinid flies parasitize caterpillars.

✔ **Trichogramma and braconid wasps:** Harmless to humans, these tiny wasps parasitize pest caterpillars, including tomato hornworm, corn earworm, and cabbage worm.

You can buy some types of beneficial insects, including ladybugs, lacewings, and praying mantids, to release into your yard. However, unless conditions are optimum for them, they're likely to fly away soon after you release them. If you choose this route, carefully follow the instructions for releasing the insects to increase the likelihood that they'll hang around. Keep in mind, too, that often simply creating an inviting habitat for beneficial insects will encourage native insects to call your yard home, saving you from having to buy them.

Choosing the nontoxic, least invasive controls

Common sense tells us that if you can prevent a pest from reaching a plant, you eliminate the risk of damage. So the first line of defense in IPM is keeping pests and plants apart. Barriers and repellents can accomplish this for some pests; trapping for others. In some cases you can physically remove pests from plants before they cause much damage. These techniques are nontoxic and cause little disruption to the ecosystem.

If you know a certain pest is likely to cause trouble on a certain plant (from personal experience or the counsel of others) you may be able to prevent problems or at least minimize them with the following techniques. If you find these controls inadequate, you always have the option of moving on to the next level of control: least-toxic pesticide sprays.

✔ **Barriers:** Sometimes a simple barrier will protect plants from pests. For example, cover plants with a *row cover* (a lightweight fabric that allows light, air, and water to penetrate) that's secured at the base of the container to keep pest insects from feeding or laying eggs on plants. Row covers are especially good for vegetables that don't require insect pollination, such as lettuce, beans, carrots, and broccoli — you can leave the row covers on the plants as long as the pests are a threat. For plants that require insect pollination, like squash plants, you need to remove the covers once the plants begin flowering or you won't have any squash to harvest.

Diatomaceous earth consists of the fossilized shells of tiny marine organisms called diatoms. Although it looks like dust to us, to small insect it feels like crushed glass. Spread it as a barrier against slugs, snails, and earwigs.

✔ **Repellents:** Like humans, many pests are repelled by certain odors and tastes. If you don't want a human to eat your apple, you can put it near some smelly socks or spray it with something bitter. Likewise, if you want to keep deer away, hang perfumed soap or bags of human hair (barber shop trimmings) nearby, or spray plants with predator urine, which you can buy at most garden centers.

✔ **Traps:** You can significantly reduce the populations of some pests by trapping them. Slug traps, for example, can significantly reduce their numbers. Spread *Tanglefoot,* a nontoxic, sticky substance, around the base of containers or on collars around tree trunks to trap crawling bugs before they can reach plant foliage.

Some Japanese beetle traps contain lures to attract the beetles. Unfortunately, studies have shown that the lures can attract beetles from all over the neighborhood, increasing rather than reducing the population in your yard.

✔ **Mechanical controls:** Many pests, such as Japanese beetles, are sluggish in the cool of the morning so it's easy to knock them off plants and into a bucket of soapy water. You can control some pests, such as aphids, by hosing them off plants with a strong spray of water every few days.

Picking an Appropriate Pesticide

If your friendly neighborhood bug-eaters, hand-picking, barriers, and traps aren't doing the trick, you can take further action against pest outbreaks by applying pesticides. Consider pesticides — even organic ones — as a last resort, because they all have some environmental impact.

When choosing a pesticide, ask yourself two questions:

1. **Is the pesticide *broad-spectrum* or *targeted* to an individual type of pest?**

   Broad-spectrum pesticides kill species other than the pest you're trying to control. When possible, choose pesticides that target only the pest species.

2. **Does the pesticide break down quickly or persist in the environment?**

   Pesticides that persist in the environment, like the notorious DDT, have long-term impacts. Most environmentally friendly pesticides degrade quickly into harmless substances once they're exposed to sunlight, air, and water. You may need to apply them more often, but that's the trade-off for being gentler on the environment.

No matter which pesticides you decide to use, you must use them safely. Always follow instructions on the product label exactly.

Both the pest you're trying to control and the plant you're spraying must be listed on the label. (Sometimes plants are listed as groups, such as simply "flowers.") Follow these additional guidelines when using pesticides:

- ✔ Wear protective gear when mixing and spraying pesticides — long sleeves, shoes, hat, gloves, goggles, dust mask. Mix only as much as you intend to use right away.

- ✔ Spray when the winds are calm.

- ✔ Avoid spraying when rain is predicted, to prevent the pesticide from washing off.

- ✔ Spray in the cool of the morning when bees are less active.

- ✔ Store chemicals in properly labeled containers well out of reach of children and pets — a locked cabinet is best.

- ✔ Dispose of empty containers as described on the label. Never pour pesticides down the sink or into storm drains. Contact your local waste disposal company for appropriate disposal sites.

In the following sections, we take a closer look at pesticide products, grouped by type.

If you're trying to grow plants organically, choosing pest control products from the array at your local garden center can be daunting. One way to determine if a product is approved for organic growing is to look for the words *OMRI-Listed* on the label. The Organic Materials Review Institute (OMRI) is a nonprofit that evaluates pesticides and determines whether or not they are approved for use in organic growing. If a product is OMRI-Listed, it has been approved.

Biological controls

These products contain living organisms that prey on or otherwise help keep pests in check. They often contain microscopic organisms that feed on specific pests. These are some of the most environmentally friendly choices for home gardeners.

- ✔ **Bt:** For years, organic gardeners have been using *Bacillus thuringiensis,* or Bt, to control caterpillars on broccoli and other cole crops. There are now several strains of this bacterium that control different pests, so read product labels carefully.

One type of Bt kills caterpillars, which are moth and butterfly larvae. Be especially careful using this product, because it kills all caterpillars, including the larvae of the butterflies that flit around harmlessly.

Other strains of Bt control Colorado potato beetle, mosquito larvae, and fungus gnats. Bt breaks down quickly in the environment and is considered safe to use around pets and humans.

✔ **Milky spore:** Another common biological control contains the bacteria that cause milky spore disease in Japanese beetle grubs. After the grubs eat the bacteria, they stop feeding and soon die. The bacteria, which, in the meantime, have been reproducing inside the grub, are released into the soil to infect other grubs.

✔ **Nematodes:** Beneficial or predatory nematodes are microscopic, worm-like organisms that live in the soil and prey on the larvae of all sorts of garden pests, including grubs, fleas, and weevils. (Don't confuse these with pest nematodes, which damage plants.) Beneficial nematodes are usually sold in packets that you mix with water and spray on the soil.

✔ **Spinosad:** This relatively new biological control is derived from the fermentation of a naturally occurring soil microbe. It controls a wide range of insect pests, including caterpillars, thrips, leafminers, some beetles, and borers. Spinosad is considered safe for beneficial insects, pets, and humans.

✔ **White muscadine fungus:** One of the most promising new biological controls contains the fungus *Beauveria bassiana,* commonly known as white muscadine fungus. This soil-dwelling fungus affects aphids, caterpillars, mites, thrips, and others.

Oils and soaps

Horticultural oils and insecticidal soaps are two of the most common and most useful all-around pesticides for home gardeners. They work on contact by damaging the insects' cell membranes, causing the insects to suffocate or dehydrate. Although these sprays can harm some beneficial insects if sprayed directly on them, they break down quickly and don't persist in the environment.

✔ **Summer oil:** When sprayed on a plant, this oil smothers pest insects and their eggs. Some summer oils are refined from petroleum; others are plant-based. Summer oil is relatively eco-friendly and short-lived. Use it to control aphids, mites, thrips, and certain caterpillars.

Double-check the product label to make sure it says that it can be used on plants during the growing season. Then follow the mixing instructions carefully. Water the plants before and after applying, and don't spray if temperatures are likely to rise above 85 degrees Fahrenheit. When it's that hot, the oil can damage plant leaves.

Don't confuse summer oil with dormant oil. Dormant oil is meant to be applied to leafless trees and shrubs during winter. It's very useful for smothering overwintering pests on roses and fruit trees and is often combined with a fungicide.

✔ **Insecticidal soaps:** Derived from the salts of fatty acids, insecticidal soaps kill mostly soft-bodied pests like aphids, spider mites, and whiteflies. Soaps can sometimes be effective against Japanese beetles. They work fast, break down quickly, and are nontoxic to humans. Soaps sometimes burn tender foliage, so carefully follow application instructions.

Botanical pesticides

For millennia people have used plant extracts to deter pests. Here are some of the most commonly available ones:

✔ **Neem:** Extracted from the tropical tree *Azadirachta indica,* neem kills young feeding insects and deters adult insects but is harmless to people and most beneficial insects. Neem works slowly and is most effective against aphids, thrips, and whiteflies, but it also repels Japanese beetles.

Neem *extract* contains azadirachtin, the key insecticidal component found in the plant. Neem *oil* is effective against insects and also two common diseases, powdery mildew and rust, so it's often a better choice for home gardeners. Neem oil gets thick when cool, so you need to warm it up before mixing it with water.

Use either kind of neem before you have a major pest problem because it acts to deter pests. Neem is most effective when applied early in the morning or late in the evening, when humidity is high. Reapply after rain.

✔ **Pyrethrins:** Derived from the painted daisy, *Chrysanthemum cinerariifolium,* pyrethrins are broad-spectrum insecticides that kill a wide range of insects — both good and bad. Use it with care to avoid harming beneficial insects.

The terminology can be confusing. *Pyrethrum* is the ground-up flower of the daisy. *Pyrethrins* are the insecticide components extracted from the flower and are common components of organic insecticides. *Pyrethroids,* such as permethrin and resmethrin, are synthetic compounds that resemble pyrethrins but are more toxic and persistent. Consequently, we prefer to avoid pyrethroids for home garden use.

✔ **Aromatic plant oils:**

- *Citrus oil* is extracted from citrus peels; products combining citrus oils and soaps are sold for controlling aphids and mites.

- *Garlic oil* repels insects and may control some fungal diseases.

- *Clove, thyme, cinnamon, and wintergreen oils* are showing promise against soil-borne pests like root maggots, wireworms, and cutworms. Repellents containing clove oil may deter deer.

✔ **Hot Pepper Wax:** Derived from a concentrate of cayenne peppers, various herbs, and food-grade paraffin wax, this product controls many insects, such as aphids, thrips, spider mites, and leafhoppers, as well as some animal pests. It can remain effective up to three weeks after spraying on plants, even if it rains.

A few botanicals have fallen out of favor because they're broad spectrum, harming beneficial insects as well as pests, and because they're particularly toxic to specific classes of animals. Avoid using these:

✔ **Nicotine:** A tobacco extract very toxic to mammals, especially if inhaled

✔ **Rotenone:** Very toxic to fish and pigs; no longer allowed in certified organic production

✔ **Sabadilla:** Very toxic to bees

Synthetic insecticides

You can successfully control most insect problems using the techniques and products we cover in the preceding sections. If, however, a pest really gets out of hand on a prized planting, some gardeners turn to synthetic pesticides. Synthetic pesticides often last longer, meaning you can spray them less often. The downside to this is that the pesticides may continue to act against nonpest species long after the pests are gone. We recommend avoiding synthetic pesticides or using them only as a last resort.

When you use any pesticide, make sure you've correctly identified the pest, and follow label instructions precisely.

Banishing Insects That Prey on Container Plants

Of the thousands of insect species that call our landscapes home just a handful pose problems for gardeners. By far, most insects you see on your plants are benign, or even beneficial, so carefully identify an insect before deeming it a pest to be controlled. Below are the most common insect pests that you're likely to find infesting your container plants and the best ways to control them:

✔ **Aphids:** Aphids are tiny, pear-shaped pests (see Figure 18-1) that come in many colors, including black, green, and red. They congregate on new growth and flower buds, sucking plant sap with their needlelike noses. Heavy infestations can cause distorted growth and weakened plants. Many plants can be infested, including annuals, roses, and many vegetables. Aphids leave behind a sticky "honeydew" substance that may in turn be colonized by black, sooty mold. The honeydew often attracts ants, too, and while the ants themselves aren't plant pests, they can signal you to look for aphids and other honeydew-producing pests.

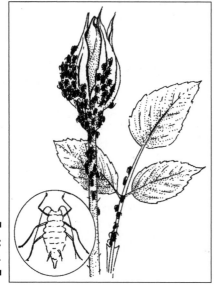

Figure 18-1:
Aphids.

Aphids are easy to control. You can knock them off sturdy plants with strong jets of water from a hose, or use insecticidal soap, spinosad, or pyrethrins. The soap also helps wash off the unsightly sooty mold. If you just wait a week or two, the aphid population boom is often followed by a buildup of beneficial insects, especially lady beetles, and they usually take matters into their own hands before serious damage occurs.

✔ **Borers:** Several kinds of beetle larvae and caterpillars tunnel into stems and wood, weakening plants and making them more susceptible to disease. The damage can also cut off nutrient flow. Borers tunnel into the wood of fruit trees, white birches, dogwoods, shade trees, and rhododendrons, among others. Other types of borers damage bearded iris and other perennials, as well as vegetables including corn and squash-family plants.

Look for borer-resistant plants. For example, if borers damage your bearded irises, try Siberian irises instead. Keep susceptible plants growing vigorously and watch for signs of borer damage — dead bark, sawdust piles, partial wilting, and poor performance. When you find borers, cut off and destroy severely infested stems and limbs. Inject Bt or parasitic nematodes into remaining borer holes, depending upon the plant and type of borer.

✔ **Caterpillars and worms:** Moth and butterfly larvae are avid eaters and can cause a lot of damage to a variety of plants. Some are hairy caterpillars; others are smooth-skinned and more wormlike. Birds and beneficial insects can keep caterpillar populations in check, so welcome these into your landscape. You can hand-pick caterpillars to reduce their numbers. If they get out of hand, the most effective way to get rid of caterpillars is to spray with Bt or spinosad.

✔ **Geranium budworms:** Geranium budworms are very frustrating pests of geraniums, nicotiana, ageratum, and petunias. The small caterpillars either bore into flower buds and eat the flowers before they open or they just feed on open blooms. The result is no flowers, just leaves. To confirm the presence of these heartless monsters, look for small holes in blossoms or the tiny black droppings the caterpillars leave behind. You may also see the worms on the flowers. To control, pick off infested flower buds and spray with Bt, spinosad, or pyrethrins.

✔ **Japanese beetles:** Japanese beetles can really be troublesome east of the Mississippi River, and they seem to be moving west. The ½-inch-long beetles have coppery bodies and metallic green heads (see Figure 18-2). They feed on both flowers and foliage, often skeletonizing leaves, eating the fleshy parts and leaving the veins. They particularly love zinnias, marigolds, and roses.

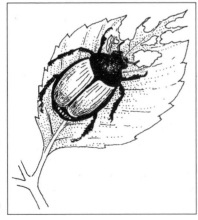

Figure 18-2:
A Japanese
beetle.

Control can be tough. Hand-pick the beetles in the cool of the morning, knocking them into a can of soapy water. Treating your lawn with parasitic nematodes or milky spore may reduce the population of the beetles' larvae (white, C-shaped grubs) but more adults may fly in from your neighbor's yard. Try to convince your neighbors to treat their lawns with the nematodes and milky spore, too.

Avoid beetle traps because, although they lure and kill beetles in your yard, they also attract beetles from surrounding areas. If you try the traps, keep them at least 100 feet from your plants.

✔ **Mealybugs:** These small, sucking insects, most common on houseplants, cover their bodies with a white cottony substance that makes them easy to identify. They usually feed in groups, forming a cottony mass on branches and stems. Wash off small numbers with a cotton ball dipped in rubbing alcohol; for larger infestations, spray with insecticidal soap or neem.

✔ **Scale:** These tiny insects look like small bumps on plant stems and leaves (see Figure 18-3). They hide under a turtlelike shell that serves as a shield. These pests suck plant sap and can kill plants if present in large numbers. The first sign of scale is often the sticky honeydew they secrete. Remove and destroy badly infested stems. Clean off light infestations with a cotton ball soaked in rubbing alcohol. Spray with dormant oil in winter or summer oil during the growing season.

✔ **Snails and slugs:** Snails and slugs are soft-bodied mollusks that feed on tender leaves and flowers during the cool of the night or during rainy weather. Snails have shells; slugs don't. (A slug is shown in Figure 18-4). Both proliferate in damp areas, hiding under raised containers, boards, or garden debris. To control snails and slugs, you can roam the garden at night with a flashlight and play pick-and-stomp, or you can trap them with saucers of beer with the rim set at ground level. You can catch a remarkable number of slugs in these traps, so check them frequently, disposing of the catch and resetting the trap.

Figure 18-3: Scale insects.

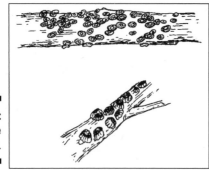

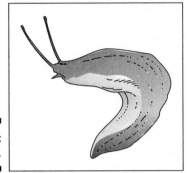

Figure 18-4:
A slug.

Snails and slugs refuse to cross anything made of copper — apparently, it gives them a mild electrical shock — so you can also surround raised beds or individual containers with a thin copper stripping or copper mesh sold in most garden centers or hardware stores. Iron phosphate-baited pellets (sold under clever trade names like Escargo and Sluggo) are another option; the mollusks eat the golden pellets and the iron phosphate kills them. The pellets are very effective and safe to use around pets and children, unlike more toxic metaldehyde baits.

✔ **Spider mites:** Spider mites are tiny, eight-legged spider relatives that you can barely see without a magnifying glass (see Figure 18-5). If the population gets big enough, you can see telltale fine webbing beneath the leaves. And as the mites suck plant juices, the leaves become yellowish with a silvery or bronze stippling. The plant may even start dropping leaves. Mites are most common in hot, dry summer climates and on dusty plants. Houseplants, tomatoes, and roses are commonly infested.

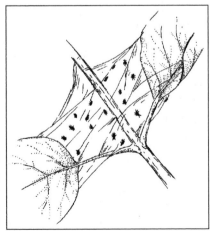

Figure 18-5:
Spider
mites.

A daily wash with a strong jet of water from a hose can help keep infestations down. You can also control spider mites with insecticidal soap and summer oil sprays.

✔ **Thrips:** Thrips are another almost-invisible troublemaker. They feed on flower petals, causing them to be discolored and the buds to be deformed as they open. They also feed on leaves, causing them to become deformed and giving them a stippled look (which can be distinguished from similar spider mite damage by the small fecal pellets that thrips leave behind). Impatiens, roses, and gladioluses are commonly infested.

Many beneficial insects feed on thrips, especially lacewings. Insecticidal soaps and hot pepper wax are also effective against thrips.

✔ **Whiteflies:** Whiteflies look like small, white gnats (see Figure 18-6), but they suck plant juices and can proliferate in warm climates and greenhouses. They tend to congregate on the undersides of leaves. You can trap whiteflies with yellow sticky traps sold in nurseries. Insecticidal soaps, summer oil, hot pepper wax, and pyrethrins are effective sprays.

Figure 18-6:
Whiteflies.

Preventing and Treating Plant Diseases

Most common garden diseases are caused by various types of fungi. As is the case with insects, most species of fungus are beneficial; they're the decomposers that help break down the vegetable scraps in our compost bin and transform mountains of fall leaves into leaf mold, a garden amendment worth its weight in gold. However, some fungus species (along with a few bacteria, viruses, and other microbes) can infect our garden plants, and when they do, we call them diseases.

Only a few diseases really do much damage to container-grown plants, and most of those can be prevented — or at least reduced in severity — with good cultural practices or by planting resistant varieties. If you know a certain disease is a problem on a particular plant in your area, simply growing something else is the easiest solution.

In the following sections, we offer some tips for heading off diseases before they become a problem, and in case they do become a problem, we give you some advice for how to take care of them.

Stopping diseases before they start

Some cultural practices can help avoid plant diseases. Some of these are similar to the pest-prevention tips we mention earlier in the chapter, but they're worth repeating here:

- **Choose resistant plants.** If you know a certain disease is common in your area, choose plants that resist it. Plant labels often will tell you if a variety is resistant to a common disease. For example, some varieties of roses are very susceptible to black spot, a disease that causes, oddly enough, black spots on the foliage. Other varieties are very resistant to infection.

- **Remove infected plants.** As soon as you notice a plant with a problem, give it the yank. Even picking off infected leaves helps prevent a disease from spreading.

- **Avoid wetting foliage.** Most plant diseases require moisture to spread. Avoid overhead watering, and apply water to soil, not foliage. Refer to Chapter 15 for information on drip irrigation and self-watering containers, both of which help reduce disease problems. Don't handle plants when the leaves are wet. If you have to use overhead watering, do so in the morning so the leaves dry quickly in the sun, rather than sitting moist all night.

- **Space plants properly.** Planting too close reduces air circulation between plants — a condition that invites disease. Set containers so the air can circulate between them. Unfortunately, planting close together is often the norm with flower-filled planters, so just be aware that diseases are more common under these conditions.

- **Keep your garden clean and tidy.** Many diseases spread on plant debris, so pick up fallen leaves and remove dead plants. Keep the spaces under containers clean.

- **Provide drainage.** Make sure your pots can drain properly. You know that your pots must have holes in the bottom so that water can drain out. But frequent checks also allow you to be sure that the openings aren't clogged with roots. And if you have a saucer under your pots, make sure you drain it after watering so plants don't sit in soggy soil — overly wet soil leads to root-rot diseases.

✔ **Keep tools clean.** Disinfect pruning tools with a 10-percent-bleach solution (1 part bleach to 9 parts water) between cuts to prevent spreading diseases.

✔ **Control insects.** Many diseases are spread by insects, including the infamous Dutch elm disease, which is spread by elm bark beetles.

✔ **Grow healthy plants.** Give your plants the right amount of light and water by putting them in a location they're well suited to. For example, when sun-loving plants are grown in shade, mildew and other diseases are more likely to take hold. When plants get exactly what they need, they stand up to disease much better.

✔ **Avoid excess nitrogen fertilizer.** Yes, you want to keep plants growing vigorously, but don't supercharge them with nitrogen. This nutrient makes plants grow quickly, but the rapid growth is weaker and susceptible to disease. Consider using slow-release or organic fertilizers to maintain healthy growth.

✔ **Use fresh soil mix.** Don't replant in used soil mix, especially if you're growing plants that may be susceptible to diseases. Compost the old, and refill with the new.

Choosing environmentally friendly fungicides

Most common garden diseases are caused by various types of fungi, and fungicides are substances used to control them. Fungicides either prevent infection or kill the fungi after infection. This distinction is important, because some fungicides must be applied before infection to prevent the disease, while others are applied to already-diseased plants. Read product labels carefully for proper application timing and technique.

Most garden diseases are caused by fungi, and most products sold to control plant diseases are fungicides. A few of these products may also help control diseases caused by bacteria, but bacterial diseases are harder to manage than fungal diseases. There are no products for controlling diseases caused by viruses. Fortunately, just a handful of bacteria and viruses pose problems for home gardeners but if they do, the best cure is often to destroy the plant so the disease doesn't spread.

The following are some of the more environmentally friendly options for managing plant diseases.

✔ **Plant extracts:** Sprays containing citric acid and mint oils control a wide range of disease-producing fungi and bacteria.

✔ **Potassium bicarbonate:** This close relative of common baking soda (sodium bicarbonate) controls powdery mildew and other diseases. Several commercial formulations are available. Homemade baking soda sprays are sometimes effective, too.

✔ ***Bacillus subtilis*** **and** ***B. pumilus:*** Fungicides containing these soil-dwelling bacteria are showing promise in controlling a number of plant diseases, including leaf blight, black mold, and powdery mildew.

✔ **Neem oil:** Especially effective in controlling black spot on roses, neem oil is extracted from a tropical tree. Flip back to the section "Botanical pesticides," earlier in this chapter, for more details.

✔ **Sulfur and copper:** These materials are strong fungicides, but they must be applied carefully to avoid harming plants and wildlife. Look for fungicidal soaps, which are easier and safer to apply than dusts.

✔ **Compost tea:** Some gardeners swear by compost tea — a liquid you brew by soaking finished compost in water, then straining off the solids. Spray it on the leaves to help prevent diseases. Compost tea is an excellent fertilizer, too.

Synthetic fungicides are some of the most toxic of all the stuff sold to spray on plants. Avoid them if at all possible. If you choose to use a synthetic fungicide, make sure you've identified the disease and that both the disease and the plant you're spraying are listed on the label. Enlist the help of local nursery personnel or a Cooperative Extension specialist for advice, and follow the label instructions exactly.

Detecting Common Plant Diseases

Plant diseases are often named by the symptoms they cause — black spot disease causes black spots; powdery mildew causes a powderlike coating on leaves. Some diseases affect just one plant part — leaves, for instance — while others can affect the whole plant. These clues can help you identify the culprit so you can take the proper control measures.

Many plant diseases are specific to their host plant. For example, the powdery mildew fungus that affects lilacs is a different species than the one that affects bee balm, so the disease can't spread from your lilacs to your bee balm.

Some plant problems that mimic the symptoms of fungal diseases may instead be caused by environmental factors. Learn to recognize these problems so you don't end up spraying fungicide in an attempt to "cure" your frost-damaged plant.

Here are some of the most common diseases encountered by home gardeners.

Diseases caused by a fungus among us

Fungi are the culprits in many plant diseases. Here are some tips on the prevention, identification, and — if possible — treatment of some common plant diseases that are caused by fungi:

- ✔ **Black spot:** Like its name suggests, this fungus causes black spots on leaves and stems (see Figure 18-7). Black spot is most troublesome on roses, but it can also attack various fruiting plants. On roses, the edges of the spots are fringed and the tissue around the spots often turns yellow. In bad infections, the plant may drop all its leaves. The disease is most common in warm, humid climates with frequent summer rain.

  The best advice for preventing black spot is to plant resistant varieties. The second-best advice is to keep your rose planters clean. Remove plant debris after pruning, clean up fallen leaves, and pick off leaves that have spots or turn yellow. Also, avoid overhead watering, or at least water early in the morning so that leaves can dry out quickly.

  The baking soda-summer oil combination that we mention under "Powdery mildew" later in this list also provides some control, as does neem oil. *Bacillus subtilis* has also been proven effective at controlling black spot.

- ✔ **Botrytis blight:** Also called gray mold, this fungal disease overwinters on plant debris and is common on strawberries as well as petunias and other flowers. The blight is most noticeable as gray fuzz forming on old flowers and fruit, turning them to moldy mush, but it can also discolor or spot foliage. It's most troublesome on older plant parts and in cool, humid weather. Make sure plants are properly spaced, and avoid overhead watering. Remove and destroy any infected plant parts.

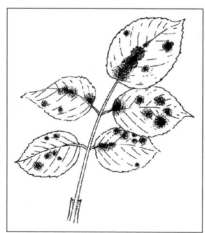

Figure 18-7:
Black spot
disease on
rose leaves.

✔ **Damping off:** A symptom caused by various fungi, damping off causes rot at the base of seedling stems, weakening them so they wilt and fall over. It's mostly a problem when you're starting seeds indoors. The best way to prevent the disease is to plant seeds in sterile potting soil and avoid overwatering. To prevent recurring problems after an infestation, clean and sanitize containers and fill them with fresh potting mix.

✔ **Powdery mildew:** This fungus coats leaves and flowers with a white powder (see Figure 18-8). Powdery mildew is most common when days are warm but nights are cool, and is particularly troublesome on zinnias, dahlias, begonias, roses, squash, melons, and peas. The disease is weather-dependent, so if you can keep plants growing vigorously through a disease cycle, they may recover just fine.

Control is difficult, but there are resistant varieties. Regular sprays of neem oil may help minimize infection. Rose growers have some success using a mixture of 1 tablespoon of summer oil and 1 or 2 teaspoons of baking soda in 1 gallon of water; you have to use the mix often to protect new foliage. A commercial version of this baking soda solution is available under the trade name Remedy. GreenCure is a similar fungicide based on potassium bicarbonate. Another rose growers' technique is to spray plants with anti-transpirants. These materials, sold with names like Cloud Cover or Wiltpruf, coat leaves with a thin, waxy film that seems to prevent the mildew from getting established — it's worth a try.

✔ **Root rots:** A number of soil-borne fungi cause similar symptoms: Plants suddenly wilt and die, whether or not the soil is moist. Vinca is notorious for checking out like this. The best way to prevent root rot is to use fresh soil mix, make sure your pots drain properly, and avoid overwatering — let the soil dry partially between irrigations. Otherwise, all you can do is remove the dead plants. Once root rot takes hold, most plants succumb.

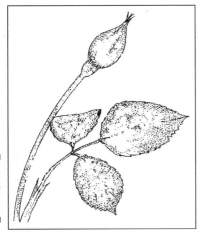

Figure 18-8: Powdery mildew.

✔ **Rust:** This fungal disease is easy to identify: It forms rust-colored pustules on the undersides of plant leaves. Gradually the upper sides of the leaves turn yellow and the whole plant begins to decline. Snapdragons, roses, and hollyhocks are common hosts. To avoid rust diseases, plant resistant varieties. Also, space plants for good air circulation, keep the garden clean, mulch around the base of plants, and avoid overhead watering. Destroy infected plants.

If a fungal disease is common on a plant in your region, choose resistant varieties or forego that plant in favor of something less susceptible. You don't want to spend all your free time applying preventative sprays or treating infections. And once a plant is infected, it's up to you to decide whether to keep treating a plant or to discard it. You may want to treat an expensive tree but toss a diseased petunia.

Abiotic diseases

The term *abiotic diseases* describes plant problems whose underlying cause is not an organism, such as a fungus, insect, or bacterium. Rule out abiotic diseases before treating plants with pesticides, which won't do any good. Instead, follow the treatment plans outlined below for the specific disease.

✔ **Salt burn:** Salt burn is caused by excess fertilizer salts building up in the soil. It's common where irrigation water is high in salts or when plants are overfertilized. Japanese maples are particularly sensitive to salt burn.

The symptoms are pretty easy to recognize — leaf edges become dry and crispy — much like what happens when a plant becomes too dry. (Excess salts affect a plant's ability to take up water, so the effect is similar to the soil drying out.) If the condition worsens, the whole leaf may dry up and drop, and tips of branches may die.

Prevent (and treat) salt burn by flooding the soil in containers with lots of water, letting it drain, and repeating up to a half-dozen times. Do this a few times during each growing season. Just be sure the container has good drainage. You may also want to reduce your fertilizing.

✔ **Sun burn:** If the foliage on plants looks bleached, your plants may be suffering from sunburn. Did you set them out without hardening them off (see Chapter 5) or move them from a shady spot to a sunnier one? Are the top leaves affected, while the ones underneath (and therefore shaded from direct sun) are fine? Most plants recover from sunburn: Just vow to harden plants off before exposing them to the elements.

✔ **Frost damage:** Chill or frost damage usually appears as blackened foliage, especially on the most exposed parts of the plant. The leaves underneath are more protected and may look fine. Some plants, such as basil, are very sensitive to cold and will be damaged even if temperatures don't drop below freezing. If a cold spell is predicted, protect tender plants by moving them to a sheltered spot or covering them with an old sheet. If plants are nipped by frost and just the top leaves are damaged, pick off the affected leaves and the plant may recover.

✔ **Wind and hail:** Plants with large, tender leaves are most likely to suffer damage from wind and hail. Leaves may have holes or be shredded. Unfortunately, damage like this, which creates open wounds, sometimes leads to fungal infections. You can't do much to treat damaged plants. If damage is limited to a few leaves, pick them off. However, the whole plant is usually affected, and all you can do is wait and hope the plant recovers on its own. If severe weather is predicted far enough in advance, move containers to a sheltered spot to wait out the storm.

Thwarting Animal Pests

Even containers located close to the house may be the targets of marauding animal pests. Wild animals will dine on container plants, especially if wild food is scarce. Sometimes domestic animals — yes, your beloved dogs and cats — can cause trouble. The first step is to identify who's causing the damage. Some critters roam around at night (raccoons, cats, and deer), while others are active during the day (woodchucks, rabbits, squirrels, and dogs). Some animals love to dig (squirrels, dogs, and raccoons), while others mostly nibble (deer, rabbits, and woodchucks).

Sometimes the only way to identify the culprit is to sit and watch, especially in the early morning and evening when many animals are most active.

Here are some common animal pest and suggested controls.

✔ **Birds:** Birds are usually beneficial in the garden, eating pest insects. But some birds dig up newly planted seeds and uproot young seedlings. Protect containers with chicken wire cages if birds are a problem — once plants are established, birds don't seem to bother them as much. One exception is fruit: Cover blueberry, strawberry, and other ripening fruits with netting to keep hungry birds at bay.

✔ **Cats/Dogs:** Cats and dogs may use a large container for their personal playground. Cats use the loose soil for a litter box. Dogs dig in containers, especially if you're using aromatic organic fertilizers, such as bone or blood meal or fish emulsion. To thwart cats and dogs, block their access to your containers with chicken wire or a gate, and use repellent sprays.

- **Deer:** As suburbs sprawl into rural areas and animals become accustomed to the presence of humans, more and more gardeners are experiencing deer damage. If they're hungry enough, deer will come right up to the house to graze on your container plantings. The best control is a tall (8-foot) fence. Barring that, you can try spraying repellents that have a taste or smell that's repulsive to deer. For containers close to your house, stick with taste-based repellents rather than the ones that smell like rotten eggs (you don't want to repel yourself!).

- **Mice/Voles:** These burrowing rodents are mostly a problem in containers planted with bulbs. Block their access with wire mesh cloth and place crushed eggshells or oyster shells around the bulbs in the container to deter their digging.

- **Rabbits:** Bugs Bunny nibbles on the tender leaves of a variety of container plants. The simplest solutions are to block rabbits' access with wire mesh cloth or a low fence or elevate your containers.

- **Raccoons/Woodchucks:** Raccoons digging in containers are usually looking for food. Prevent their activity by avoiding fertilizers with smells they like (for example, fish emulsion and bone meal). Woodchucks are only a problem on low containers and in raised beds. Fencing them out is the easiest control.

- **Squirrels/Chipmunks:** These are perhaps the most troublesome animals for container plants. Squirrels and chipmunks love to dig in the soft potting soil to find seeds or bury nuts. They uproot newly planted bulbs and plants. Once plants are established, these animals are usually less problematic. Unless you create a wire fortress, blocking their access is difficult. Try repellent sprays, and remember to reapply the sprays after a rain and as needed to protect new growth.

Avoid sprinkling ground hot pepper on or around plants to deter animal pests. If the animals get it in their eyes, it causes excruciating pain. Hot pepper wax is acceptable because it is less likely to rub off, so it acts only as a taste repellent.

Part V
Designing and Decorating

"And then it hit me — wouldn't Tyler's wagon make a wonderful container for a bunch of zinnias?"

In this part . . .

Whether you're a master artist or you're more of a paint-by-numbers kind of person — or somewhere in between — this part has something for you. Understanding a bit about color theory and how plant shapes and forms interrelate can mean the difference between a ho-hum container planting and one that stops traffic. In this part you find ideas and inspiration for designing your own planters, foolproof container combinations, and ideas for spreading your wings, container gardening-wise.

Chapter 19

Creating Eye-Catching Container Gardens

*E*ver notice how well some things go together? Like peanuts and baseball, apple pie and ice cream, stripes and plaids (just wanted to see if you're paying attention). This principle applies to the container plant world, too. A pot full of purple pansies may dazzle the eye, but watch what happens when you add a splash of fragrant white hyacinths.

Mixed plantings can range from modest to majestic. A hanging basket combining petunias and verbena is pretty. A stately urn with an evergreen Alberta spruce accented with tufts of two-toned, fragrant sweet William and surrounded by pale pink, trailing ivy geraniums can turn heads. A group of cobalt blue, oversized planters displaying a fruit-laden dwarf peach tree, a flowering mandevilla vine climbing a container-mounted trellis, and pots of blazing orange and magenta New Zealand impatiens can stop traffic.

Beyond introducing you to the wonderful world of mixed plantings, this chapter gives you a detailed road map to producing your own outstanding displays. We cover design ideas and acquaint you with the color wheel and how to effectively combine colors in a variety of ways. We look at other design basics, too — form, texture, and proportion — and show you how to incorporate these ideas into just about any decorative scheme. We also take a look at compatibility issues — between plant and planter, as well as among the plants within a container.

If you're new to gardening, the process of choosing plants can be overwhelming, so we also provide some container garden "recipes" in the chapter. Like their culinary cousins, these recipes can be tweaked to include favorite plants or to substitute plants that aren't available. For more information, refer to the chapters on individual plants (annuals, perennials, and so on).

Some of these mixed containers are provided courtesy of their developer, talented writer-designer Peggy Henry of Sonoma, California.

What Is Your Garden Style?

Choosing from among the countless plants and containers available can be daunting. Where do you begin? One way is to figure out your garden style. Consider the following questions:

- Are you drawn to blowsy cottage gardens where plants are crowded together in an informal, seemingly haphazard way? Or do you prefer tidy mounds of individual plants separated by decorative mulch?

- Do you like plants that grow this way and that, or ones that are symmetrical?

- What colors do your house, furniture, and wardrobe feature? Do you like brash and bold, subtle and earthy, or something in between?

- Do you like whimsical things — little decorations that bring a smile — or using things for an unintended purpose (like planting geraniums in an old red wagon or petunias in an old boot)? Or would you describe your gardening style as, well, more dignified (or predictable and boring, depending on your perspective)?

Answering these questions can help you get started on your mixed container plantings. If you're nervous about your design skills, start with something safe. Or throw caution to the wind — after all, you can always replant.

There are two ways to create mixed plantings. One is to use one plant per container and display multiple containers in a pleasing way. The other is to mix plants in a single container. Either way, by growing a variety of plants you're sure to have an eye-catching garden all season long.

Fun with Form, Texture, and Proportion

You can play with the basic elements of design — form, texture, and proportion — and use them to add great depth and interest to your mixed plantings.

Form refers to basic plant shape. Upright, spiky iris, for example, clearly has a different form than round-leafed, cascading ivy geranium. *Texture* is determined by the look and feel of a plant's foliage and flowers and runs the gamut from harsh and hard cactus to light and lacy ferns. Both form and texture are most effective when the elements balance each other without competing for attention.

No design discussion is complete without a word on *proportion* or scale. This comes into play in two ways: The plants should be in proportion to the container, and the container and plant together should fit the location. Making sure that everything fits together is usually a matter of balance. A tiny trailing plant in a huge tub or a wide shrub in a narrow box simply doesn't work — just as a big-leafed perennial looks odd on a small table. Disparity is okay, but just make sure that the leap isn't too great. If you're uncertain, test out potential combinations when you're shopping at the nursery. Put plants and pots together and see whether the combination appeals to you. Then imagine it on-site. Will it fill the space without overwhelming it? These tips on form, texture, and proportion apply to your mixed plantings:

- ✓ **Make sure the plant fits the pot.** A design usually looks best if small plants are used for small pots in small spaces, and larger plants are reserved for large pots in big spaces.

    Consider each plant's mature size in mind when matching plant to pot, especially when it comes to trees and shrubs. Although you can root prune plants to help control their size, it's best to use a container that can accommodate the plant's mature size. See Chapter 17 for information about root pruning.

- ✓ **Catch the eye and add balance with contrasting forms.** Combine spiky iris with rounded geraniums, for example — but be careful not to overdo it.

- ✓ **Create both a soft and pleasing feel with finely textured, lacy plants.** Lobelia, small ferns, and baby's breath are a few that fit the bill. Delicate-looking plants soften hard container edges and blend well with other textures.

- ✓ **For a bold focus, try big flowers (zinnia or dahlia) or large, dramatic leaves (hosta or elephant ear).** These are particularly effective in large pots alongside smaller plants.

- ✓ **Group similarly sized plants, but feel free to vary height.** Avoid extremes like tall shrubs and trees paired only with ground-hugging creepers.

- ✓ **Use balance and scale for container placement, too.** A huge barrel on a tiny patio looks as out of place as a tiny dish garden lost on an expansive deck.

A natural, gradual flow results from tall plants placed toward the back of the container with middle-sized plants in the center (or tall plants placed in the center surrounded by middle-sized plants), and low or trailing ones along the edges. In Chapter 7 you'll find annuals described as *thrillers* (tall, eye-catching plants), *fillers* (shrubby plants good for surrounding the taller center plant) and *spillers* (plants that tumble over the sides of the pot). Design-wise, choosing a mix of the three different types is a good place to start, whether you're planting all annuals or a combination of different types of annuals, perennials, and woody plants.

Color Is Key

Many people consider the number one design element to be color, which also happens to the most fun to play with. Look at a color wheel and examine how it works. *Primary* colors — red, blue, and yellow — are equidistant on the wheel, and all other colors result from mixing these three. Next, you find *complementary* colors opposite each other — yellow and violet or red and green, for example. Finally, you see *harmonious* colors blending gradually between two primary colors, like red to orange to yellow. *Shades* refer to lighter and darker variations of the same color. Now that you know the basics, here's a quick primer on what happens when you experiment with various combinations:

- ✔ For bold, vibrant looks, choose complementary colors (on opposite sides of the color wheel), such as yellow and violet.

- ✔ For more subtle combinations, choose harmonious blends of related colors like blue, violet, and purple.

- ✔ Create a soothing style with variations or shades of the same color — pale pink to rose-red, for example.

- ✔ Add plenty of pizzazz with energizing hot colors using red, orange, or yellow.

- ✔ Cool things down with refreshing blues, greens, and violets.

- ✔ Don't forget white. It adds welcome dimension, lightens dark areas, and works with all other colors.

- ✔ Consider foliage, too. In addition to every shade of green imaginable, leaf colors include silvery-gray, yellow, chartreuse, deep maroon, brilliant red, and variegated (multi-toned).

Remember that both the plants and the container can contribute to the color scheme. A shiny, bright blue ceramic pot will set a much different tone than a matte, terra-cotta one.

 Classic color schemes are one thing, but personal taste is your ultimate authority. The bottom line: Pick colors that you like. If you like them, they can't be wrong, whether you're going for a rainbow effect, planting orange marigolds and pink petunias, or arranging a simple, single-color display.

Compatibility Is Everything

Like a good marriage, a good container planting consists of compatible, complementary parts: in this case, the plants and the container. For the nuts and bolts of choosing containers, refer to Chapter 3. Here, we focus on aesthetics. Keep the following in mind when choosing your container:

- ✔ **Material:** Wood, terra cotta, ceramic, clay, and metal are popular choices. For that special, whimsical look, consider recycling unusual containers, including those that have been used for other things. With drainage provided, a hollowed-out tree stump, a galvanized tub, a wheelbarrow, a milk can, or even an old pair of work boots can host a small collection of plants.

- ✔ **Size:** Size is key, especially for plants that last longer than a single season and eventually reach substantial size. Be sure that the container can accommodate all the plants when their root systems are fully developed. However, don't rule out small containers: They're ideal for compact plants but need frequent watering.

- ✔ **Compatibility:** If every pot in a large grouping has a different size, shape, and color, the result might be pleasantly eclectic, but it's more likely to look haphazard. One way to provide a sense of cohesion is to keep to a single material. For example, combine terra-cotta pots in a variety of shapes and sizes, from shallow bowls to tall pots, for a classic and eye-catching display. Or, to put the focus squarely on the plants, use a row of identical pots (see Figure 19-1).

Figure 19-1:
A set of simple pots places the emphasis on the plants.

If you're planting more than one type of plant in a container, make sure the plants have similar requirements for sun/shade and soil moisture. Rosemary and thyme are good companions (both like full sun and well-drained soils); rosemary and coleus are not so good together. (Unlike rosemary, coleus likes shade and moist soil.)

Five Designs for Sunny Personalities

Place these containers on a sunny deck, porch, or front stoop and prepare to be wowed. And if you're looking for ideas for edibles in containers, you've come to the right place. These plants will grow quickly and will need regular fertilizing to look their best. Keep in mind that the soil can dry out quickly in hot, sunny weather, especially once the plants start to fill out, so you'll want to check plants daily.

Early spring bouquet

Celebrate the season with blooming bulbs and attractive annuals in this colorful little mix perfect for an outdoor table or front doorstep. The design features a repeating theme from three types of narcissus and accents from a rainbow of annuals and perennials. As shown in Figure 19-2, anchoring the bowl in the center are stunning, tall, two-toned daffodils, set off by bright yellow mini-daffodils; a third type of bulb — fragrant paper-white narcissus — adds height and continuity. Effortless violas offer compact color, and the cheery and reliable primroses provide contrasting bright colors and richly textured leaves.

- **Container:** Try a clay bowl or dish at least 18 inches across and 9 to12 inches deep. Classic terra cotta always looks good, but you may want a glazed ceramic bowl to match other decor or to add color.

- **Plants:** Five paper-white narcissus, six daffodils, six miniature daffodils, six yellow or blue violas, and six yellow or blue primroses.

- **How to plant:** Buy and plant the daffodils in fall, as described in Chapter 9. Then, when the bulbs pop up in spring, buy six-packs of violas and primroses. Space individual seedlings alternately around the rim. *Note:* If you miss the early bulb planting in fall, you can cheat and wait to find sprouted and budded bulbs for sale and plant everything all at once later in spring.

- **Special tips:** The daffodils may need a bit of help to keep them from flopping over. Use slender stakes to tie them as soon as you detect trouble. Feed plants with liquid fertilizer monthly throughout the blooming season.

Figure 19-2:
Early spring
bouquet.

Next on the menu: Herbs and veggies

You can go straight from patio to kitchen with savory vegetables and herbs just waiting to prove their worth in favorite recipes. Showing that tomatoes do well even in captivity, a caged patio variety can offer you scores of fruit (see Figure 19-3). Add to the bounty with plenty of sweet, green (or red or yellow) bell peppers. Blending beautifully with tomatoes, sweet basil adds lush and tasty leaves that are a joy to harvest. Rounding out the menu are an attractive little clump of garlic chives and the versatile, super-quick, super-pungent cilantro.

- **Container:** Go grand here, if you can, to get the most from your mini-veggie garden. Terra-cotta pots 18 inches or more in diameter can give you good space for all the edibles. And, if you choose a pot with straight rather than tapered sides, your plants' roots will have even more room. As always, terra cotta is easy to find and relatively inexpensive, and it displays well just about anywhere.

- **Plants:** One Patio tomato, one green bell pepper, one sweet basil, one garlic chives, and one cilantro.

✔ **How to plant:** Start with the tomato toward the back, planting it a bit deep by burying a few sets of leaves. Tie the tomato stem to a stake to support it. Then plant the pepper next to the tomato, and drop the basil in the center of the pot. On one side of the basil along the front, plant the chives, and on the other side, add the cilantro. Leave a few inches between all the plants.

✔ **Special tips:** Save on labor later on by mixing timed-release fertilizer granules in with your potting soil to give plants a good start. A key to success with a container of edibles is early harvest. Take ripe fruit as soon as you can, and regularly clip foliage on the basil, chives, and cilantro to keep plants under control and to ensure continuous fresh foliage.

Figure 19-3:
Next on the menu: Herbs and veggies.

Scented sensations

The wonderful fragrances that drift on the breeze add the final exclamation point in this colorful, highly textured ceramic bowl. As shown in Figure 19-4, Chocolate cosmos heads the list of unusual flowers displayed here, and its mahogany blossoms really, truly smell like chocolate. Scented geraniums spill from the bowl with delicate, dark pink flowers and richly textured foliage that releases a fruity fragrance. Dianthus is the ideal filler with masses of spicy, two-toned flowers. A handful of dazzling white nicotianas, standing tall in the background, complete the picture. Reserve a spot for this display near your outdoor seating area so that you can enjoy the subtle scents and captivating colors.

Figure 19-4:
Scented
sensations.

✔ **Container:** You have a range of colors to choose from when you select a heavy-duty ceramic bowl with a glazed finish. This one — a full 18 inches across — is big enough for a generous collection of plants. Inspect the inside of the pot because you may need to punch out or drill a drainage hole before you plant.

✔ **Plants:** One chocolate cosmos, one scented geranium, two dianthus, and three nicotianas.

✔ **How to plant:** Starting in the back, center the nicotianas along the rim. Next, plant the chocolate cosmos in the middle of the bowl, and add a dianthus on either side. Plant the scented geranium along the front rim, giving it plenty of room to spread.

✔ **Special tips:** Don't worry if it seems like the plants don't quite fill up the bowl — give them time. In fact, plan to trim back wayward stems on the geranium and snip off spent stems on the dianthus. Enjoy the scented blossoms and leaves in the house by snipping stems and leaves at their summer peak. This also helps keep plants within your container's boundaries. All the plants except the nicotiana are perennial in mild-winter climates; in cold regions the plants will need winter protection (described in Chapter 10).

Nature's bounty

This tub offers a profusion of sensory delights — including tasty fruits. The star of the show — a dwarf peach — combines with luscious strawberries spilling over the rim (see Figure 19-5). Golden hues of tall marigolds and trailing gazanias contrast nicely with masses of rich purple petunias. The dwarf tree performs well for years in the generous tub, offering the double bonus of pink spring blossoms and summer fruit. The strawberries add wonderful texture and an interesting cascading form, and the annuals fill the gaps with bright, bold color.

Figure 19-5:
Nature's
bounty.

 ✔ **Container:** A sturdy, oak half-barrel is ideal for long-term enjoyment of this collection. Be sure to drill several drainage holes. The barrel lasts longer if you coat the interior with nontoxic preservative. If the staves start to slide, use nails to hold them in place.

 ✔ **Plants:** One dwarf peach tree, three strawberry plants, three marigolds, two petunias, and two gazanias.

 ✔ **How to plant:** First, plant the tree in the center, just slightly higher than the surrounding soil level. Then add the marigolds along the back, dropping the petunias next to them toward the front. Alternate strawberries and gazanias along the front rim of the barrel where they can cascade over the rim.

✔ **Special tips:** As the tree bears fruit over the years, the peaches may become too heavy for the small branches (look forward to this problem!), so either remove part of the crop or support the branches with small stakes. The strawberry plants are perennial; however, fruit production drops after two or three years; plan to replace them with fresh plants every few years. Cut off faded blooms (deadhead) from the petunias, marigolds, and gazanias to encourage more flowers; these annuals will need to be replaced each spring. (The peach tree and strawberries will need protection in cold-winter climates; refer to Chapter 10 for overwintering tips.)

Entryway elegance

Greet your visitors in style with this glorious combination of flowers in a classic container perfect for a sunny front porch (see Figure 19-6). You can enjoy years of midsummer color from the dwarf crape myrtle shrub. Ever-reliable petunias match the deep pink of the crape myrtle. Variegated ivy cascades with wonderful grace. Daisies add bright cheer, and the contrasting deep tones of spilling lobelia complete the collection. You can keep this floral display going season after season by simply replacing the annuals as needed with fresh plants.

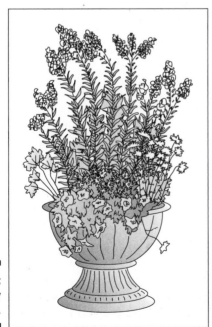

Figure 19-6:
Entryway
elegance.

✔ **Container:** Sometimes the container plays as big a role in the show as the flowers — that's the case here with an impressive cement urn. You can discover all kinds of styles, colors, and sizes in nurseries and garden centers, and although they may be more costly than traditional clay pots, urns return dividends as garden accents.

✔ **Plants:** One dwarf crape myrtle, two English ivies, one marguerite daisy, five petunias, and four lobelias.

✔ **How to plant:** Start with the dwarf crape myrtle toward the center of the urn, and surround this with the petunias. Drop the ivies along the front rim and plant the daisy in the center. Fill in the gaps along the rim with lobelias.

✔ **Special tips:** Urns that overflow with flowers look best, so make sure that all the annuals fill in evenly. Frequent applications of liquid fertilizer certainly help. Keep faded flowers groomed, and pinch back the petunias if they get leggy.

Two Designs for Shady Characters

A common lament is that nothing will grow under trees. That's not entirely true, though. It's true that tree roots growing near the soil surface can out-compete smaller plants for water and nutrients, and a shady spot does limit the selection of plants. Instead of struggling to grow shade-loving plants in the ground, why not set a few containers of plants under the tree?

Fantastic foliage

If you think green when you think leaves, this container will be a treat. These plants have striking foliage in a range of colors and patterns to rival the most eye-catching flowers (check out Figure 19-7). The combination is a classic mix of central thriller, surrounded by fillers and spillers (see the earlier section "Fun with Form, Texture, and Proportion" for more on this concept).

✔ **Container:** A deep, gently curving bowl complements this combination of spiky, shrubby, and trailing plants. Choose a bowl that's at least 24 inches in diameter for best results.

✔ **Plants:** One phormium, two Persian shield plants, two coleus plants, and four licorice plants.

✔ **How to plant:** Start by planting the phormium in the center. Place the Persian shields on opposite sides of the phormium. Place the coleus plants on the remaining sides. Then plant the licorice plants around the perimeter.

✔ **Special tips:** Pinch the growing tips of coleus and Persian shield plants to keep them shrubby. Keep the soil moist but not saturated — how much water the plants need depends on the porosity and size of the container as well as wind, air temperature, and amount of shade.

Figure 19-7:
Fantastic
foliage.

Shade-lover's delight

Dappled light, refreshing shade, and cool breezes paint the backdrop for
this winning combination featuring a flower-filled, rustic planter box. And
with scenery defined by lush plants blooming in cool, regal colors, you have
a garden retreat that's hard to resist. A combination of trailing and upright
fuchsias with striking, two-toned flowers anchors the box with long-lasting
color (see Figure 19-8). Lacy, light green fronds of maidenhair fern add balance and texture, while the impatiens provide almost constant color. The
color combination of lavender, purple, lilac, rose, and pink shades harmo-
nizes well. A classic touch of white brings life and contrast to the collection.

- **Container:** We suggest a container made of old lumber. You may find
  rustic, recycled garden containers ready-made at nurseries and garden
  centers. Or, with a hammer and a few nails, you can put one together
  yourself using planks or boards. Stick to redwood or cedar for the
  longest-lasting results. Ours is 4 feet long, 11 inches deep, and 10 inches
  wide.

- **Plants:** Three upright fuchsias, one trailing fuchsia, two maidenhair
  ferns, and nine impatiens in mixed colors.

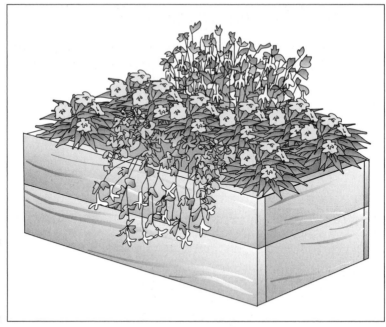

Figure 19-8:
Shade-
lover's
delight.

✔ **How to plant:** Set the tall fuchsias along the back, leaving a few inches in between plants and at the corners. Next, plant the trailing fuchsia in the center along the front rim. Now plant the two ferns on either side of the trailing fuchsia. Fill in the remaining spaces with the impatiens, varying the colors as you go.

✔ **Special tips:** It's important to keep your planter from staying overly wet, even though the shade-lovers like plenty of water. Allow the bottom to dry by raising the box a couple of inches; set it on bricks or planks. Because you need to water often, make sure you maintain a regular fertilizing schedule.

Two Designs You Can Start from Seed

If you want instant results, start your container gardens with plants. But if you can be patient, consider starting some of your plants from seed. Starting seeds is one of the most rewarding ways to garden. Plus, you'll find a much larger selection of varieties in seed form than as plants. For example, you might find a dozen zinnia varieties on the seed rack, but just a handful as seedlings in the nursery.

Annual flowers from seed

You'll have fun growing these flowers from seed (see Figure 19-9). These seeds germinate in just a few days and the plants grow quickly.

Figure 19-9:
Annual
flowers
from seed.

- **Plants:** Seeds for dwarf sunflowers, low-growing zinnias, purple basil, and nasturtium.

- **Container:** A simple 22- to 24-inch terra-cotta pot lets these beautiful plants be the focus of the display.

- **How to plant:** Sow 10 to 15 seeds of each type of plant. Plant the sunflowers in the center, surrounded by the zinnias and the basil. Plant the nasturtium seeds around the perimeter of the pot so the plants can trail over the sides. Sow sunflower and nasturtium seeds about an inch deep; zinnias, ½ inch deep; and basil, ¼ inch deep. Once the seeds sprout, thin seedlings, leaving the strongest four to six plants of each type. (If you let all the seedlings grow, the resulting crowded plants will be small and weak.)

- **Special tips:** Pinch back the growing tips of the zinnias and basil seedlings to encourage bushiness. (Don't pinch the sunflower or nasturtium seedlings.) Feel free to harvest an occasional sprig of aromatic basil for pasta sauces or peppery nasturtium leaves and flowers for salads.

Herbs in fabric pots

Freshly harvested herbs are essential in some culinary creations and are always a welcome addition to almost any homemade dish. Many herbs grow easily from seed, including basil, chives, dill, fennel, lemon balm, marjoram, parsley, savory, and thyme. In the center of the book you can find a photo of herbs in fabric pots.

- **Container:** Containers made from fabric — usually, made from a synthetic material resembling landscape fabric — are ideal for small plants like herbs. Many of the pots even have carrying handles, making them some of the most portable of all your container choices.

- **Plants:** Seeds for basil, chives, dill, and marjoram.

- **How to plant:** Sow seeds in moist soil. Sow basil, chive, and dill seed about ¼ inch deep; barely cover marjoram seed with soil. Once the seeds sprout, thin seedlings, leaving the strongest three plants of each type of herb. (If you let all the seedlings grow, the crowded plants will be small and weak.)

- **Special tips:** Keep the soil moist but not wet. Fertilize sparingly — too much fertilizer leads to weak growth with less flavor. Cut sprigs or harvest individual leaves as you need them. Herbs are at their peak just before they begin to flower; if you plan to grow extra for freezing or drying, wait until the plants are at their peak before harvesting.

Three Designs for Hanging Baskets

There's nothing at all wrong with displaying one glorious fuchsia or begonia in a hanging basket — in fact, the result can be stunning, especially when you display several identical baskets along a porch front. However, as with other containers, you can get some really special effects if you combine a variety of plants in the same basket.

The principles for combining plants in a hanging basket are similar to those for designing any mixed planting and are described earlier in this chapter. The difference is that with hanging baskets, size and weight are much more important. The larger and heavier the baskets, the sturdier the hanging chains and hooks must be (and the ceiling or siding that's supporting them).

Trailing plants are usually the showstoppers of any hanging basket combination. Baskets can beautifully display trailers of all kinds — from dazzling annuals to classic ivy to luscious strawberries. Trailers can cascade way beyond the basket (ground ivy, for example) or simply spill softly over the rim with lots of color (lobelia).

Although we describe these plant combinations for hanging baskets, they're ideal for other types of containers, too. Just be prepared for a cascade of vines that may trail onto the ground.

The following designs all use a galvanized wire basket that you can plant both from the top and through the sides. Openings allow you to insert plants just about anywhere to achieve a full, finished look. Use a 20-inch-diameter or larger basket for the best display. See Chapter 5 for step-by-step instructions on planting moss-lined hanging baskets.

Suspended animation

Full foliage and flowers take over here, completely hiding the moss-lined basket as this collection of annuals, perennials, and vines cascades from the sides and top (see Figure 19-10). Variegated ground ivy spills like a living waterfall with its two-toned leaves and exceptionally long stems. Clusters of bright pansies and deep violet lobelias fill the sides and top, a handful of ivy geraniums adds rich pink tones, and ever-reliable sweet alyssum weaves through with a fragrant white touch. The result is a blending of colors and textures — plants naturally growing together — blurring the lines that separate them.

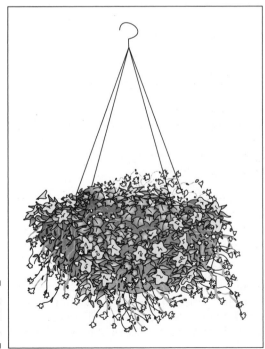

Figure 19-10:
Suspended
animation.

✔ **Plants:** Three variegated ground ivies, six lobelias, nine pansies, three ivy geraniums, and six sweet alyssums.

✔ **How to plant:** Plant the ground ivies along the basket rim. Next, gently plant through the sides, using the six lobelias and six of the pansies. This will allow space for the ground ivies to cascade. Pull plants through the sides and tuck extra moss around the roots so they're secure. Finish by adding ivy geraniums, the remaining pansies, and the sweet alyssum in the top.

✔ **Special tips:** Pick off the spent flowers on the geranium and pansy plants. If ivy stems get too long, cut them back. After the first flush of flowers passes on the lobelias and sweet alyssums, use scissors to shear off the spent flowers to encourage rebloom.

Made for the shade

This combination of flowers in rich colors and textures is sure to light up a shady spot on your deck or patio — lavenders, purples, blues, and pinks are set off by bright white. Featured are the arching stems and abundant fuchsia flowers, followed by big, bold begonias. Impatiens beautifully fill the gaps, and ivy winds its way throughout, lending texture and style (as shown in Figure 19-11).

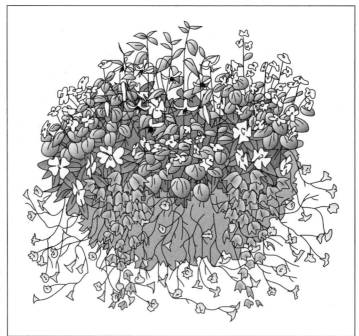

Figure 19-11:
Made for
the shade.

- **Plants:** One Cascade fuchsia, three white Nonstop begonias, nine mixed-color impatiens, twelve Cascade Mix lobelias, and three variegated English ivies.

- **How to plant:** Plant the three English ivies along the basket rim. Next, gently plant six of the lobelias and six of the impatiens through the sides of the basket, tucking extra moss around the roots to keep them in place. Center the fuchsia in the top, then evenly space the three begonias around it. Finally, fill in the rest of the top with the remaining impatiens and lobelias.

- **Special tips:** Begonia stems are fragile so be careful at planting time and during maintenance. Fortunately, if you break a stem the plants will quickly regrow. When watering, avoid wetting the foliage of the fuchsia and begonias to minimize disease problems, and pick off the spent flowers. Use scissors to cut back the impatiens and lobelia after flowering; they'll quickly regrow and produce more flowers.

Color connection

The goal for this wire basket is a mad mix of multicolored flowers. Trailing lantana sets the stage with arching stems and spectacular flower clusters in yellow, pink, peach, and orange. Another awesome trailer, ivy geranium, adds arresting red as it weaves through marigolds and lavender and purple petunias. Completing the picture, lobelias in shades from white to deep blue grow through the sides, as shown in Figure 19-12.

- **Plants:** One Confetti trailing lantana, two Mini Cascade ivy geraniums, six mixed-color marigolds, twelve Cascade Mix lobelias, three Cascade Purple petunias, three Cascade Lavender petunias.

- **How to plant:** Plant the two ivy geraniums on opposite sides of the basket rim. Next, arrange the six petunias around the sides, alternating colors. Then fill in the sides with six of the lobelias. Center the lantana on the top and surround it with evenly spaced marigolds. Finish off the top with the rest of the lobelias.

- **Special tips:** These large plants require consistently moist (but not soggy) soil. Prune back long stems to encourage plants to stay bushy. Deadhead the lantana, geraniums, petunias, and marigolds by picking off the spent flowers. Use scissors to cut back the lobelias.

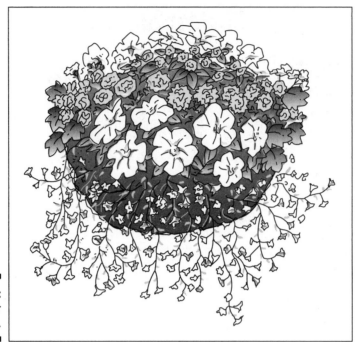

Figure 19-12:
Color
connection.

Chapter 20

Cultivating Specialty Plants in Containers

In This Chapter

▶ Choosing an easy route: Cactuses and succulents

▶ Looking for a challenge? Try bonsai

▶ Getting the lowdown on holiday and gift plants

▶ Discovering the magic of water gardening

Some plant groups are so interesting and unique they merit a section all their own. In this chapter, we finish off the design discussion with a look at some special types of plants that are perfect for container gardens, including some of the easiest and some of the most challenging.

Taking it Easy with Cactuses and Succulents

Cactuses and succulents offer advantages to gardeners who may not have all the time in the world. They usually require far less maintenance than, say, a pot of pansies. For example:

✔ Most cactuses and succulents grow slowly, and that means less time repotting plants that outgrow their containers. Of course, slow growth may also mean waiting a few years (how about 30?) before you're bowled over by the extraordinary blooms some cactuses produce.

✔ For gardeners north of zone 9, containers offer the chance to move tender varieties indoors when the temperature starts to drop.

Seeing what makes succulents special

A *succulent* is a plant that has adapted to arid conditions by creating water storage units in leaves, stems, and roots. Succulents are native to many different environments:

- ✔ Deserts that may suffer slightly cool temperatures at night (in the range of 50–60 degrees Fahrenheit) and high deserts that may get snow or frost
- ✔ Seaside areas where water-holding capacity has more to do with protection from high salinity than the dryness of the surroundings
- ✔ Dry, cold mountainside crevices
- ✔ Many temperate (neither very hot nor very cold) areas

Most succulents have evolved to store water during the rainy season and then use it during the dry season. Some succulents rely on summer rains, but for many, the wet season arrives in winter, and that's when growth occurs. The rest of the year, the plants hunker down and wait, lying dormant. As you may know from visits or pictures, the Southwest U.S. desert in spring is a sight to behold: Winter rains come, and suddenly plants everywhere are adorned in bright bursts of flowers.

Cactuses are one type of succulent and are best known for their sharp spines. These spines make them interesting to look at but challenging to handle. Keep cactuses away from footpaths, doorways, and anywhere else the spines could harm passersby. In this chapter when we refer to succulents we're including cactuses as well, unless we say otherwise.

Growing cactuses and succulents in containers

The basic rules for growing most succulents in containers are pretty simple. Just keep the following two tips in mind:

- ✔ **Shade versus sun:** Provide as much light as possible during the summer — although full sun in really warm places, including their desert homelands, can be too hot for many succulents in the confines of a container. Some types prefer part shade — see the list at the end of this chapter.
- ✔ **Shelter from the cold:** Protect succulents from cold weather in the winter. Move them indoors to a sunny window where temperatures remain above 40 degrees Fahrenheit.

If you have large, heavy containers, plan to put them on wheels — or start pumping iron.

Choosing containers

Succulents lend themselves to terra-cotta pots — both aesthetically and because terra-cotta is porous, which keeps roots from sitting in water. Feel free to use a shallow container (just 4 to 6 inches deep) if it looks best with your plants — succulent roots don't go very deep — but be sure it has drainage holes. For a plant with a rounded shape, choose a container that's 2 inches wider than the plant. For an upright plant, choose a pot that's half the diameter of the plant's height.

Selecting soil mix

Quick drainage is the most important quality of a soil mix designed for succulents. The standard mix consists of one-half organic matter (peat moss, leaf mold, or something like that) and one-half grit (crushed rock or sand). You can find many cactus and succulent mixes already bagged.

Planting

Design your succulent containers following the same principles that you apply for other plants: Combine something tall and spiky, something mounded, and something trailing. A well-balanced landscape can be accomplished by using one large container for several plants. Or, put each plant in its own container and then group the pots — this mix-and-match method gives you the freedom to rearrange on a whim.

When planting cactuses, care is the key word — for yourself and the plant. Wear thick gloves and/or wrap the cactus in a sleeve of thickly layered paper and use the ends as a handle (see Figure 20-1). (If you get stuck with a few spines, use a piece of cellophane tape to remove them.)

Most cactuses and many other succulents have shallow roots, so don't plant too deeply. Burying part of the stem invites rot to set in. Make sure that the soil level in the pot is no higher than the level of the soil in the plant's nursery container.

Maintenance

First of all, it's a myth that cactuses and succulents are maintenance-free. You do need to water them and feed them.

Water regularly during the growing season — remember that this can be winter for some species. The principles are the same as with other container plants (see Chapter 15); however, allow the soil to dry out more completely between waterings. During their dormant season and in cool temperatures (around 50 degrees Fahrenheit), most cactuses and succulents can go without water for weeks at a time. Don't become complacent and forget that the poor things are even alive. Resume regular watering just before the growing season begins.

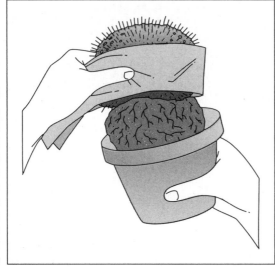

Figure 20-1:
To avoid getting pricked, use a rolled-up cloth to remove a cactus from its container.

When plants are in a growing stage, fertilize about once a month — or every other time you water, if you water every two weeks. Succulents need all the nutrients that other plants do — nitrogen, phosphorus, and potassium — plus trace elements. You can use just about any complete liquid fertilizer or a special fertilizer designed for cactuses and succulents, or try a tomato fertilizer at half-strength. For more on fertilizing, check out Chapter 16.

Selecting cactuses and succulents

Mail-order sources (see the appendix) offer tantalizing pictures and descriptions of what's available. As with any plant purchase, read carefully and plan ahead. If you live in a cold-winter area, remember to keep in mind what happens to those beauties in January. Buying cactuses and succulents locally is always possible too — check out nearby nurseries to get a feel for what different plants look like and which ones are adapted to your climate. As you shop, look for plants that aren't wrinkled or shrunken at the base near the soil. Avoid cactuses with broken spines.

Because succulents come from many different parts of the world with different altitudes, temperature ranges, and rainfall patterns, it's impossible to make blanket statements about which plants to choose and how to care for them. Pay attention to the cultural information for each species, and then group the plants in containers accordingly.

Here are just a few of the hundreds of cactuses and succulents to look for and try in containers. The plants are listed alphabetically by common name where applicable, with the botanical name given (in italics) to avoid possible confusion. Most are hardy outdoors in zones 9 and 10; in other climates, plan to move the pots indoors for winter. Remember that hardiness zones, when listed, are for plants growing in the ground, and container plants aren't that tolerant of cold.

Cactuses for containers

You may enjoy growing any of these cactuses:

- ✔ *Acanthocalycium glaucum:* Moderate-growing, small grayish mound with brown to black spines has showy yellow or orange flowers. Give it part shade in really hot areas; water in spring and summer.

- ✔ **Beehive cactus *(Coryphantha missouriensis):*** Native to Canada and the United States, this is a true cold-hardy species, able to grow as far north as zone 3. Only 3 inches tall, the beehive forms clusters with gray spines. Flowers are fragrant and green, followed by red fruit in summer. During the dormant season, beehive cactus may actually shrink so much that it retreats underground. *C. vivipara* is a cold-hardy relative with magenta flowers.

- ✔ **Bishop's cap or bishop's miter *(Astrophytum myriostigma):*** Short and rotund, its white speckles (rudimentary spines) give the plant a silvery look. Expect it to grow to the size of a large grapefruit by ten years of age.

- ✔ **Golden barrel cactus *(Echinocactus grusonii):*** A globe with golden-yellow spines, it grows slowly to 6 inches, sometimes larger. Don't wait around for flowers — they appear only after 30 or 40 years. Provide full sun.

- ✔ **Hedgehog cactus *(Echinocereus viridiflorus):*** Stems form clusters to 6 inches. Flowers are fragrant and lime-green. *E. triglochiodiatus,* a hardier species (to zone 5), has stem clusters to 1 foot, 1-inch pale gray spines, and deep pink flowers.

- ✔ **Old-man-of-the-mountains *(Borzicactus celsianus,* also listed as *Oreocereus celsianus):*** White hairs create a shaggy beard look. The plant forms a medium-size column eventually reaching a foot tall, with magenta flowers popping out here and there.

- ✔ **Orchid cactus *(Epiphyllum):*** An excellent hanging basket plant, orchid cactus resembles a wad of stems, but in bloom can be spectacular — fragrant flowers in neon colors. Provide part to full shade.

- ✔ *Parodia:* Globular plants to 1 foot tall grow by forming offsets. Flowers look like daisies. Don't water in winter. Try *P.magnifica (P. notocactus),* with white-spined ribs.

- ✔ **Pincushion cactus** *(Mammillaria bombycina):* Short cylinders up to a foot tall produce offsets covered in soft, white down and yellow spines. Pink flowers are big — at least 3 inches wide.

- ✔ **Prickly pear or cholla** *(Opuntia):* Prickly pear has flattened, oval stems, and cholla has cylindrical stems. Some are spinier than others. They tolerate more rainfall than other cactuses. Try *O. compressa, O. fragilis,* or *O. vivipara.*

- ✔ **Sea urchin** *(Echinopsis):* This is a big group of globular or columnar, medium-to-fast-growing plants. Expect a wide choice of flower colors.

Succulents for containers

These are our favorite succulents. By the way, if you're looking for the aloe plant, it's covered in Chapter 14.

- ✔ **Cub's paws** *(Cotyledon ladisminthensis):* This is a shrubby, spreading plant, about a foot high. Deciduous green leaves are toothed at the top and have a reddish margin. Provide part shade.

- ✔ *Crassula pubescens:* Tuck this small, creeping ground cover into a container. Give it plenty of sun to bring out the leaves' bright red tones.

- ✔ *Echeveria:* Choose from several species of rosette-forming plants with colorful foliage.

- ✔ **Houseleeks or hens and chicks** *(Sempervivum):* These rosette-forming plants are probably the best-known succulents. They're available with leaves in shades of green and red — cobweb-looking hairs circle some of the leaves. Plants spread by offsets; if one breaks off, tuck it into another pot, and it will root easily.

- ✔ **Jade plant** *(Crassula):* In mild climates, this shiny-leafed favorite can grow up to 6 feet tall. It produces little pink flowers in midwinter.

- ✔ *Jovibarba heuffelii:* Tuck these rosettes into fast-draining pots. Choose from many varieties with leaves of different colors — bronze, chocolate, and violet. Hardy to zone 6.

- ✔ *Lewisia rediviva:* Native to the Rocky Mountains (and hardy to zone 4), this is a colorfully blooming plant that demands very fast drainage. *L. tweedyi,* native to the Cascade Mountains, is hardy to zone 5.

- ✔ **Queen Victoria century plant** *(Agave victoria-reginae):* Spiky, short, green leaves edged in white form a dramatic 1-foot rosette. The plant is slow growing, and 13-foot(!) flower stalks take 30 years to bloom — not a century. *A. utahensis* is a cold-hardy relative.

- ✔ **Sedum** *(Sedum):* Many species are among the more versatile container plants. Check on their hardiness — certain varieties can grow in climates as cold as zone 3. Some form very showy flower heads; a popular choice is *S. spectabile* Autumn Joy.

A hanging succulent design: Textured treasures

Splendid textures, outstanding shapes, and wonderful colors give this collection of succulents special status. Succulents are easy plants to grow in hanging baskets made of wire, filling gaps and spaces ideally. Here the rosettes of hen and chicks play off the smooth texture of the jade plant. Plus, you have the interesting colors of various upright and trailing sedums, as shown in Figure 20-2.

Figure 20-2:
Textured
treasures.

> ✔ **Container:** Use a galvanized wire basket that you can plant both from the top and through the sides. Openings allow you to insert plants just about anywhere to achieve a full, finished look. Use a 20-inch-diameter or larger basket for the best display. See Chapter 5 for step-by-step instructions on planting moss-lined hanging baskets.

> ✔ **Plants:** One jade plant, one hen-and-chicks plant, one *Sedum spectabile* (upright sedum), three donkey tails, one *Sedum cauticolum,* six Cape Blanco sedums, six Ruby Glow sedums, and six Pork and Beans sedums.

✔ **How to plant:** Plant the six Ruby Glow sedums around the basket rim. Next, gently plant through the sides, using the six Pork and Beans sedums, the six Cape Blanco sedums, and the hens and chicks plant. Pull plants through the sides and tuck extra moss around the roots so they're secure. Finish by planting the remaining plants in the top.

✔ **Special tips:** Use a special soil mix for these plants, and don't overwater them. Take care handling delicate trailers such as the donkey tails. Simply tuck extra stems in bare spots, holding plants through the wire with extra moss.

Branching Out with Bonsai

On the opposite end of the spectrum from growing easy-care succulents, bonsai requires a commitment to careful watering, pruning, training, feeding, and more. In a nutshell, *bonsai* is the horticultural art of growing dwarf trees in small containers. The idea is to evoke nature in miniature — an ancient twisted pine on a rocky precipice or a forest of lacy maples with a mossy carpet underneath. Fine art is involved in selecting the plants and containers, and training and displaying the plants.

Bonsai is an engrossing hobby with dedicated followers all over the world. The pastime also revolves around an entire realm of special equipment and tools: low, flat clay pots; special shears; special wire; and so on.

You can buy bonsai plants already trained. Figure 20-3 shows a typical bonsai plant. Before taking one home, make sure you have full directions on watering, feeding, pruning, and other care. Friendly advice: Never give someone else a bonsai plant as a gift unless you know that he or she wants to take on the responsibility that goes with it.

If you want to get a taste of what bonsai is about — to just put a toe in the water — you can experiment with small plants in containers. Some succulents look at home in bonsai pots and can thrive in their shallow soil; the common jade plant is one that actually starts to take on the aged look of a bonsai.

Or, browse nurseries looking for small pines, junipers, or false cypresses *(Chamaecyparis)* that have twisted branches or other signs of character at a young age. Prune the root ball of your selected plant by as much as one-third, and plant it in a pot that's 4 or 5 inches wide, making sure that you add at least an inch of new soil around the root ball's sides. Prune the top a bit to expose some of the trunk, trimming off a few side shoots up from the base. Sorry, that's about as specific as we can get — every plant is different in terms of its requirements and responses. Keep the plant in part shade, and water often enough to ensure that the soil stays moist. If you like doing this sort of thing and you enjoy how the plant looks, launch a full-fledged trip into the details of tending to these small-scale trees. Good luck.

Figure 20-3:
A classic
bonsai.

Celebrating with Special-Occasion Plantings

Plants take on symbolic meanings at different times of the year. Here are some suggestions to help you make the most of these botanical treasures.

Live Christmas trees

The days of silver foil Christmas trees are over (at least for most of us), and people are once again returning to real trees. The most real tree of all is a living tree, roots and all, that you plant outdoors after the holidays. In all but the warmest parts of the country, you'll be looking at hardy evergreens — such as spruces, firs, and pines — which are sold in containers or balled and burlapped. If you have the yard space, it's very rewarding to plant a tree each year and be able to look back and reminisce as the trees grow — "We got that tree the year you were born."

Live trees are expensive, so before you get your heart set on one, consider the following:

✔ **Size at purchase:** Think small. Really small. If you're used to a 7-foot-tall tree commanding a quarter of your living room, think again. First of all, subtract at least 18 inches from the height of the tree for the root ball — in other words, you'd be decorating a 5½-foot-tall tree. Then consider that you'd need half a football team to carry the tree into the house. A tree that size may weigh 100 pounds or more. Head to a nursery and heft a few trees to imagine transporting one home and into the house.

✔ **Time spent indoors:** Evergreen trees don't go completely dormant in winter, but they come close to it. If you bring the tree indoors for a month, it will start to break dormancy. Then, when you plant it outside in January it may suffer freeze damage. Plan to keep your living Christmas tree indoors for a week and no more than 10 days, preferably in the coolest room out of direct sun.

✔ **Future size:** Most spruces, firs, and pines get big — really big — as in 50 to 100 feet tall. Can your yard accommodate such a large tree? You can keep these trees in containers for a few years, but they'll soon outgrow even the largest containers.

If you have your heart set on a big tree but want to plant a living one, too, here's one way to have your tree and plant it too: Buy a small live tree, decorate it, and display it outdoors, on your front porch or wherever you like. Have a second, cut tree in the house for the holidays.

Another option is to go for a dwarf evergreen. These may not have the exact same shape and aesthetic of a traditional tree, but they're a good compromise if space is limited. Dwarf Alberta spruce have that perfect conical shape and grow slowly to a mature height of about 6 feet, so they can remain in a container permanently. Other relatively small evergreens are dwarf Korean fir, dwarf arborvitae, and dwarf blue spruce. Read plant tags carefully, because the term dwarf is relative. Yet another option is to decorate an evergreen houseplant, like Norfolk Island pine. (Read more about these in Chapter 14.)

Holiday and gift plants

How many people have received holiday and gift plants — azaleas, lilies, gardenias, miniature roses, mums, rosemary "trees" — only to have them wither after a week or two? Many people then decide that they don't have a green thumb and give up on gardening. The reality is that most gift plants have been forced into bloom out of season or with such exacting conditions that even the most expert gardeners have a tough time keeping them alive. Consider these plants to be longer lasting than cut flowers, but not permanent. If you can keep them alive longer than a month, pat yourself on the back.

If you want to give a plant that will last, visit a nursery with a knowledgeable staff and ask for their advice. The answer you get will depend upon the season, what's in bloom at the time, and what grows well in your climate. Consider an easy-care houseplant, especially during the winter months. Include care instructions with the plant, too.

Working with Water-Loving Plants

All you really need for a water garden is something that holds water. By including water plants and special features like fish, stones, a small submersible pump, and maybe a fountain nozzle, you can create a container garden with tremendous appeal.

Planting a water garden

The process for planting your water garden is a simple one. First, select a decorative vessel — a large urn, a watertight barrel, a broad glazed bowl, or anything else that holds water. Find a permanent location for the container (especially if it's large), arranging the container so it's level. Then fill the container with water within 4 to 6 inches of the top, and add a few bricks to set potted plants on.

Now you're ready to plant in the pots that will be submerged. Choose special bog or water plants that prefer a wet existence. You can find these plants in nurseries and some garden centers. They range in size from tiny 3-inch guys to larger 1-gallon plants. Look for plants with outstanding flowers (Japanese iris, water lily, cardinal flower, marsh marigold) or attractive foliage (water clover, houttuynia). Some give you interesting form (horsetail, fiber-optic grass, sweet flag) or wonderful texture (shellflower, parrot's feather, waterpoppy).

For the underwater pots, use terra-cotta pots or special plastic baskets designed for water plants. Here's how you plant them:

1. **Fill the pots with heavy garden soil (lightweight potting mixes dissolve or float up), and pot the plants just as you would any container plant.**

2. **Leave room, though, for a layer of gravel or small rocks on the soil surface to keep the soil from washing away, as shown in Figure 20-4.**

3. **Rinse the outside of the pot to remove any loose soil or debris before you drop it in the water.**

4. **Submerge the pot in the water.**

   Place most plants so that the rims are at water level. Allow others to float, and set water lilies a bit deeper, lowering them as new growth appears, as shown in Figure 20-5.

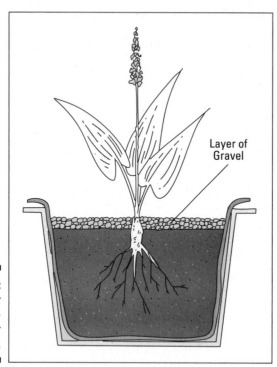

Layer of
Gravel

Figure 20-4:
Potting your
soon-to-be-
underwater
plant.

Figure 20-5:
You can
place your
containers
at different
depths.

Here are some quick tips for success with water gardens:

- Combine plants with different forms and textures for maximum interest.

- If you're using a barrel or other deep container for your water garden, elevate the submerged pots on bricks so that they don't sit too deeply in the water.

- The easiest plants to use are floating ones, and as a bonus, they help keep the water clear by using up nutrients in the water.

- Use waterproof sealant to seal cracks in barrels or holes in ceramic pots.

- Choose your location carefully: This is one container garden that you won't be moving, even if you want to, because it will be very heavy. Look for a spot with sun to partial shade.

- Select compact plants, because even with barrels, space is minimal. Many water plants become invasive; stick with smaller varieties or young plants and divide them if they grow too large.

- Add a goldfish or three if your container is at least 15 inches deep.

    Be careful with ceramic bowls or metal tubs in the summer sun — they can get hot, raising the water temperature dangerously high for fish.

Check with a garden center that handles water garden supplies for information on pumps, fish, maintenance, local factors, and other planting steps.

A water garden design: Reflective beauty

Enjoy the wonderful textures and brilliant flowers of aquatic plants in this easy-to-assemble water garden, which is shown in Figure 20-6. A watertight half-barrel can host a collection of floating and submerged plants. Japanese iris provides dramatic flair with spectacular spring blooms and deep green foliage. Parrot's feather fills the gaps with fine, delicate foliage, and shell-flower adds distinctive form from undulating petals in a rosette arrangement. Purple-leaf cardinal flower lends a contrasting note with brilliant red summer flowers on long stems. Water hyacinths finish the scene, with their unique shape and lavender summer flowers.

- **Container:** Recycled wine or whiskey barrels are ideal for an impromptu water garden that you can set up on your patio or deck. The watertight barrels are long-lasting and decorative, giving you ample space for plenty of plants.

- **Plants:** One Japanese iris, one cardinal flower, one clump of parrot's feather, one shellflower, and three water hyacinths. (These are all special aquatic plants.)

- **How to plant:** Use plastic or terra-cotta pots and heavy garden soil for the cardinal flower, iris, and parrot's feather. Plant them in individual pots, and cover the soil surface with rocks. Rinse away loose dirt and debris, and then submerge the pots in the barrel filled with water, raising them on bricks if necessary so they sit at the proper height. Simply float the surface plants — shellflower and water hyacinth — on the water toward the front of the tub.

- **Special tips:** Don't be alarmed if the water turns pea green at first. Discoloration occurs when the dissolved nutrients in the water fuel small algae. The murkiness is only temporary, and the water quickly clears. Add a special touch to your garden with a small submersible pump to give the engaging sounds of splashing water. And don't forget the fish. Goldfish (yes, the kind that you win at the county fair) are a perfect addition and give the water ecological balance — be sure to check locally for cold-weather care of fish in your climate.

Figure 20-6:
Reflective
beauty.

Part VI
The Part of Tens

The 5th Wave   By Rich Tennant

"It's my husband's idea of a drip irrigation system."

In this part . . .

Growing in containers isn't just fun, it's also one way to make gardening accessible to people who might otherwise be deprived of the joys of gardening. Chapter 21 contains tips to get you started.

The key to successful gardening is "right plant, right place," and container growing is no different. Choosing plants involves evaluating conditions and deciding what you want from your gardens, then coming up with your options. The lists in Chapter 22 will help you get started.

And finally, if your local gardening center doesn't have the exact plant you're looking for, or if you like to do research online, head to the appendix. There we list dozens of resources that you can turn to for more information.

Chapter 21

Ten Ways to Make Gardening More Accessible

*A*ge, injury, limited mobility, and other factors can pose challenges to working in a backyard garden. But that doesn't mean that gardening has to be off-limits. In fact, people who can't get out and dig in the garden are among those who benefit most from working with plants. Fortunately, tools and techniques are available to make gardening more accessible to people of all ages as well as those with limited physical, mental, and emotional abilities. And growing in containers tops the list!

Here are several ways to make gardening accessible to everyone.

Growing Plants in Containers

Choose containers that bring plants up to a height that eliminates bending and minimizes reaching. Figure 21-1 shows how a garden can be modified for folks who can't bend or stand.

Place containers in areas that are easy to access — perhaps along a paved pathway, on a patio, or indoors. Set large, heavy pots on castors to make them easier to move. Window boxes are often a good choice, because they can be tended to and enjoyed from inside and outside. Flip to the color section in the middle of this book for a photo of a container garden built to accommodate a wheelchair. (Consult the Americans with Disabilities Act (ADA) Standards for Accessible Design Web site, www.ada.gov/stdspdf.htm, for design specifications.)

Figure 21-1:
A garden can be designed for people of all abilities.

Creating Easy-to-Navigate Paths

When designing a garden that's accessible for everyone, avoid pebble paths, uneven cobbles, and mulch, all of which can be difficult for people with mobility limitations to navigate. Choose hard, smooth surfaces (but lightly textured for good traction), and keep paths as level as possible. Make paths wide enough for two people to walk side by side as well as wide enough to accommodate a wheelchair. Provide wider spots for turning. Make sure paths drain well to avoid puddles and ice buildup. Place container plants close enough to the paths so they're easily reached, but off the traveled areas so they don't hinder foot and wheelchair traffic.

Individuals with visual impairment benefit from clearly delineated paths and gardens. Use lighting and reflective materials as well as contrasting textures and colors.

Adding Areas for Frequent Sitting and Resting

Set up benches or other places to rest, preferably with shelter from the wind and sun. Elevate containers so they can be tended from a seated position. When you're working on your containers, use a garden *scooter* — a low, wheeled device that you sit on so you can roll between planters.

Using the Right Tools

You don't need full-sized tools when you're gardening in containers. Look for small, lightweight, ergonomically designed tools that minimize the stress on joints and muscles. You can also find special grips to attach to tools. Use extra padding to prevent sore hands and knees.

Simplifying Tool Storage and Watering

Use tool pouches for hands-free carrying. Provide a convenient source of water near the garden. Minimize watering chores with drip irrigation (see Chapter 15). Install a mailbox near the garden to hold hand tools, gloves, and other small items.

Growing Vertically

Grow plants up on trellises chosen to match the height and reach of the gardeners. Many flowers and vegetables adapt well to growing vertically (see the chapters in Part II, as well as Chapter 12), and you can stick a trellis right in a container to keep everything portable.

Keeping It Manageable

Start small, with easy-care plants in small pots — especially for beginner gardeners. Choose plants whose mature size fits the spot to minimize pruning chores. Look for plants with year-round interest.

Appealing to All the Senses

Include fragrant plants like herbs, plants with soft, fuzzy foliage like lamb's ears, and plants like ornamental grasses that rustle in the breeze. Hang wind chimes. Plant brightly colored flowers in contrasting containers for individuals with visual impairment.

Bringing the Garden Indoors

Place houseplants where they're easy to see and care for (see Chapter 14 for more on indoor container gardening). Create tabletop gardens accessible on all sides. Use pulleys to raise and lower hanging baskets for easy watering.

Exploring Resources for Accessible Gardening

The following companies focus on products that make daily life easier for people with limited mobility.

Charley's Greenhouse Supply, 17979 State Route 536, Mt. Vernon, WA 98273; phone 800-322-4707 or 360-395-3001; e-mail customerservice@charleys greenhouse.com, Web site www.charleysgreenhouse.com. Sells the "Down-Up Pulley" that allows you to raise and lower hanging baskets (and bird feeders) for maintenance.

Gardening with Ease, P.O. Box 302, Newbury, NH 03255; phone 800-966-5119 or 603-938-5116; e-mail input@gardeningwithease.com, Web site www.gardeningwithease.com. Large selection of tools and equipment to make gardening easier on the body.

Motus, Inc., P.O. Box 872, Winnipeg, Manitoba, R3P 2S1; phone 204-489-8280, fax 204-489-0450; e-mail info@motus.mb.ca, Web site www.motus.mb.ca. Hand grips for home and garden tools.

OXO, 1331 South Seventh St., Second Floor, Chambersburg, PA 17201; phone 800-545-4411, fax 717-709-5350; Web site www.oxo.com. Ergonomic tools for gardening, cooking, and more.

Stand Up Gardens, Ltd., P.O. Box 1080, North Hampton, NH 03862; phone 800-867-8263, fax 603-926-2226; Web site www.standupgardens.com. Indoor and outdoor garden stands.

The Wright Stuff, Inc., 111 Harris St., Crystal Springs, MS 39059; phone 877-750-0376 or 601-892-3115, fax 601-892-3116; e-mail info@thewright-stuff.com, Web site www.arthritissupplies.com. Supplies and devices for home and garden designed for people affected by arthritis.

Chapter 22

Ten-Plus Categories of Plants for Special Situations

In This Chapter

▶ Choosing the easiest flowers and veggies to grow

▶ Foiling deer with deer-resistant plants

▶ Finding fragrant flowers

*O*verwhelmed by all the plants on display at the garden center? Need some help finding just the right plant? Use the following lists to help you choose container plants for specific gardening situations. These lists are by no means complete   there are many other options for each category, so don't hesitate to experiment and try plants not on these lists.

Ten Easy Annual Flowers for Containers

If you're just starting out with gardening, give these plants a whirl. They're forgiving of mistakes.

- ✔ Coleus
- ✔ Geranium
- ✔ Marigold
- ✔ Pansy
- ✔ Petunia

- ✔ Salvia
- ✔ Sunflower
- ✔ Sweet alyssum
- ✔ Verbena
- ✔ Zinnia

Ten Easy Vegetables and Herbs for Containers

Once you get a taste of growing your own edibles, you'll be searching for more space in which to grow herbs and veggies. These are (almost) guaranteed to grow.

- Basil
- Beans
- Cilantro
- Cucumber
- Dill
- Eggplant
- Greens (lettuce, spinach, chard, and so on)
- Peas
- Peppers
- Tomatoes

Ten Easy Flowers to Start from Seed

Garden centers don't sell starter plants of every flower, but they do sell the seeds so you can do it yourself. Pick up a packet of seeds for these flowers, plant them according to the directions on the packet, and in no time you'll have more seedlings than you know what to do with!

- Alyssum
- Calendula
- Cleome
- Cosmos
- Marigold
- Morning glory
- Nasturtium
- Sweet pea
- Sunflower
- Zinnia

Ten Attractive, Edible Plants

You'll enjoy watching these plants grow and form their edible parts. Fruitful and beautiful. What more could you want from a plant?

- Blueberry
- Chard
- Eggplant
- Fennel
- Leek
- Lettuce (especially red-leaf varieties)
- Pepper
- Rosemary
- Sage
- Thyme

Ten Fragrant Plants

Place your containers sporting these plants near an open window or a door you use often. You'll be rewarded with enchanting fragrances whenever you pass by.

- Gardenia
- Heliotrope
- Hyacinth
- Narcissus
- Rose
- Scented geranium
- Star jasmine
- Stock
- Sweet olive *(Osmanthus fragrans)*
- Sweet pea

More Than Ten Deer-Resistant Plants

No plant is deer-*proof* — if they're hungry enough, deer will eat just about anything. But the following plants are less likely to be nibbled:

- Ageratum
- Cactus
- Calendula
- Catmint
- Daffodil
- Daphne
- Dusty miller
- Dwarf Alberta spruce
- Fountain grass
- Foxglove
- Holly
- Iris
- Lavender
- Lungwort
- Peony
- Salvia
- Snapdragon
- Sweet alyssum

Ten Gift Plants

Want to share your green thumb with others? These plants are nice enough to plant in a pretty container and present to a friend on a gift-giving occasion.

- African violet
- Azalea
- Christmas cactus
- Dwarf Alberta spruce
- Gardenia
- Lily
- Miniature Rose
- Oxalis
- Poinsettia
- Rosemary

Ten Plants Substantial Enough to Stand Alone

These plants are larger and have features that make them interesting to look at on their own, so you don't need to plant smaller plants around their base. Just pot 'em up, and call it a day.

- Bamboo
- Citrus
- Crape myrtle
- Dwarf Alberta spruce
- Dwarf peach
- Flowering plum
- Japanese black pine
- Japanese maple
- New Zealand flax
- Rhododendron

Plants You Can't Go Wrong with for Full Sun

Some of these plants prefer a little shade in regions with hot, sunny summers.

Annuals	Perennials	Trees and Shrubs
African daisy	Agapanthus	Boxwood
Ageratum	Alstroemeria	Chinese paperbush
Angelonia	Asparagus	Cotoneaster
Bidens	Aster	Crape myrtle
Calendula	Blanketflower	English laurel
Calibrachoa	Blue marguerite	False cypress
Celosia	Catmint	Fir
Cleome	Chrysanthemum	Flowering cherry, crabapple, plum
Cosmos	Coreopsis	Harry lauder's walking stick
Dahlia	Daylilies	Hawaiian hibiscus
Diascia	Delphinium	Heavenly bamboo
Euphorbia	Echinacea	India hawthorn
Gaura	Euryops	Juniper
Geranium	Ferns	Lantana

Lantana	Hardy geranium	Myrtle
Lobelia	Lavender	Norfolk Island pine
Marigold	Marguerite	Oleander
Ornamental kale	New Zealand flax	Pine
Pansy and viola	Penstemon	Pineapple guava
Pentas	Pinks and carnations	Pittosporum
Petunia	Primroses	Podocarpus
Portulaca	Purple fountain grass	Pomegranate
Salvia	Rudbeckia	Redwood
Strawflower	Tall sedum	Spruce
Sunflower	Yarrow	Strawberry tree
Sweet alyssum		Sweet bay
Verbena		Sweet olive
Zinnia		Thuja

Reliable Plants for Part Shade and Shade

Many of these plants can tolerate more sun in cool-summer regions.

Annuals	*Perennials*	*Trees and Shrubs*
Begonia	Astilbe	Aucuba
Browallia	Coralbells	Azalea and rhododendron
Coleus	Ferns	Camellia
Fuchsia	Foamflower *(Tiarella)*	Daphne
Iceland poppy	Foxglove	Fatsia
Impatiens	Hellebore	Fuchsia
Lobelia	Hosta	Gardenia
Ornamental kale	Lungwort	Holly
Pansy and viola	Polemonium	Hydrangea
Portulaca	Wild ginger *(Asarum)*	Japanese maple
Salvia		Lily of the valley shrub
Torenia		

Annual Flowers by Shape

An easy way to create an attractive container arrangement is to have some thrillers, fillers, and spillers. In some cases there are both upright and trailing varieties of a plant, so read the description on the plant's label.

Tall ("Thrillers")	Shrubby ("Fillers")	Trailing ("Spillers")
Angelonia	African daisy	Bacopa
Cleome	Ageratum	Begonia
Cosmos	Celosia	Bidens
Dahlia	Diascia	Calibrachoa
Dracaena	Geranium	Fuchsia
Fountain grass	Lantana	Lobelia
Gaura	Marigold	Nemesia
Salvia	Pansy and viola	Portulaca
Snapdragon	Pentas	Sweet alyssum
Sunflower	Petunia	Torenia
	Salvia	Verbena

Appendix

Additional Resources

· ·

*T*his chapter is filled with mail-order resources, Web sites, and books about container gardening. The lists are by no means complete, but they can give you a head start on your search for plants, containers, supplies, information, and inspiration.

Mail-Order Suppliers

Here is a small selection from among the hundreds, if not thousands, of suppliers of all things related to container gardening.

Seeds and plants

Abundant Life Seed Company, P.O. Box 279, Cottage Grove, OR 97424; phone 541-767-9606 (orders) or 541-767-9606 (customer service), fax 866-514-7333; e-mail info@abundantlifeseeds.com, Web site www.abundantlife seeds.com. Dedicated to the preservation of unusual heirloom vegetable, herb, grain, and flower seeds; offers organically grown and untreated seeds.

Bluestone Perennials, 7211 Middle Ridge Rd., Madison, OH 44057; phone 800-852-5243, fax 440-428-7198; e-mail service@bluestoneperennials. com, Web site www.bluestoneperennials.com. More than 1,000 varieties of perennials, grasses, bulbs, shrubs, and vines.

Bountiful Gardens, 18001 Shafer Ranch Rd., Willits, CA 95490; phone 707-459-6410, fax 707-459-1925; e-mail bountiful@sonic.net, Web site www.bountifulgardens.org. Specializes in unusual vegetable varieties.

Brent and Becky's Bulbs, 7900 Daffodil Ln., Gloucester, VA 23061; phone 804-693-3966, fax 804-693-9436; e-mail info@brentandbeckysbulbs.com, Web site www.brentandbeckysbulbs.com. Huge selection of flowering bulbs, including old standbys and new hybrids.

Busse Garden, 17160 245th Ave., Big Lake, MN 55309; phone 800-544-3192, fax 763-263-1013; e-mail `customer.service@bussegardens.com`, Web site `www.bussegardens.com`. Cold-hardy and unusual perennials and native plants.

Fedco Seeds, P.O. Box 520, Waterville, ME 04903; phone 207-873-7333, fax 207-692-1022; Web site `www.fedcoseeds.com`. A full line of vegetables including a good selection of potatoes. Also fruit trees, bulbs, books, tools, and products.

Hollow Creek Bonsai Nursery, 2124 Dutch Hollow Rd., Avon, NY 14414; phone 585-226-8593, fax 585-226-9755; e-mail `hollowcreekbonsai@yahoo.com`, Web site `www.hollowcreekbonsai.com`. Bonsai plants, plus containers, tools, supplies, and accessories.

Jackson & Perkins, 2 Floral Ave., Hodges, SC 29653; phone 800-292-4769 or 800-872-7673, fax 800-242-0329; e-mail `service@jacksonandperkins.com`, Web site `www.jacksonandperkins.com`. Excellent selection of roses, patio trees, miniatures, and containers.

Johnny's Selected Seeds, 955 Benton Ave., Winslow, ME 04901; phone 877-564-6697; Web site `www.johnnyseeds.com`. Source for seed-starting equipment; flower, herb, and vegetable seeds; and container gardening kits, seed collections, and soil mixes.

Logee's Tropical Plants, 141 North St., Danielson, CT 06239; phone 888-330-8038, fax 888-774-9932; e-mail `logee-info@logees.com`, Web site `www.logees.com`. Rare and unusual flowering plants suitable for home and patio, including cactuses and succulents, citrus trees, and tropicals.

Nichols Garden Nursery, 1190 Old Salem Rd. NE, Albany, OR 97321; phone 800-422-3985, fax 800-231-5306, e-mail `customersupport@nicholsgardennursery.com`, Web site `www.nicholsgardennursery.com`. Asian and unusual vegetables and herbs.

Nourse Farms, Inc., 41 River Rd., South Deerfield, MA 01373; phone 413-665-2658, fax 413-665-7888; e-mail `info@noursefarms.com`, Web site `www.noursefarms.com`. Wide selection of small fruits.

Park Seed Co., 1 Parkton Ave., Greenwood, SC 29647; phone 800-213-0076; Web site `www.parkseed.com`. Seeds, bulbs, perennials, trees, and shrubs.

Renee's Garden Seeds, 6060 Graham Hill Rd., Suite A, Felton, CA 95018; phone 888-880-7228; e-mail `customerservice@reneesgarden.com`, Web site `www.reneesgarden.com`. Seed varieties chosen specially for home gardeners, including flowers, vegetables, and herbs.

Spring Hill Nurseries, 110 West Elm St., Tipp City, OH 45371; phone 513-354-1510, fax 513-354-1504; Web site www.springhillnursery.com. Perennials, roses, shrubs, and vines.

Van Bourgondien, P.O. Box 2000, Virginia Beach, VA 23450; phone 800-622-9959, fax 800-327-4268; e-mail blooms@dutchbulbs.com, Web site www.dutchbulbs.com. Large variety of flowering bulbs, plus a selection of perennials, trees, and shrubs.

W. Atlee Burpee & Co., 300 Park Ave., Warminster, PA 18974; phone 800-333-5808; Web site www.burpee.com. Wide selection of flower and vegetables seeds, plus perennials, fruits, and gardening supplies.

White Flower Farm, P.O. Box 50, Route 63, Litchfield, CT 06759; phone 800-503-9624; e-mail custserv@whiteflowerfarm.com, Web site www.whiteflowerfarm.com. Hundreds of varieties of annuals, perennials, bulbs, and shrubs, plus a good selection of containers.

Small fruits and fruit trees

Bay Laurel Nursery, 2500 El Camino Real, Atascadero, CA 93422; phone 805-466-3406, fax 805-466-6455; Web site www.baylaurelnursery.com. Good selection of apples, apricots, cherries, nectarines, peaches, pears, and plums for the Southwest.

Edible Landscaping, 361 Spirit Ridge Ln., Afton, VA 22920; phone 800-524-4156 (orders) or 434-361-9134 (questions), fax 434-361-1916; e-mail info@ediblelandscaping.com, Web site www.ediblelandscaping.com. Wide variety of both familiar and unusual fruits.

Four Winds Growers, P.O. Box 3538, Freemont, CA 94539, phone 510-656-2591; e-mail cs@fourwindsgrowers.com (questions) or order@fourwindsgrowers.com (orders), Web site www.fourwindsgrowers.com. Specializes in dwarf citrus trees and other edible ornamentals.

Just Fruits & Exotics, 30 St. Francis St., Crawfordville, FL 32327, phone 850-926-5644, fax 850-926-9885; e-mail Justfruits@hotmail.com, Web site www.justfruitsandexotics.com. Temperate fruit trees suited to warm growing regions and many hard-to-find exotic trees.

Miller Nurseries, 5060 W. Lake Rd., Canandaigua, NY 14424; phone 800-836-9630; e-mail info@millernurseries.com, Web site www.millernurseries.com. Hardy dwarf fruit trees suitable for containers.

Raintree Nursery, 391 Butts Rd., Morton, WA 98356; phone 360-496-6400, fax 888-770-8358; e-mail customerservice@raintreenursery.com, Web site www.raintreenursery.com. Deciduous, tropical, and citrus trees suitable for containers.

Stark Bro's Nurseries & Orchards Co., P.O. Box 1800, Louisiana, MO 63353; phone 800-325-4180; e-mail info@starkbros.com, Web site www.starkbros.com. Wide selection of deciduous fruit trees.

Water gardening plants and supplies

Lilypons Water Gardens, 6800 Lilypons Rd., Adamstown, MD 21710; phone 800-999-5459, fax 800-879-5459; e-mail info@lilypons.com, Web site www.lilypons.com. Specialists in all aspects of water gardening.

Maryland Aquatic Nurseries, 3427 N. Furnace Rd., Jarrettsville, MD 21084; phone 877-736-1807, fax 410-692-2837; e-mail info@marylandaquatic.com, Web site www.marylandaquatic.com. Full range of plants and supplies for water gardens and fountain gardens.

Paradise Water Gardens, 14 May St., Whitman, MA 02382; phone 800-955-0161or 781-447-4711, fax 781-447-4591; e-mail contact@paradisewatergardens.com, Web site www.paradisewatergardens.com. All supplies for water gardening.

Slocum Water Gardens, 3914 S. Florida Ave., Lakeland, FL 33813; phone 863-293-7151, fax 800-322-1896; Web site www.slocumwatergardens.com. A nursery of aquatic plants.

Van Ness Water Gardens, 2460 N. Euclid Ave., Upland, CA 91784; phone 800-205-2425 or 909-982-2425, fax 909-949-7217; e-mail ponds@vnwg.com, Web site www.vnwg.com. Wide selection of water plants and supplies. Web site also provides detailed information on water gardening.

Containers, tools, and supplies

A. M. Leonard, Inc., 241 Fox Dr., Piqua, OH 45356; phone 800-543-8955, fax 800-433-0633; e-mail info@amleo.com, Web site www.amleo.com. Professional nursery and gardening supplies.

Berry Hill Irrigation, 3744 Highway 58, Buffalo Junction, VA 24529; phone 800-345-3747 or 434-374-5555, fax 434-374-0131; Web site www.berryhillirrigation.com. Drip irrigation supplies, including kits for containers and hanging baskets.

Gardener's Supply Company, 128 Intervale Rd., Burlington, VT 05401; phone 888-833-1412, fax 800-551-6712; Web site www.gardeners.com. Tools and products for gardeners, including self-watering containers and seed starting kits.

Gardens Alive!, 5100 Schenley Pl., Lawrenceburg, IN 47025; phone 513-354-1412; Web site www.gardensalive.com. A large supplier of organic pest controls and organic fertilizers.

Kinsman Company, River Rd., Pt. Pleasant, PA 18950; phone 800-733-4146 (orders) or 800-733-4129 (questions); e-mail kinsco@kinsmangarden.com, Web site www.kinsmangarden.com. Large selection of containers, as well as gardening supplies and quality tools.

Plow & Hearth, phone 800-494-7544; Web site www.plowhearth.com. A wide variety of containers and other home and garden products.

Simple Gardens, 72 Industrial Ln., P.O. Box 374, Barre, VT 05641; phone 866-460-0334, fax 802-223-0199; e-mail simplegardens@gmail.com, Web site www.simplegardens.com. Containers, window boxes, and baskets for container gardening and gardening in small spaces.

Simply Hydroponics, phone 727-531-5355, fax 727-531-6335; e-mail hydro-u@simplyhydro.com, Web site www.simplyhydro.com. Full line of hydroponic systems and accessories.

Find a Master Gardener

In the Master Gardener program, home gardeners are provided with hours of horticulture training, and in return they volunteer through their local university extension program. They conduct workshops and demonstrations, and are often available to answer homeowners' gardening questions. To find your local Master Gardener group, consult with your local university's Cooperative Extension office or visit the clickable map on this Web page: www.ahs.org/master_gardeners.

Web Sites

Web sites on container gardening abound — a Web search yields thousands of results. Sites with information specific to your region can be particularly helpful. Here are some general Web resources:

American Public Gardens Association (www.publicgardens.org): One of the best sources of information on what plants grow well in your region is your local public garden. Search this Web site for gardens near you, and browse events happening at gardens across the country.

Dave's Garden (www.davesgarden.com): With almost half a million members, Dave's Garden is a huge Web community with all sorts of user-generated resources, including a plant library and discussion forums. Garden Watchdog is a directory of mail-order gardening companies rated by members on quality, price, and service. PlantScout lets you enter the name of a plant and find sources for it.

GardenWeb (forums.gardenweb.com/forums): There are dozens of forums, including ones devoted to container gardening, balcony gardening, and bonsai. Connect with your fellow gardeners, search for information, and ask and answer questions.

National Gardening Association: The Web sites of the NGA, a national, non-profit organization, offer a wealth of resources. The site for home gardeners, www.garden.org, includes thousands of articles, message boards, an events calendar, and biweekly columns from regional experts. You can also search the Public Garden Directory to find a garden near you — these gardens are some of the best sources of information on what plants grow well in your region. The Gardening with Kids Web site, www.kidsgardening.org, has extensive resources for educators, plus Youth Garden Grants and other awards programs.

Books about Container Gardening

This is just a small sampling from among the hundreds of books on container gardening.

The Complete Houseplant Survival Manual: Essential Gardening Know-How for Keeping (Not Killing) More Than 160 Indoor Plants, Barbara Pleasant, Storey Publishing, 2005.

Container Gardening, Paul L. Williams and Nigel Marven, DK Adult, 2004.

Container Gardening: 250 Design Ideas & Step-By-Step Techniques, Fine Gardening, Taunton Press, 2009.

Instant Container Gardens, Pamela Crawford, Color Garden Publishing, 2007.

Kitchen Harvest: Growing Organic Fruit, Vegetables & Herbs in Containers, Susan Berry, Frances Lincoln, 2007.

McGee & Stuckey's Bountiful Container: Create Container Gardens of Vegetables, Herbs, Fruits, and Edible Flowers, Rose Marie Nichols McGee and Maggie Stuckey, Workman Publishing Company, 2002.

Window Boxes: Indoors & Out, James Cramer and Dean Johnson, Storey Publishing, 2004.

Index

Business/Accounting & Bookkeeping

Bookkeeping For Dummies
978-0-7645-9848-7

eBay Business
All-in-One For Dummies,
2nd Edition
978-0-470-38536-4

Job Interviews
For Dummies,
3rd Edition
978-0-470-17748-8

Resumes For Dummies,
5th Edition
978-0-470-08037-5

Stock Investing
For Dummies,
3rd Edition
978-0-470-40114-9

Successful Time
Management
For Dummies
978-0-470-29034-7

Computer Hardware

BlackBerry For Dummies,
3rd Edition
978-0-470-45762-7

Computers For Seniors
For Dummies
978-0-470-24055-7

iPhone For Dummies,
2nd Edition
978-0-470-42342-4

Laptops For Dummies,
3rd Edition
978-0-470-27759-1

Macs For Dummies,
10th Edition
978-0-470-27817-8

Cooking & Entertaining

Cooking Basics
For Dummies,
3rd Edition
978-0-7645-7206-7

Wine For Dummies,
4th Edition
978-0-470-04579-4

Diet & Nutrition

Dieting For Dummies,
2nd Edition
978-0-7645-4149-0

Nutrition For Dummies,
4th Edition
978-0-471-79868-2

Weight Training
For Dummies,
3rd Edition
978-0-471-76845-6

Digital Photography

Digital Photography
For Dummies,
6th Edition
978-0-470-25074-7

Photoshop Elements 7
For Dummies
978-0-470-39700-8

Gardening

Gardening Basics
For Dummies
978-0-470-03749-2

Organic Gardening
For Dummies,
2nd Edition
978-0-470-43067-5

Green/Sustainable

Green Building
& Remodeling
For Dummies
978-0-470-17559-0

Green Cleaning
For Dummies
978-0-470-39106-8

Green IT For Dummies
978-0-470-38688-0

Health

Diabetes For Dummies,
3rd Edition
978-0-470-27086-8

Food Allergies
For Dummies
978-0-470-09584-3

Living Gluten-Free
For Dummies
978-0-471-77383-2

Hobbies/General

Chess For Dummies,
2nd Edition
978-0-7645-8404-6

Drawing For Dummies
978-0-7645-5476-6

Knitting For Dummies,
2nd Edition
978-0-470-28747-7

Organizing For Dummies
978-0-7645-5300-4

SuDoku For Dummies
978-0-470-01892-7

Home Improvement

Energy Efficient Homes
For Dummies
978-0-470-37602-7

Home Theater
For Dummies,
3rd Edition
978-0-470-41189-6

Living the Country Lifestyle
All-in-One For Dummies
978-0-470-43061-3

Solar Power Your Home
For Dummies
978-0-470-17569-9

Internet
Blogging For Dummies,
2nd Edition
978-0-470-23017-6

eBay For Dummies,
6th Edition
978-0-470-49741-8

Facebook For Dummies
978-0-470-26273-3

Google Blogger
For Dummies
978-0-470-40742-4

Web Marketing
For Dummies,
2nd Edition
978-0-470-37181-7

WordPress For Dummies,
2nd Edition
978-0-470-40296-2

Language & Foreign Language
French For Dummies
978-0-7645-5193-2

Italian Phrases
For Dummies
978-0-7645-7203-6

Spanish For Dummies
978-0-7645-5194-9

Spanish For Dummies,
Audio Set
978-0-470-09585-0

Macintosh
Mac OS X Snow Leopard
For Dummies
978-0-470-43543-4

Math & Science
Algebra I For Dummies
978-0-7645-5325-7

Biology For Dummies
978-0-7645-5326-4

Calculus For Dummies
978-0-7645-2498-1

Chemistry For Dummies
978-0-7645-5430-8

Microsoft Office
Excel 2007 For Dummies
978-0-470-03737-9

Office 2007 All-in-One
Desk Reference
For Dummies
978-0-471-78279-7

Music
Guitar For Dummies,
2nd Edition
978-0-7645-9904-0

iPod & iTunes
For Dummies,
6th Edition
978-0-470-39062-7

Piano Exercises
For Dummies
978-0-470-38765-8

Parenting & Education
Parenting For Dummies,
2nd Edition
978-0-7645-5418-6

Type 1 Diabetes
For Dummies
978-0-470-17811-9

Pets
Cats For Dummies,
2nd Edition
978-0-7645-5275-5

Dog Training For Dummies,
2nd Edition
978-0-7645-8418-3

Puppies For Dummies,
2nd Edition
978-0-470-03717-1

Religion & Inspiration
The Bible For Dummies
978-0-7645-5296-0

Catholicism For Dummies
978-0-7645-5391-2

Women in the Bible
For Dummies
978-0-7645-8475-6

Self-Help & Relationship
Anger Management
For Dummies
978-0-470-03715-7

Overcoming Anxiety
For Dummies
978-0-7645-5447-6

Sports
Baseball For Dummies,
3rd Edition
978-0-7645-7537-2

Basketball For Dummies,
2nd Edition
978-0-7645-5248-9

Golf For Dummies,
3rd Edition
978-0-471-76871-5

Web Development
Web Design All-in-One
For Dummies
978-0-470-41796-6

Windows Vista
Windows Vista
For Dummies
978-0-471-75421-3

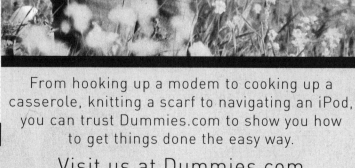

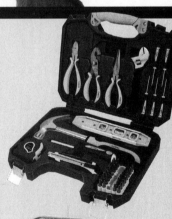

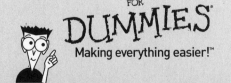